"In this fresh, engaging, and thought-provoking text, the authors explore up-to-date cases to consider the factors that have caused nuclear power to fail to deliver. Critics and supporters of nuclear energy alike will find much to ponder and reflect upon."

–Keith Baker, *State University of New York – Brockport, USA*

"*Nuclear Power in Stagnation* offers one of the most erudite and interdisciplinary assessments of the technology to date. The exploration of themes such as security, safety, and politics are rich yet readable, the national case studies carefully selected and diverse, covering France to Russia, the United States to South Korea."

– Benjamin Sovacool, *Science Policy Research Unit,*
University of Sussex, UK

"This comprehensive research study tackles critical policy, regulatory, and cultural issues, both empirically and theoretically across China, France, Russia, South Korea, UK, and the US. This important study broadens and deepens our understandings of global conundrums and more localised cultural and regulatory variabilities converging to displace nuclear energy as a viable 21st century energy source."

– Majia H. Nadesan, *Arizona State University, USA*

"This new study shows that, while safety does add to the costs of nuclear, in countries like the USA, with less strict safety regulation, nuclear power has not done conspicuously better in economic terms compared, for example, to tightly regulated France. With nuclear power now in crisis in many countries, this book provides some useful insights into what is killing it off – and it's not just the cost of trying to make it safe."

– David Elliott, *Open University, UK*

Nuclear Power in Stagnation

This book studies the extent to which nuclear safety issues have contributed towards the stagnation of nuclear power development around the world, and accounts for differences in safety regulations in different countries.

In order to understand why nuclear development has not met widespread expectations, this book focusses on six key countries with active nuclear power programmes: the USA, China, France, South Korea, the UK, and Russia. The authors integrate cultural theory and theory of regulation, and examine the links between pressures of cultural bias on regulatory outcomes and political pressures which have led to increased safety requirements and subsequent economic costs. They discover that although nuclear safety is an important upward driver of costs in the nuclear power industry, this is influenced by the inherent need to control potentially dangerous reactions rather than stricter nuclear safety standards. The findings reveal that differences in the strictness of nuclear safety regulations between different countries can be understood by understanding differences in cultural contexts and the changes in this over time.

This book will be of great interest to students, scholars, and policymakers working on energy policy and regulation, environmental politics and policy, and environment and sustainability more generally.

David Toke is Reader in Energy Politics at the Department of Politics and International Relations at the University of Aberdeen in Scotland, UK.

Geoffrey Chun-Fung Chen is Associate Professor of Political Economy at the Department of China Studies at Xi'an Jiaotong-Liverpool University which is located at Suzhou, Jiangsu Province, China.

Antony Froggatt is Senior Research Fellow in the Energy, Environment, and Development Programme at Chatham House, London, UK.

Richard Connolly is Senior Lecturer in Political Economy and Director of the Centre for Russian, European, and Eurasian Studies at the Department of Politics and International Studies at the University of Birmingham, UK.

Routledge Studies in Energy Policy

Energy Policies and Climate Change in China
Actors, Implementation and Future Prospects
Han Lin

Energy Efficiency in Developing Countries
Policies and Programmes
Suzana Tavares da Silva and Gabriela Prata Dias

Ethics in Danish Energy Policy
*Edited by Finn Arler, MogensRüdiger, Karl Sperling, Kristian Høyer Toft
and Bo Poulsen*

Mainstreaming Solar Energy in Small, Tropical Islands
Cultural and Policy Implications
Kiron C. Neale

Appraising the Economics of Smart Meters
Costs and Benefits
Jacopo Torriti

Wind Power and Public Engagement
Co-operatives and Community Ownership
Giuseppe Pellegrini-Masini

Social Movements against Wind Power in Canada and Germany
Energy Policy and Contention
Andrea Bues

Nuclear Power in Stagnation
A Cultural Approach to Failed Expansion
*David Toke, Geoffrey Chun-Fung Chen, Antony Froggatt and
Richard Connolly*

For further details please visit the series page on the Routledge website:
www.routledge.com/books/series/RSIEP/

Nuclear Power in Stagnation
A Cultural Approach to Failed Expansion

David Toke, Geoffrey Chun-Fung Chen, Antony Froggatt and Richard Connolly

First published 2021
by Routledge
2 Park Square, Milton Park, Abingdon, Oxon OX14 4RN

and by Routledge
52 Vanderbilt Avenue, New York, NY 10017

Routledge is an imprint of the Taylor & Francis Group, an informa business

British Library Cataloguing-in-Publication Data
A catalogue record for this book is available from the British Library

Library of Congress Cataloging-in-Publication Data
Names: Toke, David, author. | Chen, Geoffrey Chun-Fung, author. |
    Froggatt, Antony, author. | Connolly, Richard, 1979– author.
Title: Nuclear power in stagnation : a cultural approach to failed
    expansion / David Toke, Geoffrey Chun-Fung Chen, Antony Froggatt,
    Richard Connolly.
Description: Abingdon, Oxon ; New York, NY : Routledge, 2021. | Series:
    Routledge studies in energy policy | Includes bibliographical references
    and index.
Identifiers: LCCN 2020041796 (print) | LCCN 2020041797 (ebook) |
    ISBN 9781138341197 (hardback) | ISBN 9780429440298 (ebook)
Subjects: LCSH: Nuclear engineering—Safety measures—Political
    aspects. | Nuclear power plants—Safety measures—Government
    policy. | Nuclear power plants—Design and construction—Costs. |
    Barriers to entry (Industrial organization)
Classification: LCC TK9152 .T65 2021 (print) | LCC TK9152 (ebook) |
    DDC 333.792/4—dc23
LC record available at https://lccn.loc.gov/2020041796
LC ebook record available at https://lccn.loc.gov/2020041797

ISBN: 978-1-138-34119-7 (hbk)
ISBN: 978-0-367-71034-7 (pbk)
ISBN: 978-0-429-44029-8 (ebk)

Typeset in Times New Roman
by Apex CoVantage, LLC

Contents

Figures

Tables

Acknowledgements

We wish to acknowledge the help of Julian Cooper in reviewing the chapter on Russia, Mike Cross for helping with some statistical calculations, and Yvonne Toke for the presentation of the figures. We would also like to thank all those who gave us the time for interviews to help with the research.

1 Introduction

To date, no nuclear power plant that has begun construction in so-called Western countries (e.g. US, UK, France, Finland) this century has been completed; plants are taking much longer than expected to build and large cost overruns are being accumulated. As is indicated in Chapter 3, nuclear construction in the world as a whole has barely kept pace with retirement of old nuclear plants, and the proportion of the world's electricity supplied by electricity nuclear power was lower in 2019 compared to 2000. The issue of costs is important, since it appears as a key factor limiting the expansion of nuclear power in the West (Petti et al. 2018). The historical importance of nuclear safety issues has been much attested in the past. One much cited study dating back to the end of the 1970s commented:

> One of the principal effects of the American nuclear opposition has been the revision of numerous safety standards for light water reactors. . . . For this reason, increases in the cost of electricity from light water reactors seem probable in all countries which have chosen to develop this technology.
>
> (Bupp and Derian 1978, 170)

Later, MacKerron commented that,

> the pressure, even from within the nuclear industry, for higher safety standards continues substantially unabated. . . . To meet more stringent safety requirements and avoid ever increasing complexity, it therefore seems likely that nuclear power will need to evolve quite different designs which embody more inherent safety features than LWR [light-water reactor] designs.
>
> (MacKerron 1992, 651–652)

It is therefore important to analyse nuclear safety regimes and to examine the association of nuclear safety regulation and outcomes in the 21st century.

Indeed, the design of the type of nuclear power plant now being built in the West, the so-called 'Generation III' designs, seems fundamentally influenced by safety considerations (Fischer 2004). Elliott (2017, 2.7–2.8) argues that

> the safety problems revealed by earlier models led to the addition of ever more complex and expensive interlocks and controls, plus more backup emergency

cooling systems. Attempts have been made to reduce some of the costs and unreliability associated with Generation II reactors by redesigning operations to include passive safety features so that they are 'fail safe' with passive safety features. For example, instead of extra cooling pumps, large tanks of water are placed above the reactor to flood it using gravity should power for the pumps fail. As a last ditch safety measure (almost literally), some have 'core catchers' built into the basement –reinforced traps designed to stop a melted core from burning through the concrete floor into the top soil underneath.

It makes sense, therefore, to examine how more recent pressures for safety improvements have manifested themselves and, in order to understand the impact of differing styles of regulation, to study this process by examining different nuclear safety regimes. In doing so we focus on six countries that have at least tried in recent years to extend their nuclear power programmes (USA, China, France, South Korea, UK, Russia). This enables us to compare regulations for existing and new power plants.

Hence the overall research topic covered by this book is to examine the role played by nuclear safety in the lack of expansion in nuclear power across the world. As part of this we want to analyse the politics behind this. One particular controversy is the argument about the extent to which stricter safety regulations increase nuclear costs. This is a central part of the book. Another central part of the book is to mobilise political theory to explain the existence and nature of different regulatory outcomes.

In empirical terms we want to look at the extent to which safety regulations can be said to account for greater difficulties in the construction programmes of nuclear power, especially in terms of increased costs. The regulations themselves, of course, do not encompass all potential increases in safety-related nuclear construction difficulties – safety innovation thought up by the constructors themselves may play a part, so we need to try and separate out these factors.

If it is the case that safety factors, whether regulatory based or otherwise, do not explain much or all of nuclear power's difficulties, then there arises an expectation on us to try and spread understanding of these other factors. Finally of course we want to try to understand the political factors that have led to different nuclear safety regulatory outcomes in the different countries.

Thus, to summarise this discussion, we have an overall research question: what is the role of nuclear safety in the lack of expansion of nuclear throughout the world? This overarching question can be resolved into some sub-questions which we apply to our country case studies:

1   What role, in general, does safety play in increasing nuclear costs?
2   Specifically, what is the relative role of different nuclear regulatory systems and their safety rules in the non-expansion of nuclear power?
3   Leading on from point 2, is there evidence that national safety systems which impose less costly rules on nuclear power are associated with easier paths towards maintaining and expanding nuclear power in such countries?

4   How can we explain, in political terms, the differences between the strictness of different nuclear safety regimes?

Different political and regulatory inferences can be drawn according to different answers. If we find that different national nuclear safety systems which vary in the strictness of their safety rules produce a difference in the ability to develop and maintain nuclear power then we can say that at least part of the reason for the increase in nuclear costs is political. Whether this is something to be applauded or condemned, of course, is a different matter and will depend at least partly on value judgements. If, on the other hand, we find that differences in the nuclear safety regimes have little impact on nuclear outcomes (i.e. ability to expand nuclear power and maintain existing nuclear fleets), then this may be used as an argument in favour of stricter nuclear safety regimes. That is insofar as stricter nuclear safety regimes should not be opposed on grounds of cost.

So, we need to examine differences, and also changes in, regulatory outcomes. Given the politically controversial nature of nuclear power, we need to analyse how political processes shape outcomes. We shall examine relevant political science theories and form some hypotheses to be examined in the book.

Perhaps one of the best cited comparative analyses of nuclear safety strategies published this century was that written by Jasanoff and Kim (2009) who wrote a comparison between civil nuclear power strategies in the USA and South Korea. The paper discusses how the US nuclear power programme appeared stunted by controversies over safety, this being part of a wider dominant American 'imaginary' about 'containment' of nuclear power. By contrast in South Korea this was much less evident where an 'imaginary' of 'development' of nuclear power appeared much more prominent.

Things have changed in South Korea, of course, in the aftermath of the Fukushima accident in 2011. However, one striking aspect of this analysis is that it may reflect a more general impression that nuclear power in the USA has been seriously held back by Government policies, reflecting 'containment' concerns. According to Jasanoff and Kim (2009, 141) 'Starkly put, the US "contained" its nuclear power know-how to the point of virtual paralysis'.

Regulation is held by some to be a major contributor to the slow deployment of nuclear power deployment, at least in Western countries, in recent years. Commenting on the financial difficulties faced by the French AREVA company and the Japanese Toshiba in building reactors in Finland and the USA, Shellenberger (2017) said:

> what both Toshiba and AREVA failures underscore is that all new nuclear plants, however much they are going to be manufactured, are going to require construction according to the exacting standards of strict regulators, and it was that kind of construction that helped destroy not just one but *two* of the world's largest nuclear companies.

One of the key concerns of this book is to scrutinise such a characterisation, or at least as it may be said to apply to the system of nuclear power safety regulation.

This will be done not just in relation to the USA, but also other countries. This is necessary because we need to examine whether there is a consistent pathology of what might be called 'death through regulation' as applied to civil nuclear power, across several countries. We also need to study the possibility that particular levels and/or types of nuclear safety regulation are peculiar to one country or whether there are similar patterns in different states.

Of course, as the unpacking of our research question implied we should not take the 'death by regulation' hypothesis for granted. We still need to examine whether the US and other countries' nuclear safety regimes have contributed greatly to the difficulties of building new plants and maintaining nuclear power plants in existence.

It may be that the need to protect the public from unintended releases of radioactivity may increase costs over and above what would be the case if there was no radioactivity involved – that conclusion, at least, seems to be self-evident. The nuclear power designers certainly insist that their power plant have robust inbuilt safety measures. What is a matter of controversy is whether the safety regulations imposed by nuclear regulatory agencies act to substantially increase costs over and above what would be the case without such regulations.

Obviously, given the ubiquitous nature of nuclear safety regulatory regimes it is not possible to quantify the costs of regulation in general. There is a common set of guidelines and minimum standards promoted by the International Atomic Energy Agency (IAEA) (IAEA 2020). However, what it might be possible to do, and what is attempted in this book is to compare the relative strictness of different nuclear safety regimes. At the same time we can study the extent to which the different countries have been able a) to build new power stations and b) to keep existing power plants running. If, ceteris paribus, the countries with the strictest safety regulations also have the most difficulty in building new power plants and keeping existing plants running (compared to the countries with the less strict safety regulations) then we can say that a hypothesis that stricter safety regulations lead to substantially higher costs has not been nullified. However, if the reverse is the case, and we can find no clear link between stricter safety regulations and substantially higher costs, then we can say that the hypothesis has been nullified.

The empirical research will focus on a hypothesis that there is an association between changes in regulation of nuclear power and increases in the construction costs of nuclear power. Case studies need to look at Western and also Asiatic countries. According to Jasanoff and Kim (2009) an Asiatic case (associated with South Korea in their analysis) might be associated with a 'development' approach. A further hypothesis is that in 'development' contexts nuclear power is afforded less independent regulation than is the case with contexts associated with 'developed' phases. This difference can be observed over time and also between countries.

The theoretical dimension will be examined in the next chapter. Our analysis follows Jasanoff's (2005, 21) dictum that culture is important in influencing scientific and technological outcomes. We analyse cultural differences in order to understand differences in technological outcomes, in this case regarding nuclear power and safety. We argue that differences in outcome between the country case studies (including strictness of safety regimes and the political constraints on the nuclear power programmes) are associated with the cultural context and, crucially, changes in cultural context.

However we need a consistent measure in order to compare differences in dominant cultural influence in different countries over different times. Our measure, developed and justified in the theory chapter, is provided through cultural theory as developed initially by scholars such as Douglas and Wildavsky (1982), and later with regard to nuclear power by Baker (2017).

There the conditioning hypothesis is formed that different levels of egalitarian bias (ecological bias in short) influence the strictness of the nuclear power safety regulations – that is as opposed to 'individualist' bias which places less emphasis on ecological issues and more on cost reduction. This requires analysis of the cultural context, and the way that similar regulatory issues have been constructed and dealt with as part of the regulatory machinery in different countries. We can analyse the relevant cultural context by examining the extent of factors like anti-nuclear activities, the strength of anti-regulatory activities, and the degree of legal bias towards or away from precaution.

This key discussion concerning the importance of cultural context will be explored more thoroughly in the next chapter which sets out a theoretical framework. It may be that cultural contexts, which differ in different countries, may influence the regulatory outcomes, and this analysis will be linked to discussion of the relative influence of egalitarian activists and the type of political reactions to them.

Method

Evidence will be collected to assess, first, the nature of the regulatory regimes including their institutional nature and safety philosophy; second the outcomes of the regulations as they are applied to existing and new nuclear power plants. This will include whether or not certain technical options have been adopted, and when they were adopted; third the strength of egalitarian, individualist, and hierarchical influences with the political systems that are relevant to nuclear safety regulations.

The analysis of the empirical cases is based partly on extensive study of the rules, guidance, and other documents published by the various nuclear regulatory agencies in the different countries covered in this study. Interviews were semi-structured, but centred on the development and philosophies of the safety regimes, and in particular the degree and manner in which various technical safety measures have been recommended and/or implemented in the case of both existing, new, and planned reactors. The impacts of safety regimes on the practicalities of deploying nuclear power plants are given some priority.

The book focusses on the nuclear safety regulatory regimes as a discreet proposition, rather than on planning controversies surrounding nuclear power. This is

a) partly in order to help contain the discussion; b) partly because of an under-standing that however planning controversies may affect the timetable of building nuclear power plants, they are unlikely to constitute a major proportion of nuclear power costs, which accelerate rapidly only when construction actually begins and when large numbers of people are subsequently hired for the construction. More-over, the nuclear safety regulatory agencies in both the US and the UK have taken over more parts of the planning process (such as emergency planning and techni-cal issues) than was the case earlier in the 20th century.

Neither does the book look at issues relating to nuclear waste or decommis-sioning. Dealing with these issues does involve safety and cost issues, but we set out on the assumption that whilst these matters involve important political con-troversies, it is the issues surrounding the safety of nuclear reactors that are most likely, in practice, to provide potential barriers to building nuclear power stations in economic rather than political terms. This is because there is a tendency for costs such as decommissioning to be finessed away (by the authorities) from the costs of building new power plants or operating existing ones by a mixture of state guarantees and long-term discounting of costs.

In order to achieve this, interviews have been conducted with a range of actors including consultants advising the nuclear industry, serving and former nuclear regulatory officials, political actors, representatives of anti-nuclear NGOs, inde-pendent nuclear consultants. A large number of reports/technical documents produced by various organisations including national and international nuclear industry bodies and regulatory agencies, governmental and non-governmental bodies have been studied.

Country case studies

It would seem logical to include, in this study, those countries that are seen to be leaders in operating, building, and manufacturing nuclear power plants. The USA and France have the largest number of nuclear reactors, the USA being greatest in volume and France being greatest in terms of proportion of electricity supplied by nuclear power. It would be remiss not to include China since it has the biggest current nuclear construction programme in the world. Russia and South Korea are included as they have, or had, major nuclear power programmes and have been trying to export their technology. The UK is included since it is one of the few countries in the West trying to develop new nuclear power.

Introduction to and summary of chapters

Chapter 1 (this chapter) examines some key literature on nuclear power and safety politics. The chapter discusses the problems and questions that the book seeks to explain and answer. The method is discussed and then there is a description of the chapters in the book.

Chapter 2 sets out some theory which we can use to understand the regulatory and policy outcomes. Relevant risk, cultural and regulatory theory are considered.

We study different cultural contexts and their associations with different regulatory outcomes regarding nuclear power in general and nuclear safety in particular. In order to understand and classify these different cultural contexts we use cultural theory and its set of cultural biases. We can use these biases to explain how different sets of biases are associated with different outcomes. These biases involve a) bottom-up environmental pressures (egalitarian biases), b) individualistic biases involving opposition to rules and reliance on markets, c) biases favouring decisions by hierarchies which involve trust in top-down decision-making, and d) fatalism.

Countries will experience different combinations of biases in the nuclear regulatory field, so in order to compare the different country case studies we could use a series of metaphors. Ecological modernisation can be useful here. Ecological modernisation is an accommodation between industry and governments who seek to implement environmental policy demands in the context of economic development. Ecological modernisation can be a plausible metaphor in situations where egalitarian pressures are substantial, with bottom-up actors taking part in decisions directly in the case of 'strong' ecological modernisation, whilst 'weak' ecological modernisation reserves decision-making to elites. However other country cases may be understood as involving hierarchical or individualist biases as dominant cultural influences.

Chapter 3 examines the state of deployment of nuclear power. It does so in the context of a review of the wider energy situation and some economic/commercial/political drivers that are relevant to our analysis. Ever since the 1950s nuclear power has been promoted as a technology that will deliver affordable and necessary power in the near term and more recently that electricity that is produced by nuclear power also has very low carbon emissions associated with its production.

However, the industry has failed to become a dominant source of electricity globally; in fact its percentage contribution is diminishing year on year. This trend is likely to accelerate in the coming decades as the majority of operating reactors were built in and before the 1980s, and so will begin to be decommissioned.

As the cost of renewable energy continues to fall and it is increasingly recognised as lower than nuclear, so new build becomes less attractive both for countries that have and especially those that do not have nuclear power. Therefore, outside of those countries that have deep-rooted security, geopolitical or technological historic support, nuclear will at best make a marginal contribution to the future of the global power industry.

Chapter 4 looks at nuclear reactor politics in the USA. The USA is still the country with by far the largest number of nuclear reactors. It is also a country with public controversies about nuclear safety regulations involving multiple legal cases and claims that reactor safety rules have strangled nuclear development. This chapter examines these claims. There is a discussion of the operation of the US Nuclear Regulatory Commission and its philosophy, policies, and practices. There is an examination of how this relates to specific safety issues and also how this interacts with the USA's attempts to build new reactors this century.

We find that whilst reactor safety rules increased in the 1970s it is questionable whether safety upgrades required by the NRC have been onerous for the nuclear industry. At least that is the case if the slowness in adapting to post-Fukushima safety demands is anything to go by. It would be difficult to label the US nuclear regulatory system as one involving 'containment' of nuclear power, except in the most general sense. Rather the individualist leanings of the dominant bias in the US nuclear regulatory system could be said to be leaning towards 'development'.

Chapter 5 looks at China, crucially important since it aims for the fastest development of new reactors in the world. In this chapter, we historicise China's experience in deploying nuclear power in a hierarchical electricity system, discussing how and to what extent the idea of nuclear energy safety has shaped the institutions governing nuclear power plant development in China. In doing so we also analyse the outcomes of the regulatory regime, focussing on reactor design and the costs associated with it.

To some extent, the scientific experiments of the third-generation nuclear-technology reactors coincided with the developmental needs for the Western firms that particularly arise with Sino-foreign cooperation on China's soil. Such kinds of collaboration were built on the ground of a common interest in the political and economic imperatives of both policy elites. However pressure from local forces opposed to particular nuclear projects have slowed long-term investment in the sector.

China's safety philosophy on nuclear power plants and its cultural biases of hierarchical political norms have led to various unexpected aspects of the consequences that are unexpected by both central and local policymakers. The safety regime could be classed as weak ecological modernisation within which the emerging linkage of localism and perceived risks seemed to have made it difficult for the technology elite to implement this pursuit of a unilateral nuclear energy revival.

Chapter 6 looks at the case of nuclear safety policies and politics in France. France has the highest proportion of electricity supplied by nuclear power in the world, and has and hopes to continue to export its nuclear technology. This chapter looks at the political context in which nuclear safety regulation has developed, and the events and institutions that have been associated with the development of nuclear energy safety policy. The impact on French nuclear energy outcomes is assessed. France has engaged with a programme of retrofitting existing reactors with safety measures designed to mitigate the effects of severe accidents. Its current reactor design, the European Pressurised Reactor (EPR) includes several prominent safety features that are unique to its design.

If the French case is anything to go by we can say that countries with hierarchical systems are best placed to deliver nuclear power, but that such efforts may become more difficult if egalitarian pressures become stronger. In the case of egalitarian pressures, the regulatory result can be seen as 'weak' ecological modernisation, involving top-down regulatory pressure for more safety and the relative independence of the regulators from pressures from the nuclear industry to water down safety improvements. This is typical of weak ecological modernisation where pressures for environmental improvements are dealt with through elite negotiations between governmental agencies and leading industrial groups.

Chapter 7 examines the case of nuclear safety policies and politics in South Korea. The study of nuclear energy in South Korea is important from the point of view of this book since it represents a country that has been committed to nuclear power as part of its development strategy. Until recently, indeed, it has been included in the pantheon of nations seeing nuclear power as a key part of its development strategy. South Korea seemed to be bucking a trend towards a slowdown in building nuclear power plants.

However, in the aftermath of the Fukushima accident in 2011 a substantial anti-nuclear movement gained strength. Nuclear safety provisions were made more independent and strengthened, with safety retrofits being ordered in existing plants. Egalitarian influences seem very strong, exhibited by strong 'bottom-up' mobilisations, by heightened support for environmentalist objectives, and the use of 'bottom-up' methods to decide energy policy at a local and even at a national level. The emergence of a stronger form of ecological modernisation in the area of nuclear policy may be associated with opposition to the centralised political and economic industrial hierarchy that dominates South Korea.

Chapter 8 seeks to understand the interaction between discussions of cost and safety and nuclear power in the case of the UK. We examine the debates about the costs and Government policies underpinning nuclear power. This will be done to establish whether high costs of nuclear are a recently occurring phenomenon relating to safety demands, or merely part of the usual practice of developing nuclear power. In fact high costs seem to be pathological.

The British nuclear safety system is a hierarchy which is grounded in egalitarian norms. The original case law acted as a 'bottom-up' influence which represents a cultural disposition towards safety precaution. The hierarchy as represented by the ONR seeks to make itself the manager of this cultural tradition. It is contained within the concept of 'weak' ecological modernisation which has been described in Chapter 2.

The problem of high costs in the nuclear industry's construction programme has been a long-standing one. Unlike the French programme of the 1970s/1980s the British nuclear construction programme has never had the size needed to assure the existence of a big enough cadre of engineering specialists.

Chapter 9 examines the case of nuclear power in Russia. Specifically, we examine the evolution of nuclear safety regulation in Russia and the influence that this exerted over the evolution of the nuclear power industry in Russia. Russia is an especially important country to study in the context of nuclear power since it was the fourth-largest generator of nuclear power in the world in 2019, and had the fifth-largest installed nuclear capacity.

Over a fifth of the world's NPPs (nuclear power plants) currently under construction are being built by Rosatom, the state corporation in charge of Russia's nuclear industry. Deals have been signed for the construction of many more, although plans and deals do not always lead to completed projects. We examine such prospects. In fact, the programme of exports is likely to fall short of expectations. As such, the evolution of the Russian nuclear industry is of crucial importance to the future of the global nuclear industry. Russia is an example of a very hierarchical nuclear system in which civil and military nuclear industries are fused under the umbrella of the state-owned company Rosatom.

The final chapter, Chapter 10, is the Conclusion. In this chapter we pull the lessons of the different country case studies together in an effort to answer the research question posed earlier regarding the economic impact of nuclear safety. Whilst as a general proposition safety factors make nuclear power plant expensive, we see little evidence that raising standards over and above the general guidelines issued by the International Atomic Energy Agency makes a great difference to economic outcomes. We demonstrate using the data we have collected that the US has the weakest nuclear safety regulations compared to France, UK, South Korea, and China. However, this does not seem to have helped the US nuclear programme in economic terms.

We can compare the outcomes of nuclear power performance in two large nuclear programmes, USA and France, with France having demonstrably stricter nuclear safety rules compared to the USA. How easily have new nuclear power plants been constructed in these two countries, and how quickly are existing nuclear power plants being closed down? In fact, the US has not managed to build new nuclear plants more successfully than France, and many plants are retiring in the USA, whereas so far fewer have retired in the case of France. This is the opposite of what one might expect if regulatory strictness was a major effect on nuclear power economics. Hence we can conclude that whatever the causes of differences in nuclear power performance between the two countries may be, the strictness of nuclear safety standards is not a significant factor in causing those differences. In fact, the difference between the two countries may be explained by differences in market pressures and the relative age of the plants themselves.

The US case is influenced by anti-regulatory, individualist cultural bias. In other cases, South Korea has been recently been strongly influenced by egalitarian pressures, France, the UK, and to a certain extent China according to weak ecological modernisation practices. Russia is dominated by hierarchical biases associated with the fusion of the military and nuclear aspects of the nuclear sector.

References

Baker, K. (2017) 'Using Cultural Theory to Analyze the Metagovernance of the Nuclear Renaissance in Britain, France, and the United States', *Review of Policy Research*, 34(2), 233–254.

Bupp, I., and Derian, J. (1978) *Light Water: How the Nuclear Dream Dissolved*. New York: Basic Books.

Douglas, M., and Wildavsky, A. (1982) *Risk and Culture*. Berkeley, CA: University of California Press.

Elliott, D. (2017) *Nuclear Power: Past Present and Future*. London: Institute of Physics.

Fischer, M. (2004) 'The Severe Accident Mitigation Concept and the Design Measures for Core Melt Retention of the European Pressurized Reactor (EPR)', *Nuclear Engineering and Design*, 230, 169–180.

IAEA (2020) *IAEA Safety Standards*. www.iaea.org/resources/safety-standards

Jasanoff, S. (2005) *Designs on Nature: Science and Democracy in Europe and the United States*. Princeton, NJ: Princeton University Press.

Jasanoff, S., and Kim, S. (2009) 'Containing the Atom: Sociotechnical Imaginaries and Nuclear Power in the United States and South Korea', *Minerva*, 47(2), 119–146.

MacKerron, G. (1992) 'Nuclear Costs: Why Do They Keep Rising?', *Energy Policy*, 20, 641–652.

Petti, J., Buongiorno, J., Corradini, M., and Parsons, J. (2018) *The Future of Nuclear Energy in a Carbon-Constrained World*. Boston: MIT. https://energy.mit.edu/wp-content/uploads/2018/09/The-Future-of-Nuclear-Energy-in-a-Carbon-Constrained-World.pdf (accessed 15 November 2018).

Shellenberger, M. (2017) 'Nuclear Industry Must Change of Die', *Environmental Progress*, 17 February. http://environmentalprogress.org/big-news/2017/2/16/nuclear-must-change-or-die

2 Using ecological political theory to understand differences in nuclear safety regulation

This chapter establishes a theoretical approach which aims to help us better understand the differences between the nuclear safety outcomes in the various country case studies as they apply to nuclear power stations. I first take a brief look at some institutionalist and regulatory theory accounts that are relevant to this study, and then move onto look at an application of cultural theory to this issue of nuclear regulatory safety. I then link this to the theory of ecological modernisation.

I follow this strategy as a means of achieving a categorisation of nuclear safety regulatory regimes. This may help us compare the different country case studies, and perhaps can be used to compare other countries and changes in nuclear regulation in future studies. This categorisation focusses on outcomes that can be associated with cultural contexts. After all, according to Jasanoff (2005, 21) 'culture – more particularly political culture – matters in shaping the politics of science and technology'. If we can create some useful categories, then we have a means of comparing associations between contexts and outcomes. This could then, putatively, be applied to other countries beyond the cases looked at here.

We have a range of institutionalist approaches in political science from which to choose a basis for analysis (Hall and Taylor 1996; Peters et al. 2005; Gilardi 2004). Added to this, regulatory theory on risk issues exists as a potential way to help us understand differences in outcomes in nuclear safety regulation. This in itself encompasses a range of writings, but three especially influential are those penned by Beck (1992a, 1992b) and Hood et al. (2004).

Taking these approaches in turn, and mentioning historical institutionalism (HI) first, we can understand that different institutional arrangements for nuclear safety in different countries may result from different histories, and decisions reached at critical junctures which influence, through path dependence, the shape of institutions at a later date. Institutions, in this sense, is a term that is interpreted broadly, that is rules or agreements, whether codified or sometimes not.

Indeed, Lockwood et al. (2017, 325) argue that 'The long-standing concern with political power in HI highlights the issue of how different institutional arrangements may work for or against capture of energy sector governance by incumbents'. However as useful as this may be in understanding how institutions for the same purpose (in this instance nuclear safety) may be shaped differently, does this really have a major bearing on comparing the regulatory outcomes in different countries? In this study we need also to account for differences between outcomes, with some nuclear industry incumbents having to accept different, or changed outcomes.

In this instance the outcomes are safety measures taken to ensure that operating and future nuclear reactors does not create accidents with devastating consequences. Of course we may find that countries with similar institutional arrangements may in fact have divergent outcomes. For example, as will be discussed in later chapters China and the USA both favour a 'cost-benefit' approach to safety issues, yet they have divergent outcomes when it comes to fitting extra safety devices on nuclear reactors. These nuclear safety regulatory outcomes may also associated with the direction of, and changes in, nuclear power development (or restriction) in general, so we need also to discuss such wider nuclear power policy issues as well.

Then there is the much discussed literature on the 'risk society'. Beck (1992a) argues that late 20th-century politics moved from a debate about the distribution of wealth towards the distribution of risk. His discourse fits in well with the rise of Die Grunen in Germany in the 1980s and the focus on the perceived dangers of technologies such as genetic engineering and nuclear power. A cultural approach favoured by authors such as Douglas and Wildavsky (1983), writing largely from a North American viewpoint, also talks about the emergence of a risk society. However this discourse is much less sympathetic towards green politics than Beck. They argue that agitation against nuclear power is part of a 'sectarian' campaign that reduces the economic competitiveness of economies in favour of socially constructed and often exaggerated risks.

I mention these two theorists in particular for several reasons. First is because of their analyses of risk politics, second because they refer to nuclear power as a prime example of the politics of technological risk, and third, because they represent, in their different ways, a historical point of cultural turn for Europe and the USA. It is important to delve back into the cultural politics of technology that evolved in the 1980s to understand a transatlantic divide on environmental policies that survives until today and which may affect nuclear regulatory politics.

Douglas and Wildavsky spoke of events in the USA, especially referring to anti-nuclear activism in the 1970s, which to them represented a turn towards 'sectarian' politics at the 'border'. This had resulted in excessive regulation in order to defend against socially constructed risks, for example commenting that 'the moralism of this legislation – setting standards that could not be met, using legal orders to enforce them, refusing to consider costs – was manifestly sectarian'(Douglas and Wildavsky 1983, 163). On the other hand, in Germany (and by extension through the EU countries, to Europe) the recommended trend espoused by Beck (1992a, 234) was for risks to be limited 'through the extension and legal protection of sub-politics to exert influence' (against the influence of corporate interests).

I make this counterpoint here to illustrate a divergence of paths regarding risk politics. In the USA, in the 1980s 'Reagan' years, a backlash against regulation emerged which was sceptical about some environmental risks raised by green activists. Meanwhile, by contrast, in Europe, political sympathies turned towards green politics, especially in Germany, with anti-nuclear politics being a prime concern. In other words, contemporary patterns of anti-regulatory and green-sceptical politics in the USA emerged in the USA during this period, as represented in intellectual terms by the cultural analysis of Douglas and Wildavsky (1983). This can be contrasted to contemporary patterns of greater concern for precautionary regulation in Europe, as represented by the risk politics analysed by Beck (1992a, 1992b). This suggests that we could revisit the analyses of these writers in order to analyse contemporary risk-regulatory politics.

We can then look at how these analyses can be extended to other countries outside the West. Beck (1992a, 19–24) argued that concern with the distribution of risk has arisen in the context of satisfaction of some basic means of security among countries that had become wealthy. Given this it may not be surprising if risk politics affected technologies such as nuclear power in countries that have been developing but which have now achieved levels of wealth experienced in the West. Are these countries adopting the European or American attitudes to risk-regulation? We will examine the nuclear safety regulation of China, South Korea, and Russia to establish this.

Challenges to 'risk' politics

Another influential approach to risk politics was produced by Hood et al. (2001). They critiqued the use of the notion of 'the risk society' as an explana-tor of outcomes in different examples of risk politics. To them such 'macro-scopic and world historical perspectives on risk' usually 'do not explain, or even describe, variety *within* the putative "'regulatory state", "risk society" or "audit society"' (Hood et al. 2001, 5). Rather they use conventional analysis on political theory, giving particular attention to Wilson's (1980) typology of how in different contexts there are (four ideal) different patterns of the distribution of costs and benefits.

Certainly this approach brings with it a lot of dividends of understanding polit-ical processes. However in dismissing Beck as merely a 'macroscopic' theory which explains how risk is generally more apparent in 'late modernity', Hood et al. may miss the point that some issues (and places at different times) involve more perceptions of technological risk than others. Hence an approach, pursued here, which takes theories of cultural influence on outcomes more seriously, may offer an added level of explanatory power of outcomes.

Beck was especially referring to the rise of those technological risks given prior-ity by Beck, and not merely to regard everything in society as more 'risky'. Beck describes the attitude of ecological scepticism, for example commenting that

> Large scale nuclear, ecological, genetic and chemical hazards break in at least three ways with the established logic of risks. In the first place, they involve global, frequently irreparable damage. . . . Second, prior provision for the worst conceivable accident is out of the question for annihilation hazards. . . . Third, the accident loses its (spatio-temporal) limitations.
>
> (Beck 1992b, 109)

It can be argued that Hood et al. (2001) pay too little attention to how cultural politics have shaped risk attitudes. The fact that some (rather than other) issues involve risks that are considered for their strategic importance by green groups is evident from the case studies considered by Hood et al. Their study looked at the following nine 'risk' issues:

'Attacks by Dangerous Dogs Outside the Home' . . . 'Radon at Home and Work' . . . Benzene in the Air and Workplace' . . . Paedophile Ex-offenders Released from Custody' . . . 'Local Road Safety' . . . 'Exposure to Pesticide Risk in Food and Water'.

(Hood et al. 2001, 36–45)

Hood et al. (2001) performed a very detailed analysis looking at how the costs and benefits of regulatory action were distributed, and in doing so drew a detailed picture of how influences associated with 'market failure', opinion forming, and interest group/expert lobbies seemed to coincide with outcomes. The use of Wilson's (1980) costs/benefits interest group typology was applied in a detailed fashion. Four general distributions of costs and benefits include a) client politics where benefits are concentrated and costs dispersed, b) interest group politics where both costs and benefits are concentrated, c) entrepreneurial politics where costs are concentrated but benefits dispersed, and d) majoritarian politics where both costs and benefits are dispersed. But classifying outcomes this way says nothing about how the outcomes occurred, apart from the obvious observation that some groups appear more influential than others.

What is striking from the Hood et al. (2001) study is how few of the issues studied involved significant pressures from the green political interest groups that were the originators of much of the technological scepticism covered by Beck (1992a). One would not expect, for example, green groups to take a strong interest in dangerous dogs or paedophile policy. Others, such as benzene, were reported as being 'a low priority in their campaigns on air pollution' for environmental groups (Hood et al. 2001, 119).

The authors said that 'the interest driven explanation was the most accurate overall predictor of (regulatory) regime size. . . . When concentrated business interests were in the field, the position they could be expected to prefer over regime content was normally adopted'. But 'The main exception . . . was the defeat of UK privatised water utility interests over the maintenance of precautionary standards in EU drinking water regulation' (Hood et al. 2001, 136). This 'exception' was in the issue of pesticide risk. Certainly as far as discussion of Beckian risk theory is concerned this is a significant finding in that the only issue where green groups organised as a major campaign priority happened to be the only case where concentrated business interest were (partially) defeated. In the case of nuclear safety regulation (studied in this book rather than by Hood et al [2001), it may be found that where bottom-up anti-nuclear pressures were in evidence, this resulted in stricter nuclear safety measures. This may be contrasted to other cases where there was the adoption of relatively weaker nuclear safety standards.

One way of analysing the pressures associated with Beck-style risk theory is cultural theory. This is because it can be used to identify the mobilisation of bias on specific issues. Cultural theory involves considering four key biases, and the outcome of regulatory decisions can be associated with different mixtures of biases.

Cultural theory

Cultural theory, essentially, posits four ways of seeing regulation: hierarchical with top-down and rigid lines of oversight; 'market based' (individualist) where competition and practice in the field develop outcomes; 'bottom-up' (egalitarian) regulation where local communities or communities of practitioners develop best practice; or random and changing methods of intervention in practices (fatalistic). In particular egalitarian biases involve giving environmental objectives a maximum priority, and as such can be associated with green political tendencies.

Cultural theory has also been used to analyse energy policy outcomes in the case of the UK (Toke and Baker 2016) and in various countries (Toke 2018). Baker has used cultural theory to analyse nuclear power policy with a focus on patterns of metagovernance (Baker 2017). A literature on cultural theory can be seen in Douglas (1992), Douglas and Wildavsky (1983), Olli (2012), Rayner (1992), Swedlow (2011), Tansey and Rayner (2008), Baker (2017), Toke and Baker (2016).

As seen in Figure 2.1 the four categories of bias arise as a result of the 'grid versus group' way of visualising bias. People with a 'grid' mentality (fatalists and hierarchists) believe in following rules, those with a 'group' mentality have loyalty to groups (hierarchists and egalitarians), and individualists do not prioritise either rule following or group solidarity. This involves four biases; fatalists who follow rules about which they feel they have no influence or particular loyalty; hierarchists who follow the rules set by the leaders of a group; egalitarians who have loyalty to a particular cause but believe in equal decision-making, and individualists who are biased in favour of competitive, market-based relationships.

These biases can be said to be linked to different attitudes to the environment (Schwarz and Thompson 1990). Hierarchists will acknowledge that nature can be threatened by human activity but that this can be managed by leadership. On the other hand egalitarians see nature as very fragile requiring bottom-up action to conserve it, and not just wise leadership. Individualists see nature as being more robust and believe that as a rule the market will send signals about what environmental protection is needed. Fatalists will believe that impacts on nature are unpredictable and that there is little that we can do about outcomes.

These associations have been investigated empirically through surveys. Jones (2011, 721–723) and Kahan et al. (2007, 477) concluded that egalitarians were much more critical of nuclear power compared to individualists and hierarchists, with individualists being the least sceptical of nuclear energy.

Of course actors may not be analysed through the lens of just one bias. Olli (2012) is notable for a development of the theory in that through survey methods they conclude that cultural biases are not only influential in terms of what biases people favour but also what biases people are against. For example it might be argued that Donald Trump's statements might be often characterised by an anti-egalitarian bias considering his opposition to many objectives of the green movement. Olli comments:

> people do not only support one cultural bias, they can also *reject* or support the other cultural biases. Second, at the level of the individual, the effects of cultural biases are not additive, nor are they independent of each other; *biases must be studied in combinations*. Biases are better understood as a package of meanings rather than existing as separate items.
>
> (Olli 2012, xxi)

and:

> It is possible that rejection of a cultural bias has a strong influence on what kind of social relations or institutions we reject or do not want to be part of, what we see as the biggest political problems, which policies and political parties we abhor, and what kind of cultural alliances we are willing to enter into.
>
> (Olli 2012, 494)

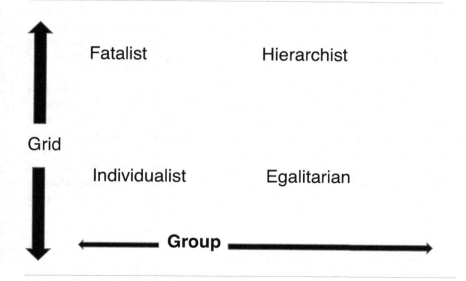

Different types of bias in social organisation

Figure 2.1 Different types of bias in social organisations

Source: Adapted from the figure prepared by Keith Baker, reproduced from Toke and Baker (2016, 447)

The risk theory divide

Today there seems to be an ideological divide between Europe and the USA about risk policies, with Europe apparently being more precautionary and the USA being more risk seeking – that is certainly the case if we take enthusiasm to sign up to climate change accords. However, this may extend to the issue of nuclear power safety. A key question then becomes, where do other countries fit in? Hence in this book's comparison we have looked at other Asiatic examples of nuclear regulatory safety regimes and outcomes.

But looking at a divide between the USA and Europe may be illustrated by a theoretical division that emerged in the early to mid-1980s, something that may have persisted since then. Certainly the modern environmental movement that focussed on the problems with industrialism and pollution grew up most prominently in the USA in the 1950s to 1970s. Douglas and Wildavsky (1983), perhaps reflecting conservative US backlash against the new environmentalism, argued that excessive concerns about risk were having a negative impact on the economy. On the other hand Beck (1992a – originally published in German in 1986) appeared to analyse the 'Risk Society' in a positive light, having written it in the context of the rise of Die Grunen in Germany.

We can further reflect on the need to spend time on works written in the 1980s. An important reason is because these works seem to have reflected a sort of cultural critical juncture, where a contrast between these works may be emblematic of a division about responses to ecological-technological threats that remains evident today. It may be seen in other issues – climate change, as already mentioned, and also attitudes to genetically engineered (modified) food. Toke (2004) talks about a cultural divide as being an explanator for much of the differences between the USA and Europe on this issue. Can we also talk about a similar divide between the USA and other countries over the issue of nuclear power safety?

It may be argued that a focus on cultural theory is misplaced given the rich veins of political science theories involving analysis of policymaking, institutionalism, and interest group influence. However, it may be that deployment of such theories do not capture a consistent understanding of the differences between nuclear safety regulatory systems. It may be that the use of cultural theory is of paramount importance simply because the political outcomes in this issue are mainly influenced by differences in dominant cultural bias, and policy changes being the outcomes of shifts in the balance of cultural bias acting in the political sphere.

Cultural theory and regulation theory

Cultural theory has been used to analyse regulation including Lodge (2009), Hood (1998), Hood et al. (2001), and Hood et al. (2004). Such studies have focussed on ways of regulation of public services in particular. This can have great advantages, especially as a consistent, easily usable tool to compare patterns of regulation across sectors and between countries. However, the cultural theory method is applied by these theorists as a means of classifying the regulatory regimes. This is different to using cultural theory as a means of categorising the biases among actors that have led to regulatory outcomes. This work chiefly uses this latter usage in that we are seeking to better understand the regulatory safety outcomes, for example the degree to which remedial safety measures have been taken in nuclear power plants. This is rather than simply classifying the organisation of the regulatory regimes itself.

Indeed, in terms of public policy analysis there is something of a contrast with (often 'classical') studies of regulation using cultural theory. These studies, such as Douglas and Wildavsky (1983) have focussed on how risk has been perceived differently, and on the impact of differences in cultural bias in risk perception on public policy practices and debates. These authors, like ourselves, have used cultural theory to analyse the pressures for safety and other environmental causes.

Moreover, there is also evidence, at least in some instances, of an apparent asymmetry between different types of cultural bias in the political context and different types of regulation regime (as categorised using cultural theory). Egalitarian pressures for more precaution can lead to more hierarchical regulatory regimes. In the issue of nuclear power safety regulation, there appears to be a particularly strong asymmetry. On the one hand, many of the most active critics of nuclear power have expressed egalitarian cultural bias, yet the regulatory regimes that have followed in the wake of such pressures have been hierarchical. Some regulatory analysis has pointed at such apparent contradictions in regulatory practices in general. Some theorists have acknowledged some degree of asymmetry. For example, Lodge (2008, 285):'We demand more hierarchical intervention exactly when the conditions for hierarchical intervention are no longer present'. Here there is an apparent contrast between demands for regulatory intervention and the trend towards greater reliance on market-based, or, in terms of cultural theory, individualist pressures.

There appears to be much room for effort to examine various types of asymmetry specifically in the case of nuclear power. One asymmetry clearly is the contrast in demands for greater intervention on safety grounds with the trend towards greater marketisation of the energy sphere. On the face of it at least, if safety concerns increase the cost of nuclear power, then in a market situation this may make the technology less competitive. However, a key aim of this book is to examine associations between cultural biases in the political context and regulatory outcomes in nuclear safety. A full examination of market pressures would require an extra book. Hence, we need to focus on country case studies with regard to the relationship of cultural pressures to nuclear safety regulatory outcomes tracing possible changing outcomes over time.

The asymmetry between egalitarian pressures for greater safety and hierarchical regulatory responses seems plausible as hierarchies themselves try to meet conflicting pressures for, on the one hand, higher safety standards, and the other, from the nuclear industry itself, solutions that do not entail big increases in costs. In short, what seems to be the case is that whilst egalitarian bias favours egalitarian regulatory designs for technologies which they prefer, when it comes to a technology which they often oppose, that is nuclear power, they press for regulatory responses that appear as hierarchical defence measures aimed to improve safety.

However, there is an issue, as the central research question posed in the first chapter implies, over whether such increases in safety regulation actually stop nuclear power plants being built, or cause them to close down earlier than they would otherwise. Such issues have, to an extent, been studied by Jasanoff and Kim (2009). They compared differing 'imaginaries' of nuclear power in the USA and South Korea, with differing priorities given to safety issues.

According to the authors, South Korea saw nuclear power in a 'development' frame whilst the USA saw this in a 'containment' frame. We would argue that development frames are associated with nuclear power being regulated more or less by the nuclear industry itself whereas 'containment' frames are associated with independent regulation of nuclear power. It should be noted that there has been, on paper at least, independent regulation of nuclear power since 1974 in the case of the USA. However it should also be noted that independent regulation of nuclear power has been put in place in South Korea since 2011 (World Nuclear Association 2019).

A key question considered in this book is the extent to which such characterisations bear up in practice. Of particular interest is the extent to which the USA does have a more safety-averse approach to nuclear power compared to other countries. We can compare the different countries' regulatory regimes by looking at the technical outcomes, that is the degree and type of safety measures taken. We can also look at the degrees of independence and transparency in decisions reached. We can also examine the safety philosophies. However, at the end of the day it is crucial to consider the relative strength of the safety measures present in the different nuclear regulatory regimes.

We also need a means of comparing the outcomes in an understandable way – in other words a typology is called for. This allows us to compare different states' outcomes in this area in a consistent way that can be easily applied to other states, and also provide a shorthand that can then be used in different analytical contexts – for example in trying to link outcomes in different areas of environmental policy. Could we use one dominant form of academic analysis of environmental politics, namely ecological modernisation, for this purpose? In order to evaluate this, we need to look at some relevant aspects.

Ecological modernisation applied to nuclear safety regulation?

In terms of organisation of nuclear regulation, all of the country case studies considered here (and all of those known) conform to hierarchies in their form, given the existence of rules or conventions about safety that are rigidly enforced by a central agency. We can study some different nuances about how the regulatory-safety machinery works. However we are also concerned with the cultural context in which these hierarchies operate, and in particular the extent of influence by ecological groups. This is where ecological modernisation comes in.

At its core ecological modernisation (EM) concerns the possibility of the reconciliation of environmental protection with economic growth (Hajer 1995, 26). This in turn is associated with business incorporating demands thrown up by civil society (with environmental NGOs and scientists acting as key actors) for environmental protection. This is done in the context of Government setting appropriate regulations and incentives so that the market adjusts to ecological priorities. A positive economic outcome is achieved as products and services meet demands from consumers for higher quality outputs.

Different forms of EM have been identified; one, called 'weak' EM, involves 'top-down' action with Governments discussing with industry how to deliver public demands and targets for ecological improvement. Another is 'strong' EM where the public, through NGOs, organise their own bottom-up initiatives to make policy on the ground in favour of radical environmental policies and practices. This makes the grass roots directly involved in determining how, in technological terms, environmental policy objectives are to be achieved (Christoff 1996).

On the other hand Dryzek et al. (2003) analysed EM in terms of how inclusive or exclusive states were compared to environmental NGOs, using four states: Germany, USA, Norway, and the UK. Paradoxically, a degree of exclusion from governmental consultation processes, as in the case of German corporatism can actually encourage NGOs to form their own 'bottom-up' networks, consequently leading to what can be described as 'strong ecological modernisation' outcomes. In Germany there has been a consistently strong grass roots anti-nuclear movement which has also spawned movements for 'bottom-up' style energy democracy. This in turn has been associated with a drive towards renewable energy with an emphasis on local and popular ownership of energy assets (Morris and Jungjohann 2016). On the other hand, the USA, whilst relatively 'pluralist' in the way it involves NGOs in decision-making, has seen environmental influence wax and (after the 1970s) wane. Stokes (2020) argues that the electricity utilities are especially effective at pursuing their interests against attempts by environmentalists to further ecological agendas.

Before we try and adopt such techniques for our purpose here, we need to consider whether EM is applicable to the issue of nuclear safety regulation. After all, the EM literature has done very little to focus on this issue. Indeed traditional EM has not dealt with nuclear power at all, except possibly indirectly in that environmental NGOs have often been active in opposition to nuclear power. Indeed, even today, despite the importance of promoting low carbon fuels, it is very difficult to find green NGOs that favour giving state support for new nuclear power plants (Toke 2018, 62).

However, the issue of nuclear safety regulation is something that transcends issues of whether people favour nuclear power in that even those opposed to nuclear energy (indeed, especially those opposed to nuclear energy) still back strong safety measures for nuclear power plants that exist or are going to be built. In the case of strong EM, which Dryzek et al. (2003) identify as being the case in Germany, it seems that a demand for bottom-up energy democracy is the response. This demand has been spearheaded by Die Grunen and for sometime was the central rallying cry of that political party. However, efforts (or at least claimed efforts) by the state to ensure that nuclear power plants are sufficiently protected to ensure that the public is buffered against radioactive releases in the case of a severe accident could be described as 'weak' EM. In many countries the demands of civil society for increased safety will be processed by nuclear regulators and translated into technical measures. This is a top-down process mirroring weak EM whereby the hierarchies implement egalitarian demands for greater nuclear safety.

On the other hand, not all nuclear safety regulatory agencies may be sufficiently put under pressure by civil society so that extra safety measures are taken, or at least the nuclear industry is successful in resisting them. This may be because a) the nuclear industry is shielded from anti-nuclear pressure by a strong hierarchy or, b) alternatively the dominant context is one of individualism in terms of cultural bias. Case a) would imply that regulators are heavily influenced by privately based industrial opposition to increased safety on the grounds that the costs are greater than the protective safety benefits. Perhaps, to aid wider understanding we could call this individualist bias a 'developmental' approach, which is more widely understood to put more stress on development when trade-offs have to be done between cost and ecological protection.

Hence we emerge with four basic categories of nuclear safety regulatory outcome: individualist/developmental, hierarchical, weak ecological modernisation, and strong ecological modernisation. The countries that are being studied here are, unlike Germany (which is not a prime focus of study in this book) all countries with an active nuclear power industry where plants are being built. Nevertheless it may be that elements of strong EM may be found if it is the case that a dominant nuclear industry is in fact in the process of being confronted by a strong grass roots movement that opposes nuclear power.

Of course, as part of the explanation, we shall look at the political context, to see how civil society has interacted with the authorities in terms of concerns about nuclear safety and support/opposition for nuclear power in general. It may be that individualist/developmental regulatory outcomes are more associated with the political pressures against strong regulation, whilst EM outcomes are more associated with pressures from civil society for greater nuclear safety.

It is to be noted that the cultural-bias-driven nature of the theory adopted here means that the prime focus is on relating dominant bias to that of regulatory outcomes. This does not mean we ignore institutional attributes – such as degree of independence of regulatory agencies, degree of transparency, modes of deciding safety rules, philosophies behind making safety decisions, and nature of the safety rules themselves. This is to assume however that the most important factor is cultural bias. We hope that this emphasis will be borne out by the discussion of the different country case studies. A plausible way of falsifying the notion that cultural bias is the most important driver of safety regulatory outcomes is the extent to which the outcomes are consistent with alternative, institutional, or interest group explanations as opposed to cultural contexts as measured by our framing of cultural theory.

Conclusion

This chapter attempts to utilise risk theory, regulatory theory, cultural theory, and ecological modernisation theory to generate a category schema to help analyse nuclear safety regulatory regimes by way of outcome. This is different to how cultural theory has been used in regulatory theory earlier in that the schema aims to analyse nuclear safety regulatory regimes according to their outcome and context rather than their institutional mechanics.

This analytic approach offers us a further layer of understanding of regulatory regimes on top of approaches such as those based on institutionalism or interest group politics. It represents a way of using risk theory more precisely by linking it to the mobilisation of egalitarian bias (which drives eco-technological politics) and analysing the extent to which such bias triumphs over pressures through other cultural biases. The setting of categories which allows us to better compare country case studies involves using cultural theory and applying it through ecological modernisation theory to help us categorise different regulatory outcomes according to context.

All nuclear safety regulatory regimes share a common nature in that they are hierarchical with complex conventions or rules that the regulatory regime (in theory) enforces. This is done in order to attempt to mollify public concerns about nuclear safety. The problem here is to explain differences between the regime outcomes. We can do this by reference to differences in cultural context. We need tools to allow us to analyse differences in cultural contexts. Cultural theory, as discussed in this chapter, with its set of biases, allows us to do this.

Outcomes may be characterised as being a consequence of differing dominant cultural biases. Those regimes with relatively stricter regimes, but which involve decision-making solely reserved to elite hierarchies will be classed as 'weak ecological modernisation'. On the other hand the existence of alternative movements for 'energy democracy' that succeed in achieving grass roots decision-making possibilities may imply elements of 'strong' ecological modernisation. Those with relatively weaker nuclear safety regimes will be classed as either 'individualist' or hierarchical' in terms of dominant cultural bias. Individualist indicates successful resistance from privately organised nuclear interests whilst hierarchical implies weaker safety regimes resulting from strong hierarchies, for existence from military/authoritarian pressures.

References

Baker, K. (2017) 'Using Cultural Theory to Analyze the Metagovernance of the Nuclear Renaissance in Britain, France, and the United States', *Review of Policy Research*, 34(2), 233–254.

Beck, U. (1992a) *Risk Society: Towards a New Modernity*. London: Sage (original published in 1988).

Beck, U. (1992b) *Ecological Politics in an Age of Risk*. Cambridge: Polity Press (original published in 1988).

Christoff, P. (1996) 'Ecological Modernisation, Ecological Modernities', *Environmental Politics*, 5(3), 476–500.

Douglas, M. (1992) *Risk and Blame: Essays in Cultural Theory*. London: Routledge.

Douglas, M., and Wildavsky, A. (1983) *Risk and Culture*. Berkeley, CA: University of California Press.

Dryzek, J., Downes, D., Hunold, C., Schlosbergy, D., and Hernes, H.-K. (2003) *Green States and Social Movement*. Oxford: Oxford University Press.

Gilardi, F. (2004) 'Institutional Change in Regulatory Policies: Regulation through Independent Agencies and the Three New Institutionalisms', in J. Jordana and D. Levi-Faur (eds.) *The Politics of Regulation: Institutions and Regulatory Reform in the Age of Governance*. Cheltenham: Edward Elgar, pp. 936–957.

Hajer, M. (1995) *The Politics of Environmental Discourse*. Oxford: Oxford University Press.

Hall, P., and Taylor, R. (1996) 'Political Science and the Three New Institutionalisms', *Political Studies*, 44(4), 536–557.

Hood, C. (1998) *The Art of the State*. Oxford: Oxford University Press.

Hood, C., James, O., Peters, B.G., and Scott, C. (eds.) (2004) *Controlling Modern Government: Variety, Commonality, and Change*. Cheltenham: Edward Elgar.

Hood, C., Rothstein, H., and Baldwin, R. (2001) *The Government of Risk*. Oxford: Oxford University Press.

Jasanoff, S. (2005) *Designs on Nature*. Princeton, NJ: Princeton University Press.

Jasanoff, S., and Kim, S. (2009) 'Containing the Atom: Sociotechnical Imaginaries and Nuclear Power in the United States and South Korea', *Minerva*, 47(2), 119–146.

Jones, M. (2011) 'Leading the Way to Compromise? Cultural Theory and Climate Change', *PS: Political Science and Politics*, 44(4), 720–725.

Kahan, D.M., Braman, D., Gastil, J., Slovic, P., and Mertz, C.K. (2007) 'Culture and Identity Protective Cognition: Explaining the White-Male Effect in Risk Perception', *Journal of Empirical Legal Studies*, 4(3), 465–505.

Lockwood, M., Mitchell, C., Kuzemko, C., and Hoggett, R. (2017) 'Historical Institutionalism and the Politics of Sustainable Energy Transitions: A Research Agenda', *Environment and Planning C: Politics and Space*, 35(2), 312–333.

Lodge, M. (2008) 'Regulation, the Regulatory State and European Politics', *West European Politics*, 31(1/2), 280–301.

Lodge, M. (2009) 'The Public Management of Risk: The Case for Deliberating among Worldviews', *Review of Policy Research*, 26, 395–408.

Morris, C., and Jungjohann, A. (2016) *Energy Democracy*. London: Palgrave.

Olli, E. (2012) 'Rejected Cultural Biases Shape Our Political Views: A Migrant Household Study and Two Large-Scale Surveys', Bergen: PhD thesis for the University of Bergen, http://bora.uib.no/handle/1956/6103

Peters, B.G., Pierre, J., and King, D. (2005) 'The Politics of Path Dependency: Political Conflict in Historical Institutionalism', *Journal of Politics*, 67, 1275–1300.

Rayner, S. (1992) 'Cultural Theory and Risk Analysis', in S. Krimsky and D. Golding (eds.) *Social Theories of Risk*. Westport, CT: Praeger, pp. 83–116.

Schwarz, M., and Thompson, P. (1990) *Divided We Stand: Redefining Politics, Technology and Social Choice*. New York: Harvester Wheatsheaf.

Stokes, L. (2020) *Short Circuiting Policy*. New York: Oxford University Press.

Swedlow, B. (2011) 'A Cultural Theory of Politics', *PS: Political Science and Politics*, 44(4), 703–710.

Tansey, J., and Rayner, S. (2008) 'Cultural Theory and Risk', in R. Heath and H. O'Hair (eds.) *Handbook of Risk and Crisis Communication*. London: Routledge, pp. 53–77.

Toke, D. (2004) *The Politics of GM Food*. London: Routledge.

Toke, D. (2018) *Low Carbon Politics*. Abingdon, Oxon: Routledge.

Toke, D., and Baker, K. (2016) 'Electricity Market Reform: So What's New?', *Policy & Politics*, 44(4), 445–461.

Wilson, J. (1980) *The Politics of Regulation*. New York: Basic Books.

World Nuclear Association (2019) 'Nuclear Power in South Korea'. www.world-nuclear. org/information-library/country-profiles/countries-o-s/south-korea.aspx

3 Nuclear power – the missing 'renaissance'

This chapter examines the state of deployment of nuclear power. It does so in the context of a review of the wider energy situation and some economic/commercial/political drivers that are relevant to our analysis.

Power demand

The creation and use of energy has been the foundation of the development of modern societies. Initially fire was used to create warmth and enable the consumption of foods that were otherwise indigestible. Then the burning of fossil fuels enabled the development of machines to undertake functions faster and more efficiently than with animals. While the development of electricity systems has created a cleaner environment for the end user and a much greater variety of fuel sources, there is a disconnect between production and consumption of energy.

However, despite some obvious advantages, such as the lack of direct pollution for the final end users, electricity use is today still not universal. As of 2016, approximately 13 per cent of world's population does not have access to electricity, although a considerable increase from 1990 when 29 per cent lacked power. In high-income countries access is effectively universal, with significant differences and changes in low-and middle-income countries (Ritchier and Roser 2020). Since 1990 India has seen access increase from 43 per cent to 85 per cent by 2016. Universal electrification was a key pledge in the election campaign of Prime Minister Modi in 2017, and by 2019 according to the Indian Government less than 20 000 households were without, at least partial, electricity access (Nazmi 2019).

Per capita consumption varies significantly between countries, with a global average of just over 3 MWh per year, with the highest consumers found in the wealthiest countries with extreme weather, such as Norway (23 MWh); Bahrain (20 MWh), or Canada (16 MWh), compared around 750 kWh in the lower middle-income countries, such as Zambia. Globally per capita electricity consumption has grown from the turn of the century from 2.3 MWh/year to 3.2 kWh/year in 2017 (IEA 2020). Total consumption of electricity has grown faster than total energy consumption. Over the last decade the annual growth rate for electricity consumption has been 2.5 per cent, compared to 1.5 per cent for energy (BP 2019).

The further electrification in low-and middle-income countries, particular in rural areas, along with the increase in GDP, leading to greater consumption of electricity-producing products, is expected continue the increase in global electricity consumption at a relatively modest pace. However, the electrification of transport, with the rise of electric vehicles (EVs), heat, and in the slightly longer-term industrial processes, could rapidly accelerate overall electricity consumption. According to the International Renewable Energy Agency (IRENA and China State Grid 2019) the global share of electricity in total final use of energy could rise from 20 per cent today to nearly 45 per cent by 2050 (IRENA 2019). In the IEA's most ambitious roll-out of EVs, penetration of cars reaches 30 per cent globally by 2030, with 250 million vehicles consuming 1100 TWh (IEA 2019a) – compared to 26600 TWh globally in 2018.[1] The electrification of passenger vehicles and light goods vehicles offers an opportunity to relatively easily reduce GHG (greenhouse gas) emissions and air pollution which is seen as a policy objective for many countries, such as UK, Norway, and France, all of which have put in place targets for the mid-term (before 2040s) phase-out of internal combustion engines for these categories of vehicles.

The electrification of heating would have an even more significant impact on electricity consumption as the sector accounts for 50 per cent of global final energy consumption. About half of the total heat produced was used in industrial process, with the vast majority of the rest going to the heating of buildings. However, electrification is only one option with radical energy efficiency, hydrogen, and direct renewable energy consumption all offering options to mitigate GHG emissions created in the production of heat.

It is therefore clear that decarbonising and enabling greater access to energy services globally is likely to lead to greater electricity consumption in the medium term. However, what is also clear is that the current Covid-19 pandemic has already reduced energy and electricity consumption and the subsequent global recession will radically change short- to medium-term electricity consumption patterns. Rapid changes to energy consumption patterns have a significant impact on the price, but particularly so in power sector, as electricity is expensive to store. Therefore, it is difficult to forecast how power demand will change in the short term and the impact that this will have on the nuclear sector.

Decarbonisation

There is global recognition that urgent action is needed to reduce GHG emissions in order to attempt to avoid the most dangerous consequences of climate change. The 2015 Paris Agreement states that its

> central aim is to strengthen the global response to the threat of climate change by keeping a global temperature rise this century well below 2 degrees Celsius above pre-industrial levels and to pursue efforts to limit the temperature increase even further to 1.5 degrees Celsius.

While António Guterres, Secretary General of the United Nations, stated at the December 2019 meeting of the UN Framework Convention of Climate Change (UNFCCC) that 'the world is getting hotter and more dangerous faster than we ever thought possible. Irreversible tipping points are within sight and hurtling towards us' (Guterres 2019).

The energy sector is responsible for nearly three-quarters of annual GHG emissions, with the power and heating sector producing around 31 per cent of the total, the largest of any sector. Consequently, reducing emissions from these sectors has been seen as a priority. Despite this, emissions directly from the energy sector in 2018 grew 1.7 per cent to reach a historic high of 33.1 GtCO2. It was the highest rate of growth since 2013, and 70 per cent higher than the average increase since 2010. Coal-fired power plants were the single largest contributor to emissions growth in 2018, an increase of 2.9 per cent compared with the previous year and surpassing annual total emissions of 10 GtCO2 – with non-energy coal use also significant, producing 4.5 GtCO2 (IEA 2019b).

In order to review the impacts and potential for restricting global temperature rises to only 1.5 degrees, the International Panel on Climate Change (IPCC) have undertaken taken a special report. In the chapter on mitigation the IPCC review the role of different energy technologies and are clear that in order to have a high degree of confidence in meeting a 1.5 degree target that the share of primary energy from renewables (including bioenergy, hydro, wind, and solar) needs to increase by 2050 so that they supply between 52–67 per cent of primary energy. The role for nuclear power, as the only other significant non-fossil fuel, is much less certain, with the suggestion that by 2050 primary energy supplied by nuclear would range from 3–66 EJ/year (median of 24 EJ) – in comparison nuclear supplied 27.8 EJ in 2015. Furthermore, the IPCC state that 'some 1.5°C pathways with no or limited overshoot no longer see a role for nuclear fission by the end of the century' (IPCC 2018).

The demands of the decarbonisation are changing the global power mix, although fossil fuels continue to dominate – in 2018 coal provided 39 per cent, gas 24 per cent and oil 3 per cent of the mix (BP 2019).

However, over the last decade there has been a significant increase in the deployment of renewable energy as a result of the combination of national and subnational policies and falling technology costs. There has been a significant increase in the past decade of power coming from gas and coal, although there has been an even greater increase from a combination of non-hydro renewable energy sources, such as biomass, solar, and wind. What is also significant is that the contribution of nuclear has not significantly changed, which is, in part, a result of a decrease in production in 2012, following the Fukushima accident in Japan and subsequent closure of reactors in Germany and Japan. Since the signing of the Kyoto Protocol in 1997, the annual output from nuclear power has increased by just 245 TWh, while for solar PV and wind power by 440 TWh and 1100 TWh respectively (BP 2019).

Global status of nuclear power

The first reactor that was used to generate electricity was connected to the Russian grid, from the Obninsk reactors in 1954. Over the following decades the deployment of nuclear power continued at relative pace until the early 1980s when the annual number of reactor start-ups started to decrease, a process which accelerated following the Chernobyl accident in Ukraine in 1986. As of the end of 2019, the total number of reactors operating globally was 414 reactors, well below a peak of 438 in 2002 and even below that at the end of the 1980s (418 reactors).[2] However, as those reactors that are being completed are larger than those being closed, the total generating capacity of the world nuclear fleet is likely to reach a global record in 2020, of over 367 GW – exceeding the previous record set in 2006.

Consequently, in 2019, more nuclear electricity was generated than in any other single year – as a result of this increase in global capacity and more efficient operation of the reactor fleets. However, as a percentage of global electricity production, nuclear's share continues to fall, due to ever-increasing demand. In 1996 nuclear power provided 17.5 per cent of global electricity and in 2019 just 10.15 per cent (Schneider and Froggatt 2019).

Analysis of the orders, construction, and closure of reactors shows clearly the impact of the world's most significant nuclear accidents, Three Mile Island (1979) in the United States, Chernobyl, and Fukushima (2011) in Japan. In each case the impact was not restricted to the host countries, and globally reactors construction projects have been shelved or extended (as adjustments were made to designs) and, often older operating reactors have been closed.

However, it is not just nuclear accidents that have affected the global trends for nuclear power deployment. The oil shocks in the 1970s were a significant driver of the ordering of new nuclear power plants. In 1973 25 per cent of global electricity was generated by oil; the rising price of oil, its value for transportation and as a chemical feed stock and the subsequent policies of governments to reduce dependency on imported oil, led a cancellation of oil-fuelled power plants and greater interest and ordering of nuclear power plants (Toth and Rogner 2006). It was in these years that significant ordering of reactors occurred especially in Europe, primarily France, and in the United States.

Despite rising power demand there has not been a significant spread of civil nuclear power technology in order to meet security of supply concerns. In the last three decades only four countries, China, Iran, Mexico, and Romania, have successfully started new civil nuclear power programmes; however, Belarus, Turkey, and the United Arab Emirates are constructing reactors for the first time. During this period a number of countries also totally withdrew from the civil nuclear field, such as Italy (1990), Kazakhstan (1999), and Lithuania (2009). Each of these programmes was shut for a different reason. In Italy, following the Chernobyl accident in Ukraine in 1986 a referendum was held in November 1987 that led to the abandonment of construction at three reactors and eventual closure of four operating units. Kazakhstan operated a Soviet-designed fast breeder reactor, the BN 350 at Aktau between 1972 and 1999 and was closed for technical and economic reasons. Despite various attempts to restart a nuclear power programme, it remains without an operating reactor. Lithuania also operated Soviet-designed reactors, two massive RBMK (similar to that deployed at Chernobyl) – 1500 MW – units at Ignalina. These were closed (along with reactors in Bulgaria and Slovakia) as part of the EU enlargement process in the early 2000s.

Furthermore, of the 31 countries that operate nuclear power plants, around one-third of these have specific policies in place to limit the operational life of their current reactor fleet and/or pledges to build no new reactors, while the lack of new build is forcing nuclear operators to seek to extend the operating lives of their existing assets to maintain market share (Schneider and Froggatt 2019).

Argentina has three reactors in operation and one, the CAREM-25 reactor, under construction. This has been under construction since February 2014 and is a small modular reactor which was originally expected to be finished in 2018. Discussions have been ongoing for decades about the construction of additional larger reactors, but lack of political will and financing have stopped any serious proposals developing.

Armenia has one of the oldest Soviet reactor designs (VVER 440–230) in operation within 30 km of the capital Yerevan. It started operation in 1980 and provides around a quarter of the country's electricity. Regional concerns have been raised about its ongoing operation, but the lack of alternatives have enabled its operational life to be extended on several occasions.

Belgium has seven reactors providing around one-third of the county's power. There have been ongoing political debates about the phase-out of nuclear power for decades and in January 2003, legislation was passed to close all of them after 40 years of operation so that the plants would be shut down progressively between 2015 and 2025. However, this process has not started and some of the units are being given an additional ten years of operation.

Brazil operates two reactors that provide less than 3 per cent of the country's power, with construction of the third suspended in 2015 due to a corruption scandal and the high financial cost of nuclear.

Bulgaria used to have six operating reactors, but four were closed as part of the agreement to join the EU. The two remaining Soviet designed reactors have been licenced to operate until 2029. Over the decades various attempts have been made to build additional reactors, but financing problems, changes in Governments, and changing negotiations with suppliers have all acted to stop any serious proposals being developed.

Canada operates 19 CANDU (natural-uranium-fuelled reactors) reactors providing 15 per cent of the country's power. It is not envisaged that additional large-scale reactors will be built in Canada, although there remains research interest in small modular reactors.

China has become the dominant force in the global industry, with 48 reactors in operation and a further ten under construction, as of early 2020. This gives it the third largest fleet in the world, behind France and the United States. However, with nuclear only providing 4.2 per cent of the country's electricity, its domestic contribution is marginal. China also dominates the global nuclear build statistics and over the last decade, of the 63 reactors that have started up, 37 were in China, with the next highest Russia (eight), South Korea (six), and India (five). Despite this, post the Fukushima accident, China has dramatically slowed down the ordering of new reactors, with ten new construction starts in 2010 and there hasn't been another one since 2017. China is also interested in exporting reactors, and a Chinese-designed reactor, Hualong 1, is currently going through the licencing process for construction in the UK, having already been exported to Pakistan.

The **Czech Republic** has six Russian-designed reactors in operation at two sites, Dukovany and Temelín. The Dukovany reactors started operating in the mid-1980s and Temelín in 2000. There are ongoing discussions about the construction of more reactors, although little concrete progress has been made regarding the essential element of financing.

Finland was expected to be in the vanguard of a new generation of nuclear nations at the turn of the century, as it ordered the first European Pressurised Reactor (EPR) from the French company AREVA (Orano). However, the country's fifth reactor at Olkiluoto is now expected to be 12 years late, coming online in 2021 and with an estimated cost of over €8.5 billion, it is one of the most expensive reactors ever to be built – but still expected to be cheaper than similar reactors being built in the UK at Hinkley Point. Despite this experience Finland is planning a sixth reactor, to be built by Rosatom of Russia, at Hanhikivi, although progress is extremely slow and physical construction is yet to begin.

France operates nearly 50 per cent of all the reactors in the EU, with 57 units providing over 70 per cent of the country's electricity. However, there is a political acceptance that the contribution of nuclear will come down over time and the latest governmental energy strategy foresees that nuclear power would provide 50 per cent of electricity by 2035 even with the closure of 14 reactors. The EPR reactor at Flamanville is also suffering from considerable cost overruns and delays, as the reactor is seven years late and three times over budget (€12.4 billion).

Germany has also historically been one of Europe's most significant nuclear players but is now committed to totally phasing out the use of nuclear power by 2022. Following the accident at Fukushima the Government suspended and then closed the oldest eight reactors and that June Parliament agreed to an overall phase-out plan for the remaining units. At its peak nuclear power provided over 30 per cent of the country's electricity.

Hungary has one nuclear power plant at Paks, which provides nearly half of the country's electricity. Despite agreement of life extensions allowing the four reactors to operate until the mid-2030s, plans are underway to build an additional, Russian designed and financed, power station.

India has one of the world's oldest nuclear fleets, starting in the 1960s and has 22 operating reactors which provide less than 5 per cent of the country's power. Officially there are seven reactors under construction, although some are experiencing delays.

Iran has a single reactor operating at Bushehr with construction at the site having officially begun in October 2017 for a second unit.

Japan suffered one of the world's nuclear accidents in 2011, which totally changed its nuclear industry. Prior to the accident government policy was to enable nuclear power to provide 50 per cent of the country's power by 2030. In 2019, although 33 reactors are officially in operation, in reality only nine are producing electricity providing about 8 per cent of the country's power. The restart of the remaining reactors is being decided, often locally, and on a case-by-case basis.

The **Republic of Korea** has a strong state-backed nuclear industry which operates 24 reactors providing 24 per cent of the country's electricity, less than half of its contribution in 1987 – as growing power demand is outstripping any additional reactors, in part due to recent extended maintenance of the existing reactors due to corrosion.

Mexico has two reactors which have operated since the 1990s and provide about 5 per cent of the country's power. The operator intends to run the units for 60 years.

The **Netherlands** operates a single reactor at Borselle, which provides 3 per cent of the country's electricity. The unit is expected to operate until 2033, but it may struggle to compete in an increasingly competitive power market if maintenance costs are not kept under control.

Pakistan has a growing nuclear sector with five reactors providing nearly 7 per cent of the country's power. Further expansion is expected with the construction of the most modern Chinese-designed Hualong 1 reactor near Karachi – the reactor is financed by Chinese investment institutions.

Romania has two Canadian-designed reactors in operation at Cernavoda which provide 17 per cent of the country's power. Originally, there were to be five units and various parties have been in negotiation to fund and complete the remaining reactors, the latest involving China's General Nuclear Power Corporation (CGNPC), but this too was halted in early 2020.

Russia has a powerful domestic industry, with 39 operating reactors and a further four under construction. Over the last two years it completed four reactors, including two of the world's first 'floating' nuclear power reactors, small (32 MW) ship-based units designed to bring power to isolated communities. Russia is also active in exporting reactors, with highly competitive financial packages and, according to the industry, with an order book worth over $100 billion with 36 separate projects, although less than ten are actually under construction.

Slovakia has four operating units at Bohunice and Mochovce, with a further two reactors under construction at the latter plant. Construction at Mochovce 3 and 4 has been plagued by cost overruns and delays and policy investigations into corruption, but the first of the units is expected to enter service in 2020.

Slovenia has a single reactor, jointly owned with Croatia, operating at Krsko. If permitted it could operate for 60 years, until 2043. No serious attempts have been made to build additional reactors in the country.

South Africa operates the continent's only commercial nuclear reactors at Koeberg. These French-designed reactors provide less than 5 per cent of the country's power. The current administration has abandoned plans to build any more nuclear reactors.

Spain now operates just seven reactors which provide 20 per cent of the country's power – around half of the maximum in 1989 – and it has permanently closed three reactors. It is currently expected that all the country's reactors will be closed by 2035.

Sweden has seven operating reactors, having closed six other units. A referendum in 1980 agreed to close all the country's reactors by 2010, but it is currently expected that formal phase-out will not happen until 2040, although economics may lead to closure of some or all of the reactors before then.

Switzerland operates four reactors, with an average age of 44 years, with two reactors permanently closed. A referendum in 2017 prohibited the construction of additional reactors, but put no operational limit on the current fleet.

Taiwan has four reactors. A government proposal to close the reactors by 2025 was overturned in a referendum in 2018, although construction has not commenced on two reactors at the Lungmen facility.

The **United Kingdom** has 15 remaining operating reactors, as 30 units reactors already closed. The UK has two reactors under construction at Hinkley Point, which are EPR designed, with construction expected to cost in excess of £19.5 billion (US$25 billion). Further plans have been prepared for further EPRs at Sizewell, as well as additional reactors from CGNPC at Bradwell, while other nuclear constructors have developed plans, but are currently put on hold.

The **United States** has the largest number of operating reactors, 96, with 37 closed and two under construction at Vogtle. The cost of construction of these AP1000-designedreactors has risen to US$28 billion for both units. However, key to the industry is maintaining the existing reactors, through a mixture of life extensions though relicencing and additional financial support through tax breaks and zero emission certificates, which could be worth upto US$100 million per unit.

It is difficult to see a single country where the nuclear sector is thriving to an extent to which the industry would be comfortable; the exception could be China, but even here the lack of new orders – and in particular no construction inland – indicates a relative slowdown in the future. While in the past the industry has argued that it is a lack of public support that has halted their development, this is no longer the primary reason. Rather the continual decline in new reactors orders is now a combination of market liberalisation, which enables new actors to enter the market and the high costs of nuclear new build relative to other non-fossil fuel generators.

Economics of non-fossil electricity generators

Technology costs

Over the past decade the costs of electricity produced by renewable energy have fallen rapidly and consistently. According to an International Renewable Energy Agency (IRENA) estimate, the global weighted average LCOE of utility-scale PV plants has fallen by 74 per cent between 2010 and 2018, from USD 3 300–7 900/kW range in 2010 to USD 800–2 700/kW in 2018. The utility-scale solar PV projects commissioned in 2018 had a global weighted average LCOE of USD 0.085/kWh, which was around 13 per cent lower than the equivalent figure for 2017. While for wind in 2018, new capacity was commissioned at a global weighted average LCOE of USD 0.056/kWh, which was 13 per cent lower than the value for 2017 (IRENA 2019). On the other land, the costs of electricity produced by new nuclear power plants has remained static or has risen. The IEA stated in their recent assessment of nuclear power that

> Today, the high capital cost of nuclear makes it significantly more costly on a levelized costs basis than wind power or gas fired generation in both the

European Union and United States. By 2040, in the United States, the LCOE for nuclear power is projected to be around USD100 per MWh, double that of solar PV and wind. In the European Union, the gap is smaller as nuclear's LCOE averages around USD 110 per MWh compared to wind and solar PV in range of USD 85–90 per MWh.

(IEA 2019c)

The annual assessment by Lazard of the levelised cost of energy in the United States shows in 2019 that costs for nuclear are in the range of US$118–192/MWh, compared to US$66–152/MWh for coal; US$44–68/MWh for combined cycle gas turbines; wind $28–54/MWh and for thin film utility-scale solar PV US$32–42/MWh (Lazard 2019). Importantly for the future of the nuclear industry, the falling costs associated with new build renewables are increasingly challenging the operating costs of nuclear power, meaning that it may become cheaper for utilities to close units rather than extend their operating lives.

The different economic directions that nuclear and solar and wind power are taking are a result of a variety of factors, some of which are inherent to the technologies and others which are due to the current state of the sectors.

Technology types

Solar PV and wind are by their very nature modular power plants, made up of hundreds or millions of generating units and factory manufactured and assembled on site. This enables improvements to be routinely be made in the manufacturing processes. A 2018 study produced by MIT on the cost reductions of solar PV found that there were a number of factors that led to the dramatic falls in costs, including that increasing module efficiency resulted in a quarter of all cost reductions between 1980–2012. The study further found that costs reductions were achieved through greater economies of scale as well as through the use of government and private research and development as did market-stimulating policies (Kavlak et al. 2018). Solar units have compared to processing chips, which have exhibited falls in costs directly proportionate to the volume of production volumes, the Moore's Law, whereby doubling of production leads to a halving of costs.

Nuclear power plants are in many ways at the other end of technological development. They are only manufactured by a handful of companies around the world. In fact, there are so few reactors being built outside of China it is impossible to see any significant learning curve. Between 2009–2019 a total of 64 reactors were completed, of which 37 were in China. China has historically purchased overseas reactors while also designing and building domestic designs. The imported reactors include two of the French European Pressurised Water Reactors (EPRs) at Taishwan as well as four Westinghouse-designed AP1000s, two each at Sanmen and Haiyang. The domestic designs are split between two competing designs, the CAP 1000 and the Hualong 1 reactors. There are two main reactor operators in China, CNNC (China National Nuclear Corporation) and CGNPC (China General

Nuclear Power Corporation). Russia completed ten over the last decade, the next largest number of reactors, but of four different designs, followed by India with five reactors and two different designs. It takes decades to design, site, and construct a nuclear power plant and therefore any experienced-based design improvements will be very difficult and slow to implement in future reactors.

An assessment by Arnulf Grubler in 2009 noted that even in the French fleet, the second largest in the world and one where a single builder has been responsible for the construction of all units, that between the first and last reactor generations being built the cost per installed capacity increased threefold (Grubler 2009). While in the United States, the cost of new construction is so high that, according to Peter Bradford, a former member of the federal Nuclear Regulatory Commission, 'new nuclear is so far outside the competitive range . . . not only can nuclear power not stop global warming, it is probably not even an essential part of the solution to global warming' (Smith 2019). A historical assessment by Rangel et al. suggested that the overnight construction costs (ONC) of the first reactors built in the early 1970s was about $1000 per kW and has increased steadily ever since reaching $5000 per kW for the recent reactors built in the early 1990s. In other words, a one-to-five ratio in constant USD. While the construction time during this period nearly doubled (Rangel and Leveque 2013).

Construction costs and delays

The costs of electricity generated from new nuclear power plants is largely determined by the costs occurred during construction, accounting for upto four-fifths of the total cost (with fuel cycle costs 10 per cent, operating and maintenance 8 per cent, and decommissioning 3 per cent). This means that delays in construction and subsequently high costs and higher interest payments can have a materially significant impact on the cost of electricity over the subsequent decades.

Due to the lack of experience of building any one reactor design and the sheer degree of complication in construction it is not surprising that there are delays in construction globally. As of July 2019, the 46 reactors that were being built had on average been under construction for 6.7 years, with at least 27 projects officially delayed. Most of the units which are nominally being built on time were begun within the past three years or have not yet reached projected start-up dates, making it difficult to assess whether or not they are on schedule.

It is also important to note that the actual lead time for nuclear plant projects includes not only the construction itself but also lengthy licencing procedures in most countries, complex financing negotiations, site preparation, and other infrastructure development (Schneider and Froggatt 2019).

A new approach?

The output from nuclear reactors has increased over time. The initial commercial reactors, built in the 1950s were in the 10s of MW, such as the Calderhall Magnox reactors in the UK which were 50 MW each; these designs are often referred to as Generation I. The later versions of these designs were increased in size and the Oldbury reactor's capacity was 280 MW. The subsequent reactor designs, in particular the Pressurised Water Reactors, were larger, starting at 200 MW and rapidly scaling up to 600 and then 900 MW in the 1970s; these designs are often referred to as Generation II. The increase in size was economically driven, as the cost of power was seen to be lower in the larger units. However, higher production levels also increased market share and were therefore also important in the politics of the power sector.

This trend has largely continued until today, as reactors have gotten larger and larger, with most reactors in the range of 1000–1400 MW. The Westinghouse AP1000, its most modern and classified as Generation III+, was originally a 600 MW design, but it was enlarged for economic reasons. AREVA's showcase reactor, the EPR, is 1600 MW. However, as both the Westinghouse and EPR experiences have continued to show, the industry suffers from cost overruns and delays and in these larger reactors the economic implications of this are even more significant, due to greater economic risks – translating into higher borrowing costs – and larger interest payments.

As a consequence of these greater financial risks and the potential for exporting reactors to new markets, often with smaller demand and where 1000 MW reactors are too large and will unbalance the grid, attempts are being made to develop Small Modular Reactors (SMRs). These may not be that small, being up to 300 MW, but a key difference is that any one site will have a larger number of individual units. Furthermore, in theory they can be built quicker and with more uniformity as a much larger percentage of the facility can be manufactured in the factory and then installed on the site. Many of these SMRs are also described as Generation IV reactors.

However, most of the SMR designs remain purely theoretical or are at the very early stages of development and despite strong pressure from the industry many governments are reluctant to accelerate the programme's development through additional government financial support. Exceptions to this are in Argentina, which is building a CAREM-25 unit; Russia, which has competed two floating reactors; and China, which is constructing a high-temperature reactor at Shidaowan. While in the United States, the Department of Energy (DOE) has been an important and persistent supporter of SMRs. The most substantial DOE investment was providing support for first-of-a-kind engineering, design certification, and licencing for two SMR designs, the mPower design in 2012 and the NuScale design in 2013, both of which were awarded up to US$226 million. While the mPower investment was scaled back in 2014 due to lack of customers, the NuScale reactor has continued to be developed and is expected to complete the licencing processes in 2020. NuScale are optimistic that they will build the pilot project in Idaho, where 12 units are expected to be sited, with operation in the mid-2020s (Parshley 2020). However, as with the existing nuclear power plants, key to deployment will be the economics and if they can compete with the falling costs associated with renewable energy.

In the UK Rolls-Royce is leading an industry initiative with the Government and in November 2019, UK Research and Innovation provided £18 million of match funding to develop an SMR in the UK, with a deployment target of 2029. However, once again economics may be a stumbling block, with the initial costs of SMRs in the UK expected to be £60/MWh (NEI 2020), which is well above the current cost of offshore wind.

Conclusions

Ever since the 1950s nuclear power has been promoted as a technology that will deliver affordable and necessary power in the near term. Over the last couple of decades, the industry's supporters have added a rationale for its existence, that electricity that is produced by nuclear power also has very low carbon emissions associated with its production.

However, despite these claims the industry has failed to become a significant source of electricity globally; in fact its percentage contribution is diminishing year on year. This trend is likely to accelerate in the coming decades as the majority of operating reactors were built in and before the 1980s, and so will begin to be decommissioned.

As the cost of renewable energy continues to fall and it is increasingly recognised as lower than nuclear, so new build becomes less attractive both for countries that have and those that don't have nuclear power. Therefore, outside of those countries that have deep-rooted security, geopolitical or technological historic support, nuclear will at best make a marginal contribution to the future of the global power industry.

Notes

1 An approximate 4 per cent increase in consumption, with a full roll-out equating to an increase of less than 15 per cent.
2 This number of calculated reactors in the World Nuclear Industry Status Report excludes those reactors in long-term outage which have not generated power for a year. Other bodies, such as the International Energy Agency, continue to classify these facilities in operation.

References

BP (2019) *Statistical Review of World Energy*, June.

Grubler, A. (2009) *An Assessment of the Costs of the French Nuclear PWR Program 1970–2000*. Laxenburg, Austria: International Institute for Applied Systems Analysis.

Guterres, A. (2019) *Remarks at COP25 Event on Climate Ambition*, 11 December. www.un.org/sg/en/content/sg/speeches/2019-12-11/remarks-cop25-event-climate-ambition

IEA (2019a) 'Global EV Outlook 2019, Scaling Up the Transition to Electric Mobility', *International Energy Agency*, May. https://webstore.iea.org/download/direct/2807?fileName=Global_EV_Outlook_2019.pdf

IEA (2019b) *Global Energy & CO2 Status Report*. www.iea.org/reports/global-energy-co2-status-report-2019 (accessed 22 February 2020).

IEA (2019c) *Nuclear Power in a Clean Energy System*, May. https://webstore.iea.org/download/direct/2779?fileName=Nuclear_Power_in_a_Clean_Energy_System.pdf (accessed 29 March 2020).

IEA (2020) *Electricity Per Capita Consumption Data*. www.iea.org/fuels-and-technologies/electricity (accessed 28 February 2020).

IPCC (2018) *Global Warming of 1.5°C: An IPCC Special Report on the Impacts of Global Warming of 1.5°C Above Pre-Industrial Levels and Related Global Greenhouse Gas Emission Pathways, in the Context of Strengthening the Global Response to the Threat of Climate Change, Sustainable Development, and Efforts to Eradicate Poverty*, V. Masson-Delmotte, P. Zhai, H.O. Pörtner, D. Roberts, J. Skea, P.R. Shukla, A. Pirani, W. Moufouma-Okia, C. Péan, R. Pidcock, S. Connors, J.B.R. Matthews, Y. Chen, X. Zhou, M.I. Gomis, E. Lonnoy, T. Maycock, M. Tignor, and T. Waterfield (eds.). In Press.

IRENA (2019) 'Renewable Power Generation Costs in 2018', *International Renewable Energy Agency*, May. www.irena.org/-/media/Files/IRENA/Agency/Publication/2019/May/IRENA_2018_Power_Costs_2019.pdf?la=en&hash=1C7553C3BFD997DEA36D07149D60005258C9C8A8 (accessed 29 March 2020).

IRENA and State Grid Corporation of China (2019) 'Electrification with Renewables, Driving the Transformation of Energy Services', *International Renewable Energy Agency and State Grid Corporation of China*, May. www.irena.org/-/media/Files/IRENA/Agency/Publication/2019/Jan/IRENA_RE-Electrification_SGCC_2019_preview.pdf

Kavlak, G., McNerney, J., and Trancik, J. (2018) 'Evaluating the Causes of Cost Reduction in Photovoltaic Modules', *Energy Policy*, 123, December, 700–710.

Lazard (2019) *Levelized Cost of Energy Analysis –Version 13.0*, November. https://www.lazard.com/media/451086/lazards-levelized-cost-of-energy-version-130-vf.pdf (accessed 28 February 2020).

Nazmi, S. (2019) 'India Election 2019: Bringing Power to the People', *BBC Reality Check*, 26 March. www.bbc.co.uk/news/world-asia-india-47499917 (accessed 28 February 2020).

NEI (2020) 'Rolls Royce Targets UK SMRs for 2029', *Nuclear Engineering International*, 28 January. www.neimagazine.com/news/newsrolls-royce-targets-uk-smrs-for-2029-7743730 (accessed 11 April 2020).

Parshley, L. (2020) 'The Countries Building Miniature Nuclear Reactors', *BBC, Future Planet*, 9 March. www.bbc.com/future/article/20200309-are-small-nuclear-power-plants-safe-and-efficient (accessed 11 April 2020).

Rangel, L.E., and Leveque, F. (2013) 'Revisiting the Nuclear Power Construction Costs Escalation Curse', *The Energy Forum*, 3, 14–15.

Ritchie, H., and Roser, M. (2020) *Access to Energy: Published online at OurWorldInData.org*. https://ourworldindata.org/energy-access [Online Resource].

Schneider, M., and Froggatt, A. (2019) *World Nuclear Industry Status Report*, September. www.worldnuclearreport.org/-World-Nuclear-Industry-Status-Report-2019-.html (accessed 13 April 2020).

Smith, G. (2019) 'Nuclear Power Is Economically Obsolete', *EcoWatch*, 9 January. www.ecowatch.com/nuclear-power-cost-renewables-2625524662.html (accessed 4 April 2020).

Toth, F.L., and Rogner, H.-H. (2006) 'Oil and Nuclear Power: Past, Present, and Future', *Energy Economics*, 28, 1–25. http://citeseerx.ist.psu.edu/viewdoc/download?doi=10.1.1.173.3505&rep=rep1&type=pdf

4 Nuclear reactor safety politics in the USA

Nuclear reactor safety in the USA

In this chapter we look at the nature of nuclear safety regulation in the USA, explanations for the outcome of the regulations, and also the impact of the safety regulations on the costs of nuclear power. We want to discuss the extent to which US nuclear safety regulation can be characterised as involving excessive strictness, over-containment prompted by pressure from anti-nuclear activists, or, alternatively, a proclivity towards favouring nuclear development. The issue of the costs of nuclear power will be an important issue, both in terms of the impact of safety issues on costs of existing and also on new nuclear power plants.

The chapter will consider first the context of nuclear safety in the USA, then examine the nature of the Nuclear Regulatory Commission's (NRC's) regulatory approach. There will be then study of specific cases of nuclear regulation. Two cases are chosen because of their contested nature showing the development of politics of safety. These are the cases of aircraft protection and also post-Fukushima accident reforms.

In looking at the case of nuclear safety regulation in the USA we should bear in mind that previous characterisations have often seen concerns about nuclear safety as having been taken very seriously, to the extent of increasing costs unreasonably (Douglas and Wildavsky 1983). Jasanoff and Kim (2009) framed the US 'sociotechnical imaginary' of the deployment of civil nuclear power as 'containment', implying, amongst other things, a desire to put nuclear safety at the top of this agenda.

However, another interpretation of the discourses around whether there was excessive, economy-killing regulation is that such claims reflected a dominant conservative narrative. This narrative, which may have become more pronounced in the 1980s, was opposed to what had, in the 1950s–1970s, been an environmental movement of growing importance. Certainly in the early 1980s the Republican administration, under Ronald Reagan, promoted efforts to roll back regulatory environmentalism (Layzer 2012). This anti-regulatory narrative has, more recently, been reinforced during the Trump era.

Of course it may be argued that there is another, egalitarian, Democratic Party and Green Party green narrative. Such narratives are influential if not dominant in some states, especially California, and some north-eastern states. But this dominance does not extend to Republican-leaning states, nor Republican administrations. The Trump administration remains not just pro-nuclear power but also pro-coal, and has attempted to aid existing nuclear and also coal-fired power plants. Such a policy is redolent of an individualist and anti-egalitarian cultural approach, as is argued by Toke (2018).

However, it does seem that in many other parts of the world (certainly including Western Europe), an egalitarian narrative has become, if not dominant, at least absorbed sufficiently by hierarchies to generate consensus governmental objectives on issues such as climate change, and a precautionary approach towards nuclear safety.

The USA has by far the largest amount of nuclear reactors and reactor capacity in the world, although by no means the largest proportion of electricity supplied by nuclear power (France holds that record). At the time of writing (February 2020) the USA had 96 operating nuclear reactors with around 98 GW of capacity. This constituted around 30 per cent of total world nuclear capacity (World Nuclear Association 2020). A succession of the reactors have been closing in recent years – nine closing since 2013 (USEIA 2019). Indeed a total of 35 reactors had been closed by 2020. However this in itself should not be seen as too much of a surprise if one assumes that nuclear reactors may come to the end of their useful economic lives after around 40 years or more. It has to be remembered that the USA built up its reactor fleet early compared to many other countries and already had a total of 84 reactors in operation by the end of the 1970s (IAEA 2020).

The majority of the nuclear reactors now in operation in the USA are Pressurised Water Reactors (PWRs), or what is known as second-generation (Generation II) reactors. These were developed in the aftermath of the successful use of a pressurised water reactor in a nuclear submarine soon after WW2. Most recently, there have been (problematic) attempts to build more advanced, so-called Generation III, reactors in Georgia and South Carolina through the Vogtle and V.C. Summer plants respectively.

Most of the nuclear power plants now operating were ordered in the 1960s and early 1970s. However, as Peter Bradford (a former NRC Commissioner) commented: 'New orders in the US stopped well before the Three Mile Island accident [in 1979], entirely because utilities experienced declining growth in [electricity] demand and continuing inability to control runaway costs [of building nuclear power plants]' (interview 04/06/2018).

Interest in building nuclear power plants began to perk up in the early 2000s as oil prices increased. As part of the 2005 Energy Policy Act, loan guarantees for building six nuclear power plants were offered by the Federal Government. Several companies expressed interest in the idea. In the events that transpired there were few serious proposals for new reactors. Three states (Georgia, South Carolina, Florida) issued their own support programmes for nuclear power plants, consisting of arrangements where the electricity companies developing the plants receive payments (raised from electricity ratepayer bills) to cover construction costs before the plants become operational. Indeed in the case of Florida, Florida

Power and Light received payments for several years even though no construction has ever been started.

There have only been four power plants which have begun construction in the 21st century (two different twin sets) in the USA, two in Georgia (Vogtle 3 and 4) and two in South Carolina (Virgil Summer 2 and 3). These plants are all of the same Advanced Pressurised Reactor (APR) 1000 design and construction began under the leadership of Westinghouse. Westinghouse went bankrupt in 2017 as a result of problems associated with building these plants. All have been subject to long delays and cost overruns, to the extent that two of those plants, those in South Carolina, have been formally abandoned.

Certainly, with the possible exception of a very small number of US states, it is difficult to pinpoint legal or regulatory bans in US states that have prevented nuclear power plant construction. Rather there are economic explanations. For a start, around half of US states practise liberalised wholesale markets for electricity sales. This means that companies in these states cannot pass on the costs of the higher construction costs that nuclear power plants entail to their consumers without making themselves less competitive compared to companies who do not do this. But more generally the privately owned utilities that dominate the US power market have put their money behind fossil fuel and (more recently) wind and solar projects rather than nuclear power. These projects have proved much more financially predictable and able to produce a revenue stream compared to building nuclear power plants.

According to the US Government the proportion of electricity generated from coal-fired power stations has fallen greatly in recent years whereas generation from natural gas and non-hydro renewable energy plants has increased. Generation from nuclear power has remained almost constant (EIA 2020).

USA NRC

In the earlier phase of the US nuclear power programme, responsibility for nuclear safety rested with the Atomic Energy Commission (AEC). However, critics of the safety of nuclear reactors questioned the ability of the AEC to simultaneously perform its function of promoting the technology and being in charge of safety. The result was that the AEC's safety regulatory duties were divested to the Nuclear Regulatory Commission, which started work in 1975 (Walker and Wellock 2010; Petti et al. 2018). The rules for nuclear safety were set down from 1970 onwards in a very detailed fashion and are publicly accessible using Freedom of Information requests. Documents such as detailed licences awarded to nuclear power developers are also available for public inspection.

A system was established whereby there was public consultation for proposed rule changes, and public groups could petition for rule changes, although in addition the NRC can also make 'orders' without going through a rule-making process. The number of rules expanded greatly during the 1970s. These are tabulated as Commission Federal Regulations (CFRs). As can be seen in Figure 4.1 the number of CFRs relating to reactor safety dramatically increased in

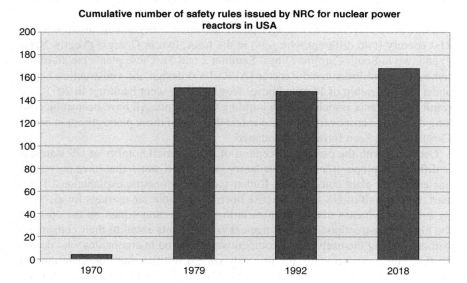

Figure 4.1 Cumulative number of safety rules issued by NRC for nuclear power reactors in the USA.

Source: US Nuclear Regulatory Commission

the 1970s. However since then there has been only a modest increase of extra CFRs to deal with issues such as new 'Generation III' designs for nuclear reactors and proposed 'advanced' nuclear reactor technology. Rule changes occur as a result of processes initiated by the NRC itself, after petitions made by a range of groups, representing both anti-nuclear and pro-nuclear interests, or a mixture of these pressures.

Analysis by Komanoff (1981) suggests that the increase in safety measures was associated with a substantial increase in the costs associated with building nuclear power stations. The increase in CFRs levelled off thereafter, but has seen a slight increase since the 1990s.

Certainly, in the 1970s, there was an increasing pressure for the nuclear industry to adopt what would now be regarded as basic provisions such as containment shielding (which was lacking in adequacy in the case of Chernobyl), some level of redundancy of key components, adequate fire protection engineering, and engineering practice which took account of the uniquely high specifications needed for nuclear power stations. The growth of regulations reflected these, and such things have become global standards recommended by the International Atomic Energy Agency (IAEA 2016). One can debate the extent to which the increase in safety regulations are merely a reflection of what the nuclear power industry felt necessary to reflect, or whether they actually resulted in changes in safety design. However it is difficult to specify a method of analysis that could achieve this.

As an NRC report put it, written by the NRC Executive Director for Operations R. W. Borchardt:

> A key element of the design of nuclear power plants is the inclusion of multiple barriers to prevent or contain potential release of radioactive materials created within the fuel by the fission process. In the United States, multiple structural barriers always have been required to confine the fission products to the plant should an accident lead to a compromise of one or more of the barriers provided by the fuel design, the reactor coolant pressure boundary, and the containment.
>
> (Borchardt 2012, 4)

It is difficult to characterise such things as regulatory excess to general publics around the world today given that there appears to be a consensus that the consequences of accidents such as Chernobyl and Fukushima need to be avoided. Moreover, largely as a response to the Three Mile Island and Chernobyl accidents the nuclear industry themselves decided upon, and implemented, the task of designing a new generation of so-called 'passive safety' Generation III reactors to hopefully more cheaply accommodate the public expectations for safety of nuclear power plants. The success or otherwise of this technological initiative therefore may be largely in the hands of the nuclear industry rather than nuclear regulators or anti-nuclear activists.

Peter Bradford, who served as a Commissioner of the NRC from 1977 to 1982 said:

> The Atomic Energy Commission (AEC) prioritised the promotion of nuclear power above safety regulation. Though the AEC was responsible for both, it viewed light water reactors as a transient technology. The greater goal was to develop reprocessing and breeder reactors. Inadequate attention was paid to such issues as proliferation of weapons based on power reactors spreading to many countries, waste disposal, emergency cooling as reactors grew in size and emergency planning outside of reactor sites. Following a number of siting controversies and a serious accident at the Brown's Ferry site, Congress in 1975 grew exasperated with the performance of the AEC and divided up that Commission, placing responsibility for safety regulation in the newly created Nuclear Regulatory Commission (NRC). Although the NRC had no promotional responsibilities, this change made less difference than many had hoped. The NRC adopted most of the AEC's regulations and hired most of its regulatory personnel.
>
> (interview, 18/06/2018)

A key facet of the NRC's *modus vivendi* is quantitative cost-benefit analysis (CBA). This procedure was established as a basis of regulatory activities in general during the Reagan era (i.e. not just restricted to the NRC) (Shapiro and Morrall 2012, 190). According to Shapiro (2011, 386), 'Reagan had campaigned on a deregulatory platform' and,

> supporters of regulation have blamed CBA for deregulation and for playing an important role in reducing environmental protections and American health and safety. Opponents of regulation have regularly called for greater use of CBA, citing the immense cost that regulation imposes upon American business.
>
> (Shapiro 2011, 385)

The NRC guidelines for choosing levels of safety hinge first on the notion of 'adequate protection'. According to the NRC (2004, 7): 'regulatory action is necessary to ensure that the facility provides adequate protection to the health and safety of the public'. The term 'adequate protection' comes from the 1954 Atomic Energy Act (NRC 2013). It can mean many things. The notion of adequate protection is concerned with setting rules that will govern the terms and conditions of issuing new licences to operators, that is for new nuclear power stations.

Probabilistic Risk Analysis (PRA) is applied to examine the likelihood of accidents and, according to the NRC (NRC 2004, 13), 'regulatory initiatives involving new requirements to prevent core damage should result in a reduction of at least 1.0×10^{-5} in the estimated mean value CDF' (core damage frequency). PRA is itself a contested concept; according to nuclear critics, it can artificially limit the assessments of risk, given that many risks are simply unknown.

Downer (2017) discusses these limits in a comparison with the aircraft industry. He argues that their risks are discovered through practice and overcome through the learning that ensues rather than through PRA. He points out that, in the case of the nuclear industry, practice is orders of magnitude lower than that which occurs in the aircraft industry, and says that this renders PRA inadequate in identifying risks, as later reflected in nuclear accidents or near accidents.

Secondly, there is the principle that any safety requirements proposed on top of this (adequate protection concept) should be subject to cost-benefit analysis. This applies to projects that have already been given licences to operate (and, usually they will already be operational). This is set out in NRC rules and explained at length in NRC (2004). In terms of reactor or operating safety, this means that if safety improvements are to be made, then a formal cost-benefit analysis (CBA) – involving monetary analysis – must be performed to justify this as a positive gain (i.e. it must show that monetised benefits exceed costs). According, for example, to Commission Regulation 50.109 on backfitting,

> the Commission shall require the backfitting of a facility only when it determines . . . there is a substantial increase in the overall protection of the public health and safety or the common defense and security to be derived from the backfit and that the direct and indirect costs of implementation for that facility are justified in view of this increased protection.
>
> (NRC 2017a, para (a (3)))

According to the NRC, the equation used to calculate the cost-benefit analysis is:

{(Public Health_Accident) + (Public Health_Routine) + (Occupational Health_Accident) + (Occupational Health_Routine) + (Property_Offsite) + (Property_Onsite)} − {(Industry Implementation) + (Industry Operation) + (NRC Implementation) + (NRC Operation)}

(NRC 2012)

The values associated with some key variables mentioned here will be subjects to differing interpretations. One obvious one is the benefit to public health in avoiding an accident. Regulators cannot know in advance what this may be, so estimates tend to be based on quantified risks to the public from a given radiation dose, with standardised assumptions being made about the extent of the radiation discharges. But there is a wide range of possibilities for both the extent of radiation discharges and their effects. One can be conservative or precautionary about such calculations.

This also applies to the benefits of avoiding 'public health routine'. This may include, in particular, questions about when and whether there should be evacuations. But even if this can be precisely determined, in practice many people (in the event of a nuclear accident) may flee, making any exercise in quantifying the impact very difficult. Again, one can be conservative or precautionary in such assessments. That is even before we come to consider the costs of making adjustments to the safety technology.

In practice, uncertainties in assessing the probabilities of accidents occurring and the impact of such accidents mean that both the term 'adequate protection' (used for deciding rules for new reactors) and cost-benefit analysis (used for assessing upgrades to existing reactors) is subject to political interpretation. Certainly the way that CBA is deployed in practice seems to protect existing operators from frequent changes in their licence conditions.

The rule-making decisions are made by the majority of (when full-strength) five Nuclear Regulatory Commissioners, albeit advised by their staff. Commissioners are political appointees, often appointed in the context of partisan considerations by the President in office. According to Nesbit and Dickman (2015, 43),

> The historical insulation of commissioners from partisan politics appears to have worn away. Six of the 14 first commissioners were affiliated with neither political party, but since 1986 there have been 21 confirmed commissioners, only one, the current chairman, was an independent. . . . Commission turnover has increased recently and the current trends are for commissioners with less background in technical areas but more attuned to political considerations and issues.

As such, decisions made by the NRC may be inherently political, rather than (just) based on quantitatively led judgements. Critics will point out that even the apparently quantitively based judgements are based a patchwork of assumptions about costs and benefits which can be more or less conservative or precautionary, as discussed earlier.

T. S. Kress, a former Chairman of the IAEA's Advisory Committee on Reactor Safeguards (ACRS) Subcommittee on Future Reactors, commented on the US nuclear safety arrangements by saying:

> Because of the complexity and relative lack of coherence of the system and the somewhat legalistic and bureaucratic circularity associated with the concept of 'adequate protection', it is not apparent to the general public that the level of safety is acceptable, nor do they have a firm understanding as to what level of safety has actually been achieved.
>
> (Kress 2002, 234)

In short the US nuclear regulatory system relies on a system whereby a) the philosophical basis for ensuring safety in new designs for nuclear power plant is a vague one and b) once a nuclear power plant has been given a licence it is very difficult, both in theory and practice, to upgrade safety measures beyond the 'design basis' of the licence conditions that were originally granted.

An additional factor is the tendency that is especially pronounced in the USA of regulatory judgements being challenged, or even pre-empted, by action in the courts. Baumgartner and Jones's (1993) notions of 'venue shopping' come into play here in that both the nuclear industry and its critics can resort to this as a political bargaining technique. It could be argued, however, that the political context in which courts make decisions has been favourable towards nuclear interests in that the nuclear industry has been successful in challenging, through court action, the ability of the NRC to enact tough regulations that can be said to involve significant extra costs.

For example, fire safety rules became a battleground in the courts following the Brown Ferry nuclear power plant fire in 1975. The NRC attempted to set clear safety rules, but these were challenged in the courts in successive actions by the nuclear industry (Jaczko 2019, 43–48). According to the former (Obama-appointed) NRC Chairman, Gregory Jaczko, whilst definitive fire rules were established in 2004, following all the court battles,

> Safety rules would no longer be simple and clear, like those earlier requirements for twenty feet of separation between systems or barriers that could withstand fire for three hours. In place of rules there would now be computer programs the industry itself developed and ran.
>
> (Jaczko 2019, 48)

The fear of action by the courts, in conjunction to the fact that the nuclear industry could appeal to sympathetic politically appointed NRC Commissioners and Senators has led to pressure on the NRC to rely on 'voluntary' safety codes with the nuclear industry. This drift towards reliance on voluntary action by the nuclear industry as opposed to reliance on rules established by the NRC is something that applies not just to fire safety but other issues, including post-Fukushima safety measures (Lyman 2016).

This notion that it is the nuclear industry that has a strong resource in that it can constrain the NRC through recourse to the courts is at odds with any idea that US nuclear power is struck down as a result of legalistic hounding by anti-nuclear groups. Certainly anti-nuclear groups take legal action sometimes, but it is by no means clear that they obtain a relative advantage over the nuclear industry in such venues. What may be visible is a shift in activity since the peak days of anti-nuclear activism in the 1970s in that it is difficult to find today the sort of mass activism that used to be the case. Elite level lobbying seems to be the game that counts, and there the nuclear industry has an advantage.

Direct action by green groups is nowadays more often directed at targets such as oil pipelines being built. Although green groups are still largely unsympathetic to building new nuclear power plants, their opposition to nuclear power in general may have been dulled by their desire to put climate change at the top of their political agenda. The political 'contagion' may have shifted away from anti-nuclear activism and towards pro-nuclear activism in and around Capitol Hill in the shape of Republican support for the nuclear industry in their fight to avoid what they see as excessive safety measures being forced upon them.

Although the NRC is nominally independent from the Federal Government, this independence is subject to a key formal constraint. The formal constraint is that the NRC is governed by Commissioners who often react in partisan ways. According to Jaczko (2019, 125), speaking about the post-Fukushima report recommendations on strengthening safety measures, 'There is little doubt that the Republican Commissioners would oppose much of the report because they believed that Fukushima was a Japanese problem and that U.S. plants were sufficiently protected'.

Jaczko (2019, 122) says that until the Fukushima accident

> the industry had been able to avoid dealing with some accident scenarios because they were deemed too remote or too vague. The industry had also been able to avoid making improvements because the NRC had to prove that the accidents the improvements were intended to guard against *could* occur.

Yet, despite the Fukushima accident, many of the suggested safety improvements were still not accepted by the nuclear industry and it was the NRC that was forced to row back on initial recommendations made by its Task Force. The problem is clearly political. If the nuclear industry can rely on Republicans to support their objections to making safety improvements then it is difficult for the NRC to ensure the implementation of its preferred technical changes.

Aircraft protection in the USA

It may be helpful to understand the dynamics (or lack of dynamics) in achieving increased safety measures if we study a particular issue, that of protection against terrorist attacks. There was for many years (prior to September 2001) a campaign by anti-nuclear campaigners for greater protection at nuclear power stations against the threat of terrorist attacks, but this led to little revision of safety protocols. Following the 9/11 attack, the NRC issued orders to strengthen security of nuclear power stations, but these measures did not include the need to install aircraft protection sufficient to maintain reactor integrity in the face of a strike by a large commercial aircraft. Rather, orders issued on 29th April 2003 merely instructed that 'physical security plans, safeguards contingency plans, and the guard training and qualification plans . . . be revised to provide protection against this revised DBT'[1] (Federal Register 2003, 24518 Column 1).

However, anti-nuclear groups energetically campaigned for effective aircraft protection, saying both that the design-based threat did not include proper attention to terrorist attacks, let alone measures to deal with such eventualities. Such campaigns were spearheaded by the 'Committee to Bridge the Gap' (led by Daniel Hirsch) and featured campaigns about truck bomb attacks as well as strikes by aircraft. In 2004, they petitioned the NRC to ensure that nuclear power plants were protected against such threats, including fitting full aircraft protection to nuclear power plants. The petition was supported by a range of (anti-nuclear) groups. However, the petition was rejected, with the NRC response saying that 'the NRC concludes that the requirements imposed by the April 29, 2003, DBT orders, which are being incorporated into proposed §73.1 remain adequate' (NRC 2005, Annex page 61, Table 1 Comment Response 1).

The Nuclear Energy Institute, which represents the US nuclear power industry, commented that,

> the petitioner states that nuclear power plants were not designed to withstand the attack by a fully loaded jumbo jet nor the intentional use of airplanes for terrorist purposes . . . the nuclear industry and the NRC have conducted independent studies of such an attack on a nuclear power plant and concluded that it is unlikely that significant harm to the public would result from such an attack. This is due to the measures taken by the Federal government to reduce the likelihood of attack, the robustness of nuclear plant structures, the multiple safety systems designed into the plants and the practiced and proven ability to carry out emergency plans.
>
> (NEI 2005)

However, the appointment of a new (Nuclear Regulatory) Commissioner, Greg Jaczko, led eventually to the adoption of an aircraft protection rule. According to Daniel Hirsch from the Committee to Bridge the Gap:

> I met with NRC Commissioner Greg Jaczko. Previously, while he was a Congressional staffer, he and I had worked together to draft legislation that would have required upgrading the DBT requirements for all nuclear plants. Now that he was a Commissioner, however, he was proposing regulations on aircraft protection that would only apply to new plants, not existing ones.

I presumed – although he did not say – that this was based on a calculation that he didn't have the votes to require protection of existing plants. In discussing his proposal that only new plants be protected from aircraft impacts, I asked him the logical question, if there were around 100 older nuclear plants without protection from air attack and a handful of newer ones that were so protected, why a terrorist wouldn't attack the older, unprotected plants. He got angry and essentially threw me out of his office, although shortly thereafter had an aide call to apologize.

(interview with Daniel Hirsch22/06/2018 and
email communication 26/06/2018)

The NRC's new Federal Regulation (NRC 2017b), adopted in 2009, effectively required developers of new nuclear power plants to include aircraft protection in their designs, although, as implied in the previous quote, the rule failed to satisfy nuclear critics. In addition to the lack of attention to existing nuclear power plants, critics complained that under the new regulation, nuclear developers were required to perform assessments and it was not specifically stated that the protection had to be adequate against strikes from large commercial aircraft.

The nuclear industry, in delaying the imposition of an aircraft protection rule, which implied a requirement for shielding for new nuclear power plants necessary to prevent core damage, may not necessarily have secured an advantage. This is because there was room for uncertainty over what was required for nuclear developers, leading to inconsistent application of NRC rulings on aircraft protection for new schemes. Hence it could be argued that the nuclear constructors increased their own costs not so much by having to follow the rules set by the NRC, but in attempting to resist rules requiring them to reach higher safety standards. This may be borne out when one looks at the arguments about costs which occurred during this controversy.

US safety regulations and costs

Do the rules increase costs?

According to a nuclear industry consultant, referring to problems in constructing new nuclear power plants in the USA:

The problem in the US is many organisations there are regulated by the NRC, are unwilling to publicly criticise the NRC and make them look bad. The NRC has almost total control over their life. Different regulators can take offence. They can start making things harder, all of the approvals they have to give can be withdrawn. . . . There is a real reluctance to go out and say NRC, 'you killed us here'. That is part of what has driven the cost, in my view, without really affecting safety at all.

(interview 09/09/2018)

On the other hand, according to a former NRC Commissioner, Peter Bradford:

> The experience of the 1970s and 1980s was repeated at Vogtle and Summer. For reasons having nothing to do with environmental opposition or regulatory excess these plants and several others now cancelled experienced major costs that they were unable to manage. Ultimately Westinghouse, which had no experience as a constructor despite its storied history as a reactor designer was driven into bankruptcy by the interplay between the cost overruns and its fixed price contracts.
>
> (interview 04/06/2018)

In April 2008, Georgia Power (a subsidiary of Southern Company) contracted with Westinghouse to build the Vogtle 3 and 4 nuclear power plant. The constructors (Stone and Webster, who were implementing the Westinghouse design work) received permission to begin work in August 2009 (Southern Company 2018). This allowed them to undertake preparatory work pending final approval of the site design. However, the constructors' original plans, drawn up in 2008, proceeded on the basis that the aircraft protection needed was rather less robust than what the NRC later decreed was necessary. However, during the course of 2009 the new aircraft protection rule had been approved. What's more, the constructors had designed an external shielding that did not meet the heightened expectation of aircraft protection of the NRC. According to Southern Nuclear Company, 'we began to excavate the foundations for the 5 nuclear islands and turbine buildings in 2009' (NRC 2011b, 21).

The NRC looked at the plans for the shielding and issued a violation notice in October 2010 (NRC 2010). This is because the constructors had failed to adequately meet the new (2009) rule requiring assessment of risks of aircraft protection. This resulted in serious delays to the project, as new designs for shielding had to be prepared and presented. This had knock-on effects for the construction process that were very costly, especially as work had to be suspended and some work already completed had to be changed.

In fact, the NRC had been discussing the design certification of the AP1000 since 2005 (Westinghouse 2011). Indeed the NRC had issued a generic certification of AP1000 designs in January 2006. It was, at that time, assumed by all sides in the nuclear industry that aircraft protection against crashes by large commercial aircraft was not needed for this new plant. From this, it seems plausible to say that the US nuclear safety policy initially resisted aircraft protection ultimately later had a negative unintended consequence by introducing inconsistency into the process. The unintended consequence manifested itself, to a greater or lesser extent, in cost problems for nuclear construction projects. By contrast the UK's nuclear safety regulators (the Office for Nuclear Regulation, ONR) have required aircraft protection for new reactors since 2001. If the NRC had adopted the same strategy as the UK's ONR, then Westinghouse would have had to incorporate this measure from the start and thus avoid the costs that it later suffered.

Westinghouse sued Georgia Power Company (who had issued the contract for the Vogtle power plant to be built) for $900 million to cover the cost of the new shielding arrangements (United States District Court for the District Of Columbia 2013; Litvak 2012). As the court judgement put it: 'Plaintiffs contend that the NRC-imposed Regulatory Changes they made constitute compensable changes under the terms of the EPC (Engineering Procurement and Construction) Agreement, entitling them to adjustments to the contract price and project schedule' (for $900 million) (United States District Court for the District Of Columbia 2013, 3). However, the judgement dismissed the constructors' case. An implication of the judgement was that it was the constructor's problem that they did not get the regulatory requirements right.

Other regulatory problems have beset the construction of the Vogtle and Summer plants. These included problems with filing the correct documentation for parts, a problem with 'backfilling' at the start of the project, and a delay of six months because of a 'rebar' problem (Hals and Flitter 2017). This 'rebar' problem involved fitting part of the foundations in a way that was seen by the NRC as being inconsistent with the plans submitted as part of the licence (O'Donohue 2012). This resulting six months' delay in construction is likely to be very expensive, for the reasons discussed earlier in this paper.

Various (non-regulatory) issues have also been raised to explain cost overruns at these plants and it is debatable what proportion of cost overruns can be ascribed to regulatory issues (Reuters 2017). However, whatever the contribution of regulatory issues, it could be argued that the US regulatory approach could have been more pre-emptive and consistent with regard to the aircraft rule issue. This could have significantly reduced the costs of building the nuclear power plant. In this sense the influence wielded by the nuclear industry over the NRC (insofar as it delayed and confused NRC efforts to make an early, clear, decision) may have been counterproductive to their very interests. Less costs would have been incurred by the nuclear constructors if a prompt intervention soon after 9/11 had been made by the NRC to adopt a rule prescribing comprehensive aircraft shielding.

In the case of the construction of V. C. Summer plant being supervised by the South Carolina generation company SCANA, corruption allegations emerged concerning a lack of candour about delays that the project was facing. A case was brought against executives of SCANA by the Securities and Exchange Commission (SEC). The SEC said that

> SCANA and its senior executives repeatedly deceived investors, regulators, and the public over several years about the status of a $10 billion nuclear energy project. When the truth was revealed, it resulted in hundreds of millions of dollars in losses to SCANA's investors and to South Carolinians.
> (Securities and Exchange Commission 2020)

Following the bankruptcy of Westinghouse in 2017 it seemed touch and go whether the nuclear plants in Georgia and South Carolina would be completed. Indeed V. C. Summer in South Carolina was abandoned, but a decision was made by Georgia Power (which is rather larger than SCANA) to continue building Vogtle 3 and 4. This latter decision was aided by the granting of federal loan guarantees of $3.7 billion (Ciampoli 2019).

At the time of writing (early 2020) the date set by the developers for first generation from Plant Vogtle was said to be sometime in 2021–2022. The total cost of the double reactor plant (2.5 GW in all) was said to be $25 billion (Walton 2018), although it remains to be seen whether this adjusted figure will require further (perhaps considerable) adjustment in an upwards direction. This compares with the original cost estimate for the plant of $14.3 billion. It should also be mentioned that when the earlier Vogtle nuclear power plant was built (completed in the late 1980s), costs escalated around ninefold between original estimate and completion (Patel 2018).

Whatever the arguments about the impact of regulatory decisions, a very big contribution to whether plants are more or less expensive is the amount of time that the developers take to build the plant. As will be discussed in Chapter 8 on the UK, cost overruns due to delays in building plants are said to be the biggest cost killers for nuclear power. For instance, if the plant is projected to be finished in, say five years, a delay of three years will lead to a cost overrun of in excess of at least 60 per cent and perhaps a lot more depending on interest rates applicable to the project.

This leads on to arguments that the problem with nuclear power, at least in the West, is that the sheer complexity and the lack of specialist expertise to deal with the unique engineering problems posed by building nuclear plants is the major problem facing nuclear developers. This discussion will be expanded in Chapter 6 on France and rounded off in the concluding Chapter 10.

US post-Fukushima measures

Soon after the Fukushima nuclear accident, the NRC, now led by Greg Jaczko as the Chairman of the Commission, established a Task Force to examine the safety lessons from the accident and to bring forward proposals to improve reactor safety. The recommendations (NRC 2011a) were similar to those reached in the review established by the UK's ONR (see Chapter 8). In the case of France (Chapter 6), it could be argued that many or most of the recommendations had already been implemented well before the Fukushima accident. Key recommendations included having a stipulated minimum period of redundancy for power and water systems that would allow reactors to be securely cooled in the absence of power from other sources. In addition, there were recommendations requiring backfitting existing light water reactors to ensure hydrogen mitigation and containment venting and also recommendations that stress tests for seismic and flooding risks be conducted.

However (in contrast to the UK), many of the recommendations were later watered down or rejected by the NRC and/or its staff. For example, when it came to 'cooling the spent fuel, preventing a loss-of-coolant accident, and preventing containment failure', the Task Force originally said that licensees would need an extended coping capability to maintain these functions 'for at least 72 hours' (NRC 2011a, 36). However, under a 'FLEX' plan agreed with the Nuclear Energy Institute, this was changed so that it was agreed merely that, 'on-site resources will be used to cope with the first two phases of the casualty for a minimum of the first 24 hours of the event' (i.e. loss of external power event) (NEI 2012, 58). As Lyman (2016, 9) put it: 'plans only have to show that the plants can be self-sufficient for 24 hours – an easier requirement for plant owners to meet than the 72-hour period recommended by the task force'.

Although the NRC Task Force recommended a review of beyond design basis flooding and seismic risks, this was later watered down and, according to Lyman,

> only a few plants may have to proceed with comprehensive flooding assessments. Even those plants may not be subject to new regulatory requirements if owners can show that the cancer risk to the public from meltdowns caused by super floods would still be 'acceptable'.
>
> (Lyman 2016, 12)

Indeed, even these recommendations were undermined when, in early 2019, the NRC voted down even the idea that some plants who face 'bigger floods and earthquakes than they are now required to withstand' (UCS 2019) would automatically be expected to upgrade their safety measures. The NRC recommendations were voted down by a 3–2 majority of Republicans on the NRC (UCS 2019), illustrating how what could be described as anti-egalitarian, individualist cultural biases pervade decisions of the NRC.

Such issues illustrate, at least to critics of US nuclear safety systems, how the emphasis on bias in favour of original licence conditions, and against upgrading safety measures later, limits the ability of the nuclear regulatory system to upgrade safety systems. The discourse of opposition (from the nuclear industry) to deal with circumstances called 'beyond design basis', is strong and generally successful in practice.

The US nuclear industry successfully opposed the installation of filtered containment venting systems (FCVS) in the PWRs. FCVS allows gases that build up in the contained section of the reactor to be released while filtering out the more dangerous radioactive materials so that these are not released. It was argued that the costs of such work would be greater than the benefits. A version of this system has been ordered by the NRC to be installed at the boiling water reactors (BWRs), but BWRs constitute a minority of nuclear reactors in the USA compared to PWRs, and in any case the Union of Concerned Scientists has criticised the orders issued by the NRC even in this respect as being inadequate (Lochbaum 2012).

The US nuclear industry also successfully resisted having to install additional hydrogen mitigation. Hydrogen released from reactors was a key part of the Fukushima accident because it ignited, leading to explosions. This hydrogen mitigation would be achieved via the fitting of Passive Autocatalytic Recombiners (PARs). The NRC staff conducted a cost-benefit analysis and concluded that the 'impact' cost of not adopting the backfit would be a little over three times the 'value' of doing so. The proposed PAR fitting was thus judged not to be cost-effective (NRC Staff 2012).

The cases of the FCVS and the PAR demonstrate, again, how the discourse of opposing measures to upgrade safety on the grounds of 'beyond design basis' considerations proved successful. Efforts by the then NRC Chairman Jaczko to insist that new reactor licences be only granted with measures that fully took account of lessons from Fukushima were rejected by the other members of the NRC members. The NRC Chairman (at the time of writing) Kristine Svinicki has said that 'where the agency (NRC) needs to act quickly rule-making is not the means to act quickly' (Svinicki 2018).

As yet, no post-Fukushima safety rules have been discussed and the prospects of discussions emerging in the near future (at the time of writing) have been set back by the pronounced anti-regulatory atmosphere in the Trump administration. The NRC has relied instead on issuing a few orders which, as discussed, have been criticised for weakening the recommendations of the Task Force.

Conclusion

It might be argued that the institutional setup of the NRC inclines it towards dominance by the nuclear industry. This is because of the political control exercised over the NRC through its governance arrangements, which involves the NRC Commissioners being political appointees. The NRC can be said to lack independence from government as a result since the NRC officials do not take the final decisions, but political appointees do. Attempts by NRC staff to propose measures unacceptable to the nuclear industry have to overcome a steep barrier of likely opposition by NRC Commissioners sympathetic to the specific objections of the nuclear industry. The Commissioners likely to back the positions of the nuclear industry (against what otherwise are the wishes of the NRC officials) will almost always include Commissioners appointed by the Republican industry and often, even, also Commissioners appointed by the Democrats.

The ability of the public to make representations on proposed, or even for new, rule changes can be seen in this context merely as a check on the nuclear-dominated NRC governance structure that they do not move egregiously out of line with that of public opinion. Even correcting this may take time, as possibly was the case with the delays in adopting an aircraft protection rule.

However to adopt a purely institutional focus for the explanation of the resistance by US nuclear regulators to adopt a precautionary approach would be to ignore the impact of cultural context. The point is that if even if a weakly precautionary, ecological modernisation approach to nuclear safety regulation was consensus in the USA, it would seem much less likely that NRC Commissioners would give such strong support to the nuclear industry in their resistance to safety measures. Rather, the existence of sometimes strong anti-egalitarian bias amongst Republicans undermines possibilities for consensus in favour of precautionary safety measures.

On the other hand, anti-nuclear militancy has long since subsided in the USA. To the extent that extent anti-nuclear scepticism still exists it is rarely manifested in terms of civil resistance, and exists mainly still at the level of court actions. Yet in the area of the courts the nuclear industry appears to have copious abilities to influence outcomes for its own objectives.

Arguably the nuclear industry may have too much influence over nuclear safety regulations for their own good. For example, the relative early weakness and inconsistency of the NRC's approach to aircraft protection may have had unintended consequences. Although the NRC initially followed the preferences of the nuclear industry, this proved to have much more costly consequences in the longer run than if the NRC had adopted a policy similar to that of the ONR in the immediate aftermath of 9/11. The changing rulebook and the uncertainties that were associated with this arguably cost the developers a lot of money.

Certainly, in the light of this it would be difficult to label the US nuclear regulatory system as one involving 'containment' of nuclear power, except in the most general sense. Rather the individualist leanings of the dominant bias in the US nuclear regulatory system could be said to be leaning towards 'development'. The fact that nuclear development seems very difficult to obtain in the US, however, may have a lot, ironically, to do with developmental factors. This developmental fact is that nuclear power is less economic compared to other energy technologies. That seems a more plausible explanation for the lack of new nuclear development – as opposed to legal barriers preventing nuclear development.

The argument that strict regulatory standards have been a major reason for the lack of completion of building of nuclear power plants seems to have little weight in view of our analysis in this chapter. Many would argue that the uncompetitive economics of nuclear power appear to be the main factor preventing nuclear development. It is even possible to argue that the sheer inconsistency of US nuclear regulatory standards owing to industrial pressure to relax them has increased costs (with some evidence to that effect in the aircraft protection controversy).

In order to make a full judgement on the issue of whether US nuclear safety regulations are preventing the construction of new plants and the continued operation of existing ones, there really needs to be a comparison with one or more regulatory regimes that clearly have weaker, or, alternatively, stricter standards to see if this variable has an effect. In that case we need to analyse other countries in order to make a firmer conclusion on this. This will be part of the objective in succeeding chapters.

Interviews quoted in this chapter

Interview with Daniel Hirsch (Committee to Bridge the Gap), 22/06/2018 and email communication 26/06/2018

Interview with Peter Bradford, former NRC Commissioner, 04/06/2018; 18/06/2018

Anonymous interview with US nuclear industry consultant, 09/09/2018

Note

1 Note that DBT refers to 'design base threat'.

References

Baumgartner, F.R., and Jones, B.D. (1993) *Agendas and Instability in American Politics.* Chicago: The University of Chicago Press.

Borchardt, R. (2012) 'Policy Issue Notation Vote: Consideration of Additional Requirements for Containment Venting Systems for Boiling Water Reactors with Mark I and Mark II Containments'. www.nrc.gov/reading-rm/doc-collections/commission/secys/2012/2012-0157scy.pdf

Ciampoli, P. (2019) 'DOE Reaches Final Close for Additional Loan Guarantees for Vogtle', *Public Power*, 22 March. www.publicpower.org/periodical/article/doe-reaches-financial-close-additional-vogtle-loan-guarantees

Douglas, M., and Wildavsky, A. (1983) *Risk and Culture*. Berkeley, CA: University of California Press.

Downer, J. (2017) 'The Aviation Paradox: Why We Can "Know" Jetliners But Not Reactors', *Minerva*, 55, 229–248.

EIA (2020) 'Short Term Energy Outlook'. www.eia.gov/outlooks/steo/report/electricity.php

EIA–US Energy Information Administration (2019) *Despite Closures, U.S. Nuclear Electricity Generation in 2018 Surpassed Its Previous Peak*, 21 March. www.eia.gov/todayinenergy/detail.php?id=38792

Federal Register (2003) *Federal Register/Vol. 68, No. 88/Wednesday, 7 May, Notices*. www.govinfo.gov/content/pkg/FR-2003-05-07/pdf/03-11302.pdf (accessed 15 November 2018).

IAEA (International Atomic Energy Agency) (2016) *Safety of Nuclear Power Plants: Design, Specific Safety Requirements, No. SSR-2/1 (Rev. 1)*. Vienna: International Atomic Energy Agency. www-pub.iaea.org/MTCD/Publications/PDF/Pub1715web-46541668.pdf

IAEA (International Atomic Energy Agency) (2020) *USA Country Profile*. https://cnpp.iaea.org/countryprofiles/UnitedStatesofAmerica/UnitedStatesofAmerica.htm

Jaczko, G. (2019) *Confessions of a Rogue Nuclear Regulator*. New York: Simon and Schuster.

Jasanoff, S., and Kim, S. (2009) 'Containing the Atom: Sociotechnical Imaginaries and Nuclear Power in the United States and South Korea', *Minerva*, 47, 119–146.

Komanoff, C. (1981) *Power Plant Cost Escalation*. New York: Komanoff Energy Associates.

Kress, T. (2002) 'Trends and Needs in Regulatory Approaches for Future Reactors', *International Atomic Energy Agency*. https://inis.iaea.org/collection/NCLCollectionStore/_Public/33/024/33024735.pdf (accessed 15 November 2018).

Layzer, J. (2012) *'Open for Business: Conservatives' Opposition to Environmental Regulation*. Cambridge, MA: MIT Press.

Litvak, A. (2012) 'Westinghouse and Georgia Power Sue Each Other over AP1000 Units', *Pittsburgh Business Times*. www.bizjournals.com/pittsburgh/blog/energy/2012/11/westinghouse-and-georgia-power-sue.html (accessed 15 November 2018).

Lochbaum, D. (2012) 'To Filter or Not to Filter, That Is the Question (with Only One Sane Answer)', *Union of Concerned Scientists*, 17 September. https://allthingsnuclear.org/dlochbaum/to-filter-or-not-to-filter-that-is-the-question-with-only-one-sane-answer

Lyman, E.(2016) *Preventing an American Fukushima*. Washington, DC: Union of Concerned Scientists. www.ucsusa.org/sites/default/files/attach/2016/03/Preventing-American-Fukushima-full-report.pdf

NEI (2005) 'PRM-73–12, Comments on the Petition for Rulemaking Submitted by the Committee to Bridge the Gap', Letter from Douglas J. Walters on behalf of Nuclear Energy Institute to Secretary, US Nuclear Regulatory Commission, (Comment 126), 24 January. https://adamswebsearch2.nrc.gov/webSearch2/main.jsp?AccessionNumber=ML050270207 (accessed 15 November 2018).

NEI (2012) *Diverse and Flexible Coping Strategies (Flex) Implementation Guide*. Washington, DC: Nuclear Energy Institute. www.nrc.gov/docs/ML1222/ML12221A205.pdf (accessed 15 November 2018).

Nesbit, S., and Dickman, P. (2015) 'The NRC: Observations on Commissioner Appointments', *Nuclear News*, July, 40–44.

NRC (2005) *Rulemaking Issue Notation Vote: Proposed Rulemaking to Revise 10 Cfr 73.1, Design Basis Threat (Dbt) Requirements*. www.nrc.gov/reading-rm/doc-collections/commission/secys/2005/secy2005-0106/2005-0106scy.pdf (accessed 15 November 2018).

NRC (2010) *Letter to Westinghouse from Robert Sisk of NRC*, 28 October. www.nrc.gov/docs/ML1029/ML102980583.pdf (accessed 15 November 2018).

NRC (2011a) *Recommendations for Enhancing Reactor Safety in the 21st Century: The Near-Term Task Force Review of Insights from the Fukushima Dai-Ichi Accident*. Washington, DC: Nuclear Regulatory Commission. www.nrc.gov/docs/ML1118/ML111861807.pdf (accessed 15 November 2018).

NRC (2011b) *Hearing on Application for a Combined License (COL) to Build Vogtle 3&4*, 27–28 September. Washington, DC: Nuclear Regulatory Commission. https://adamswebsearch2.nrc.gov/webSearch2/main.jsp?AccessionNumber=ML11276A145 (accessed 15 November 2018).

NRC Staff (2012) *Passive Autocatalytic Recombiner (PAR) Requirements for PWRs: Value Impact Assessment*. Washington, DC: NRC. www.nrc.gov/docs/ML0210/ML021090022.pdf (accessed 15 November 2018).

NRC (2013) *Nuclear Regulatory Legislation*. Washington, DC: Nuclear Regulatory Commission. www.nrc.gov/docs/ML1327/ML13274A489.pdf (accessed 15 November 2018).

NRC (2017a) *NRC Regulations Title 10, Code of Federal Regulations CFR§ 50.109 Backfitting*. www.nrc.gov/reading-rm/doc-collections/cfr/part050/part050-0109.html (accessed 15 November 2018).

NRC (2017b) *Code of Federal Regulations Title 10 (CFR 10) § 50.150, Aircraft Impact Assessment*. www.nrc.gov/reading-rm/doc-collections/cfr/part050/part050-0150.html (accessed 15 November 2018).

NRC NUREG/BR-0058 (2004) *Regulatory Analysis Guidelines of the U.S. Nuclear Regulatory Commission*. Washington, DC: U.S. Nuclear Regulatory Commission Office of Nuclear Regulatory Research. www.nrc.gov/reading-rm/doc-collections/nuregs/brochures/br0058/br0058r4.pdf (accessed 15 November 2018).

O'Donohue, K. (2012) *Letter from NRC to B. Ivey of Southern Nuclear Company Concerning Notice of Violation*, 18 May. https://adamswebsearch2.nrc.gov/webSearch2/main.jsp?AccessionNumber=ML12139A192 (accessed 15 November 2018).

Patel, S. (2018) 'How Vogtle's Nuclear Expansion Plan's Costs Escalated', *PowerMag*, 18 September. www.powermag.com/how-the-vogtle-nuclear-expansions-costs-escalated/

Petti, J., Buongiorno, J., Corradini, M., and Parsons, J. (2018) *The Future of Nuclear Energy in a Carbon-Constrained World*. Boston: MIT. https://energy.mit.edu/wp-content/uploads/2018/09/The-Future-of-Nuclear-Energy-in-a-Carbon-Constrained-World.pdf (accessed 15 November 2018).

Securities and Exchange Commission (SEC) (2020) United States Securities and Exchange Commission, Plaintiff, v. Scana Corporation, Dominion Energy South Carolina, Inc. (f/k/a South Carolina Electric& Gas Company), Kevin B. Marsh, and Stephen A. Byrne, Defendants, 27 February, Columbia, South Carolina. www.sec.gov/litigation/complaints/2020/scana-complaint-022720.pdf

Shapiro, S. (2011) 'The Evolution of Cost-Benefit Analysis in US Regulatory Decision Making', in D. Levi-Faur (ed.) *A Handbook on the Politics of Regulation*. Cheltenham: Edward Elgar, pp. 385–396.

Shapiro, S., and Morrall, J. (2012) 'The Triumph of Regulatory Politics: Benefit: Cost Analysis and Political Salience', *Regulation & Governance*, 6, 189–206.

Southern Company (2018) *Plant Vogtle 3&4*. www.southerncompany.com/innovation/nuclear-energy/plant-vogtle-3-and-4.html (accessed 15 November 2015).

Svinicki (2018) *RIC 2018: Keynote Speaker: NRC Chairman Kristine L. Svinicki*. www.youtube.com/watch?v=uLw22qyxD28

Toke, D. (2018) *Low Carbon Politics*. Abingdon: Routledge.

Union of Concerned Scientists (2019) *Press Release: NRC Guts a Critical Safety Regulation, Recklessly Disregarding the Critical Lessons of the Fukushima Disaster*, 24 January. www.ucsusa.org/about/news/critical-lessons-fukushima-disaster

United States District Court for the District of Columbia (2013) *Stone & Webster, Inc. Et Al V. Georgia Power Company Et Al, United States District Court for the District of Columbia, Civil Action No. 12–1783 (Ckk), Memorandum Opinion*, 30 August. https://Cases.Justia.Com/Federal/District-Courts/District-Of-Columbia/Dcdce/1:2012Cv01783/156731/33/0.Pdf?Ts=1411526530 (accessed 15 November 2018).

Walker, J., and Wellock, T. (2010) *A Short History of Nuclear Regulation, 1946–2009*. Rockville, MD: US Nuclear Regulatory Commission.

Walton, R. (2018) 'Vogtle Cost Upgrade Causes Rethinking of $25B Nuclear Plant's Future', *Power Engineering*, 9 August. www.power-eng.com/2018/08/09/vogtle-cost-upgrade-causes-rethinking-of-nuclear-plant-s-future/

Westinghouse (2011) *Report on AP1000 Design Certification and Design Finalization Project*. www.nrc.gov/docs/ML1307/ML13074A028.pdf (accessed 15 November 2018).

World Nuclear Association (2020) *Nuclear Power in the USA*. www.world-nuclear.org/information-library/country-profiles/countries-t-z/usa-nuclear-power.aspx

5 Nuclear power and safety in China

Incremental growth of nuclear capacity in historical context

China's nuclear power development began before the start of the reform and opening-up policy which took place after the end of the 1970s. The initial nuclear power infrastructure was developed in line with the development of the national nuclear weapons strategy (Fiori and Zhou 2016, 161). The ruling Chinese Communist Party (CCP) began to build the first nuclear power plant against the backdrop of the national craving for a so-called *endogenous innovation* campaign, which had taken root at the founding of the People's Republic of China. This development rule emphasises a need of national economic policies no longer controlled by other foreign states. Such beliefs or notions are rooted in the thinking of the key political figures, from Chiang Kai-shek to Mao Zedong to Deng Xiaoping (Lampton 2014, 160–161).

To some extent, economic nationalism facilitates the possible resistance and counter-preparation necessary to defend against the return of colonialism and imperialism. Such ideas, although gradually loosened after the reform and opening-up policy of 1979, are still to a certain extent embedded in the core of the country's industrial policy. Its implicit value stipulates the development strategy while limiting and forging the development trajectory of nuclear power generation.

In the 1960s, science and policy elites began to plan the application of atomic energy in military- and industrial-power generation. The planning and construction of the Daya Bay nuclear power plant, China's first nuclear power station, was carried out under the supervision of Peng Shilu, who had successfully participated in the overall design of China's first-generation nuclear-powered submarine. Pressurised Water Reactors (PWRs) were successfully placed during the time of development. The endogenously designed nuclear power, which policymakers praised, was finally connected to the grid in 1991 (Stevenson 2016), and its capacity reached 298 MWe (Zhu et al. 2016, 142–143). This achievement to some extent seemed to acknowledge the policymakers' value of conviction, given the absence of nuclear power over the years. It also seemed to meet the policymakers' value orientation, which reflected their inclination to promote domestically produced reactors although such a tendency does not value and appreciate the use of the 'best technology'.

The policy and scientific elites incrementally targeted and advanced the innovative adaptation of nuclear power plants, which was initially seen as a relatively reliable strategy. After the Qinshan Power Plant came the successful grid-connected power generation of the Ling Ao Nuclear Power Plant in Shenzhen, Guangdong Province. Its reactor is a domestic M310-CPR-1000, and the capacity of the Ling Ao Nuclear Power Plant's two units has reached 2052 MWe (Zhu et al. 2016, 143). However, the extension of nationalism in this field did not imply the possibility of commercialisation of nuclear power utility.

After the complexity of nuclear power as a uniquely sensitive industry was realised by the policy elites, the pursuit of endogenous design gave way to the mentality of 'catching up' with the West. In 1994, China's first commercial nuclear power station was completed in Daya Bay, Guangdong Province. In the following two decades, the nuclear power project in China has been developed parallel to conventional energy and has been aimed at combining military and civilian purposes, so the project has been developed in a complementary way. On one hand, the policy elites require independent research and endogenous development to provide research outcomes.

On the other hand, the policy elites were also reluctant to stand still and were lured into connecting with the international community with limited scope. France, Canada, and Russia also cooperated with China during this period, and policy elites have sought to introduce foreign nuclear power technology, in part to ameliorate domestic nuclear capacity. These cooperative projects have since opened up the construction of a number of large-scale commercial nuclear power plants, which have undergone the bidding processes and contract management system. Until 2004, the nature of the development of nuclear power was slow exploration. Not many policy elites were willing to engage in such business development, mainly because of its thorny technical and political nature (Xu 2010). As of 2004, China had only 9.1 GWe of installed capacity, accounting for only 2 per cent of the country's electricity generation (Fiori and Zhou 2016, 161).

Investments in new nuclear power generation

The incremental increase has changed since the beginning of 2000. A more noticeable policy shift emerged in 2004, a watershed year, when China's policy elites actively started to pursue nuclear energy as a perceived 'alternative energy' worthy of cultivation. In the policy paper introduced that year, we see that the development's tone changed from a slightly conservative description of 'moderate' to 'active development' (Zhang 2015, 58). This year can be considered a critical juncture, marking a watershed in the trajectory of nuclear power generation. The energy shortages encountered in early 2000 seem to have encouraged a new policy preference among politicians: it seems that to ensure the diversity and reliability of energy security, the Hu-Wen administration began to seek new alternatives. The state economic planning body, the National Development and Reform Commission (NDRC), issued a new policy document specifying the state's opinion on nuclear energy industry policy on acquiring new technologies, moving from a conservative endogenous overprotection of key security industries to the new idea of participation in global competition by acquiring the world's most cutting-edge technology.

The NDRC aims to deploy an industrial policy that facilitates the export of Chinese technology to the developing world to compete with the forerunners in the market through the learning networks built by advanced economies. The central government's policy elites around that time started to focus on the possibility of introducing to China the AP1000-model reactor Westinghouse had produced (Zhu et al. 2016, 142), which implies that the ruling party pays less attention to the previous imperative of endogenous innovation emphasising 'domestic technology' and turns the future of China's nuclear power plants toward relying on the third generation of technology so that, as some academic elites and technocrats expect, China can be better integrated into global standards in terms of safety requirements and productivity.

As one of the biggest beneficiaries of this policy transformation process, Westinghouse won the bid to do key strategic business with China, installing the first AP1000s in Sanmen, Zhejiang Province, and Haiyang, Shandong Province. These third-generation AP1000 nuclear power units were the first AP1000 units in the world under construction. This strategic business operation allowed China to explore the most advanced experimental field of this latest third-generation reactor. To some extent, the institutional change seems to satisfy the two parties' perceived interests. Chinese policy elites look forward to cooperating with advanced Western technology innovators, seeking a curve overtaking the development of technology, and Westinghouse has sought to obtain the funds to test the latest technology on the ground that has never been adopted elsewhere to demonstrate the innovative technology's availability.

To meet the third-generation security standards, the central government, through the NDRC, has begun to lead and intervene in the policy options and development of reactor technology. During this period of active nuclear power development, the National Development and Reform Commission (NDRC)[1] issued the Medium- and Long-Term Development Plan for Nuclear Power (2005–2020), in which it was pointed out that by 2020, the main design of new nuclear reactors should adhere to the standards by which nuclear power plants operate in the advanced economies. Therefore, the main design indicators for all nuclear power plants under construction must be 'close to or meet the equivalent requirements of the US Nuclear Power User Requirements Document (URD) or the European Nuclear Power User Requirements Document (EUR)', also known as an advanced level of organisation recognised by the World Association of Nuclear Operators (NDRC 2007, 9).

On the assumption that the most advanced Western standards are guaranteed to be the safest, China's policy elites expected that China's security risks could be largely reduced with the introduction of the new third-generation nuclear power reactor units. Such expectations have indirectly led to the official conservative attitude in approving the old domestic second-generation plants, which were driven by endogenous research and development efforts in reactor technology. The policymakers have clarified that only the latest third-generation reactor technology is favourable for construction although China has developed several models of domestic reactors, such as the CNP-300, CNP-600, CNP-1000, CRP-1000, CAP1400, and Hualong 1 (Chen et al. 2018, 82).

The types of third-generation nuclear power reactors present in China include three cooperative projects with three different countries: the AREVA M310 reactor in cooperation with France; the AP1000 reactor in cooperation with Westinghouse in the United States (Fiori and Zhou 2015, 247); and the BN-800, VVER-1000, and VVER-1200 reactors in cooperation with Russia (Chen et al. 2018, 82). Among them, the ACPR-1000+ revision of No. 5 and No. 6 units of the Tianwan Nuclear Power Plant near Lianyungang, Jiangsu Province, has a reactor with the world's first core-melt trap (or 'core catcher'). Its main function is to collect and cool the core during an accident to prevent it from penetrating the floor, thereby effectively preventing leakage of radioactive materials in a severe accident. Such a new design is meant to prevent serious consequences while having the ability to resist aircraft impact. However, these projects (from No. 3 to No. 8 units in Tianwan) are still under construction, which has been delayed and has exceeded the expected due date for many years. We will elaborate on it later.

The safety philosophy and nuclear regulatory regime

Policymakers believed that China's regulations before the Fukushima nuclear accident in Japan were not sufficient enough to prevent a similar incident. Before that, the People's Republic of China Radioactive Pollution Prevention and Control Law (*Zhonghua renming gongheguo fangshexing furan fangzhi fa*) was the main regulation governing nuclear power safety. However, as stated by Zhao Chengkun, the current Deputy Director of the National Nuclear Safety Administration (also the Executive Deputy Director of the Expert Committee of the China Nuclear Energy Industry Association), the law lacks the establishment and implementation of basic guidelines, principles, legal measures for nuclear safety. Major issues such as the responsibility for nuclear safety have not been stipulated, and they cannot be 'adapted to the needs of the safe and efficient development of nuclear energy' (Zhao 2018, 11–15). The Medium- and Long-Term Development Plan for Nuclear Power (2005–2020), launched in March 2006, to some extent marked China's watershed of nuclear power development.

Before the Fukushima accident, nuclear energy was situated in the strategic energy industry, emphasising the consideration that both the economy and safety must be taken into account, which to some extent foreshadows the necessary trade-off between economic costs and security measures. Such a redemption implies a step towards the localisation of equipment so that rapid development can be implemented without being restricted by foreign safety regulations. To achieve this purpose, the following year, the State Council promulgated the Regulations on the Supervision and Administration of Civil Nuclear Safety Equipment (*Minyong he anquan shebei jiandu guanli tiaoli*) to pave the way for this consideration.

Such new regulation clarified the State Council's Department's supervision and inspection duties and processes. In addition, in 2012, the State Council's executive meeting passed the '12th Five-Year' Guidelines for Nuclear Safety and Radioactivity Prevention and Vision 2020 (*He anquan yu fangshexing fangzhi 'shierwu' guihua ji 2020 nian yuanjing mubiao*), in which nuclear power was included in the national strategic emerging industry plan, considered as an alternative energy mix for energy transition. Since the central government promulgated the Nuclear Safety Law in 2017, a new nuclear safety concept has taken shape in the written documents of the regulation for the first time.

This new regulation increases the legal liability of enterprises through explicit and severe penalties, such as increasing fines and corresponding costs. The discourse regarding the safety philosophy seems to focus on the 'cost-benefit' idea. Although Zhao Chengkun, the former director of the National Nuclear Safety Administration and the current deputy director of the National Nuclear Safety Administration (also the deputy director of the Expert Committee of the China Nuclear Energy Association), stated that the safety philosophy is 'strict management, defense in depth, independent supervision, and comprehensive protection', Xi Jinping advocated that 'China shall put equal emphasis on development and security, equal rights and responsibilities, autonomy and cooperation, and symptoms and root causes' (Zhao 2018, 11–15). The statement is reflective, albeit with ambiguity, of Article 2 of the Nuclear Safety Law: China shall 'take adequate precautions, protection, mitigation, and supervision of nuclear facilities, nuclear materials and related radioactive waste to prevent technical, human, or natural disaster'.

This law applies to nuclear accidents and activities where one seeks to minimise the radiological consequences. On the one hand, it puts forward the statement of safety in laws and regulations regardless of cost. On the other hand, it emphasises that safety and development are equally important, which seems similar to the safety philosophy of the US cost-benefit argument.

Indeed, such laws and regulations seem to contain a discretionary space for interpretation and variant enforcement. After the Fukushima accident, China carried out repairs and improvements based on its reactors' conditions and different reactor types, combining economic and safety considerations. The actions and inactions of each nuclear power plant were not coordinated with each other, and the central government seemed to have no one-size-fits-all regulatory requirements. However, looking at the increased accident prevention and mitigation measures, we can identify that some plants have increased safety and advanced measures, such as measures for responding to earthquakes, tsunamis, and large aircraft collisions. For instance, Tianwan Nuclear Power Station introduced special safety measures in the new containment, the purpose of which is mainly to remove hydrogen in the containment under conditions exceeding the design basis accident (Guan et al. 2012; Jiang et al. 2015, 66).

As pointed out by three Jiangsu Nuclear Power Co., Ltd., engineers at Tianwan Station, the Passive Autocatalytic Recombiner ensured that under the dehydration design basis accident, the hydrogen volume concentration in the containment can be controlled to be less than 4 per cent. In the case of a super-design basis accident, the hydrogen gas volume concentration generated by the reaction in the containment shall not be able to exceed 10 per cent (Guan et al. 2012, 155). At Tianwan Nuclear Power Plant, as described by Yiao Gang, director of the Nuclear Safety Division of Jiangsu Nuclear Power Co., Ltd., the reactor unit has been equipped with a core catcher to ensure that the core melt does not leak under severe accident conditions (Yiao 2011, 33). However, it must be noted that not every nuclear power plant has been equipped with a core catcher, and the central state does not mandate that all nuclear power plants should install such a facility. According to Liu Yu, an engineer at Taishan Nuclear Power Joint Venture Co., Ltd., efforts are only being made at present to study whether it is necessary to design and modify existing structures. After all, installation of such a facility will add complexity and the redesign process is difficult (Liu et al. 2012, 35–38). It must be noted that the potential high cost of the redesign process may impede the decision requiring all reactor units to comply with a national standard.

Such a challenge is reflected in the price of Taishan Nuclear Power Plant's EPR unit, which, to some extent, marked the difficulty of installation of relevant backfitting measures. As described by Hong Cui, a Tianjin Electric Power Construction Company engineer, the high requirements for the quality of complex constructions, such as the construction of core structures and the double-layer safe construction of the EPR, have increased the construction difficulty (Cui 2009). In addition, after the Fukushima nuclear power disaster, with regard to backfitting existing PWRs, especially FCVS, China's various nuclear power plants also have various arrangements due to different reactor units.

Generally speaking, the central government has not mandated FCVS. As described by Shengjie Li and Laing Wen, two engineers from CGNPC Engineering Co., Ltd. in Shenzhen,

> whether the FCVS is installed or not varies depending on the reactor type of the nuclear plant. First, the second-generation plus nuclear power plants that are based on the M310 model are all equipped with FCVS; while the other third-generation nuclear power plants are different: Hualong 1 set up FCVS, but the EPR of Taishan Nuclear Power Plant did not set up FCVS.
>
> (Li and Liang 2019, 66)[2]

Furthermore, the plants with AP1000 reactors are not equipped with FCVS (Li and Liang 2019). It must be noted that although the Taishan Nuclear Power Plant's EPR reactor does not have FCVS, it has added a new core catcher, which is an important safety design for EPR (Cui 2009).

In addition to the backfitting measures, the central government has been prudent in developing new nuclear projects. From 2015 to 2018, China's nuclear power plant development projects stagnated, and all nuclear power plants were under review. The Chinese nuclear power industry has experienced what they called a state of 'zero approval', which means that new proposals, including inland nuclear power plants, have not been further operated. However, in early 2019, this situation quietly began to change. On 30 January 2019, China National Nuclear Corporation (CNNC)'s Zhangzhou Nuclear Power Plant Phase I Project No. 1

and No. 2 units and CNNC's Huizhou Taipingling Nuclear Power Plant Phase I Project No. 1 and No. 2 units were approved (People's Daily 2019). After such a period, it seems that the central government is preparing to restart the development of nuclear power. The Chinese White Paper on Nuclear Safety, released in September of that year, details many new policies on nuclear safety.

After the Fukushima nuclear accident, new backfitting also played a part in the development of the iconic Hualong 1 reactor. To realise the development of a Chinese independent brand for markets in emerging countries, China's National Nuclear Safety Administration revised the Safety Regulations for the Design of Nuclear Power Plants (*He donglichang sheji anquan guiding*, HAF102–2016). Such an effort was also aimed at matching the updates of the International Atomic Energy Agency (IAEA) standards. In terms of safety principles and concepts, HAF102–2016 is a detailed regulation based on the rules of SSR-2/1 (Rev. 1) that the IAEA issued.

The entire article is divided into five parts, each of which is relevant to the safety goal, the concept of defence-in-depth, design safety management, technical requirements, overall civilian nuclear power design, and nuclear power plant system design. In the regulation of HAF102–2016, Article 6.3.5.4 stipulates that 'design measures must be taken to prevent the loss of the integrity of the containment structure in all states of the nuclear power plant'. This implies that the requirements for physical protection are more stringent. In particular, the design provides requirements for resisting malicious impact from commercial aircraft. However, SSR-2/1 (Rev. 1) by the IAEA does not seem to require this, and it was not required in the previous version of HAF102–2004. As engineers Chengwen Hao, Baojian Gao, and Dapeng Gong of China Nuclear Engineering Consulting Co., Ltd. pointed out, such new measures are also required in the Hualong 1 technical agreement.

> The major design of Hualong 1 uses an aircraft-resistant APC [airplane crash] shell protection. The mechanical properties of the APC shell are very high, which can resist anti-aircraft impact. In addition to meeting the general technical specification for Steel Bar Mechanical Connection (JGJ107–2016), it must also meet the instant load impact test, aka [also known as] the anti-aircraft impact test.
>
> (Hao et al. 2019, 276)

The new regulations clearly require that at the initial stage of design, the design extension conditions beyond the scope of the design basis accident should be considered. That is, the new regulations propose requirements for a comprehensive safety assessment known as Design Extension Conditions (DEC). In more detail, the safety condition should be as low as reasonably achievable and mitigate the radiological consequences of such an accident to the greatest extent possible. At present, DECs are already used in some nuclear power plants under construction in China, such as the Taishan Nuclear Power Station as well as the Fangcheng gang and Fuqing Nuclear Power Plants (Li et al. 2017). In general, Hualong 1, as

China's first third-generation nuclear power technology with independent intellectual property rights, has adopted the safety design concept of 'the combination of active and passive power'. It has 177 fuel assemblies, a single stack arrangement, and a double-layer safety shell (Yi and Gu 2016).

As for the design of the containment, as Wen Fan and Bo Yuan, two engineers at Fujian Fuqing Nuclear Power Co., Ltd. pointed out,

> compared with the reactor AP1000, Hualong 1 requires a *lower cost*. For the concrete structure, the heat extraction is completed by a dedicated heat exchanger inside the containment of Hualong 1, whereas for the AP1000, there is a gap between the steel containment and the outer concrete containment. Such steel containment not only requires great strength and good thermal conductivity but also it needs to have a sufficient capacity of resistance to electrochemical corrosion and thermal stress corrosion, so AP1000 steel containment has high requirements for materials and processes. The production and operation costs are extremely high.
>
> (Fan and Bo 2017, 168–169)

Safety regulator, stakeholders, and nuclear power institutional system

It is necessary to clarify several important stakeholders and understand the relationship between the safety regulator and specific stakeholders in China's nuclear power governance structure. The safety regulators (i.e. the National Nuclear Safety Administration and the Atomic Energy Authority) belong to different ministries. The National Nuclear Safety Administration is under the jurisdiction of the Ministry of Ecology and Environment and is responsible for the supervision of nuclear safety, radiation safety, and radiation environment management nationwide. The National Atomic Energy Authority is a governmental unit under the Ministry of Industry and Information Technology's jurisdiction, and it is responsible for formulating development guidelines, plans, and industry standards for the use of civilian atomic energy. The National Atomic Energy Authority's responsibilities also include drafting policies and regulations, researching nuclear energy business and development plans, setting industry standards, organising nuclear safety and nuclear material control, monitoring nuclear technology equipment imports and exports, decommissioning nuclear facilities, and managing radioactive waste.

In accordance with the White Paper on Nuclear Safety published in 2019 (People's Daily 2019), the director of the National Nuclear Safety Administration is also the deputy minister of the Ministry of Ecology and Environment and assumes the main responsibility for safety supervision. In this government apparatus, the staff coordinate the National Nuclear Safety Expert Committee to supervise and review various safety statute licences. The staffs of the National Atomic Energy Authority and the National Nuclear Safety Administration are technical bureaucrats. Although the two agencies have ostensible linkages, in recent years, one can identify that the National Nuclear Safety Administration's responsibility in the administrative reorganisation process seems to be clearly separated from that of the past. The National Nuclear Safety Administration was established in October 1984. At that time, its responsibility was to conduct independent nuclear safety supervision and management of Chinese civilian nuclear facilities. When the unit was established in 1984, it was affiliated with the State Scientific and Technological Commission (*Guojia kexue jishu weiyuanhui*), a former Ministry of Science and Technology government apparatus. Since 1990, the deputy director of the National Science and Technology Commission has also been the director of the National Nuclear Safety Administration.

However, in 1998, the National Nuclear Safety Administration merged into the State Environmental Protection Administration (the State Environmental Protection Administration was later upgraded to the Ministry of Environmental Protection), and since 1998 the agency's director has also been the deputy director of the State Environmental Protection Administration (Zhu 2009, 98). The head of the National Atomic Energy Authority is also the deputy head of the unit to which he or she belongs, which is also the deputy minister of the Ministry of Industry and Information Technology. To some extent, the heads of these two organisations are not affiliated with each other and belong to different organisations, even if they are both technocratic appointees (for their expert knowledge), nominated and appointed by the Central Organization Department (*Zhongzu Bu*). The Central Organization Department appoints China's civil servants. Generally speaking, the appointment and removal process is secretive and opaque, and the Party Central Organization Department arranges personnel.

An organisation, whether it is the National Nuclear Safety Administration, the National Atomic Energy Authority, the Ministry of Ecology and Environment, or the Ministry of Industry and Information Technology, has the political power to influence the appointment and removal of personnel under its jurisdiction. Bureaucrats govern this method of cadre management. The party chooses the perceived suitable candidates based on their professional and technical backgrounds and experience (Brødsgaard 2012b, 2017). For example, Hua Liu, Deputy Minister of the Ministry of Ecology and Environment and Director of the National Nuclear Safety Administration, who took office in 2018, is an engineer with a bachelor's degree in nuclear radiation physics from the National University of Defense Technology and a master's degree in radiation protection and nuclear safety at the Chinese Academy of Atomic Energy. In the past, most of his service experiences were in nuclear-related departments. Before taking this position, he served in the National Nuclear Safety Administration, the Nuclear Safety Center of the National Science and Technology Commission, the Nuclear Safety Center of the Environmental Protection Administration, the Nuclear Safety Management Division, the Nuclear Safety Supervision Department, etc.

Although there has emerged an increasingly independent safety regulatory system in China's nuclear energy governance structure, several economic and political actors in such system seem to have begun to demonstrate more vexing interests interlinked with each other because nuclear power generation is considered a strategic industry. Four nuclear power groups are important economic entities in the policy network encouraging diversified use of energy sources: CNNC; CGNPC; China Nuclear Engineering Corporation, Ltd.; and State Nuclear Power Technology Corporation, Ltd., which was in 2015 merged and restructured with State Power Investment Corporation, Ltd. The NDRC directed and introduced this policy. Each of them has played a unique role in the history of China's nuclear power development. All of them belong to a few key central state-owned enterprises, whose assets are supervised by the state-owned Assets Supervision and Administration Commission (SASAC), which acts as a shareholder-monitoring asset manager (Brødsgaard 2012a).

The most important entity among these state-controlled firms is the China Nuclear Industry Corporation. As a large state-owned enterprise, it was transformed from the former Ministry of Nuclear Industry. It is now composed of more than 100 affiliated companies or government research institutes affiliated with their group, including China Nuclear Industry Construction Group Co., Ltd., which the central command transferred to CNNC, Ltd. in early 2018. China Nuclear Industry Construction Group Co., Ltd. was originally one of the central enterprises SASAC managed. It is not only the main investor and owner of many nuclear power plants in China; it has also led the way for the technical development of nuclear weapons and nuclear power since the mid-1960s. The China Nuclear Industry Corporation was given the mission of independent technological innovation (i.e. the aforementioned endogenous innovation) (Forrest and Braun 2017, 32). Headquartered in Beijing, its business includes but is not limited to research and development or construction and operations in the fields of nuclear weapons, nuclear power, nuclear fuel technology, etc. Its business covers the initial projects of Qinshan and Tianwan and even the construction of the Chashma nuclear power plant in Pakistan.

Another strong competitor of this group is CGNPC, located in southern China and headquartered in Shenzhen, Guangdong Province. CGNPC also consists of more than 30 major member companies. The purpose of its establishment was to build another nuclear power plant in Daya Bay to supply electricity to Guangdong Province and Hong Kong. It was listed as a central state-owned enterprise in 2012, and the SASAC supervises it. Similar to CNNC, CGNPC's business includes nuclear power production, engineering construction, technology research and development, nuclear fuel-supply security systems, and even the development of renewable energy, such as wind power, hydropower, and solar energy, as well as energy-conservation technology solutions.

However, unlike the CNNC, CGNPC was more inclined to purchase reactor technology directly from overseas at the beginning of its establishment. The reactor deployed in Daya Bay in 1994 was the M310 reactor Framatome, a French enterprise, had designed (NTI 2011; Forrest and Braun 2017, 33). This does not mean that CGNPC does not design. After the completion of the nuclear power project in Daya Bay, CGNPC created a domestically produced reactor design (model CPR-1000), which China's preparatory electric field later used. The emergence of the technological innovation resulted from the introduction of and learning from overseas technology.

In addition to the previously mentioned two important power groups related to the design and development of reactor technology, a new strategic central state-owned enterprise, State Nuclear Power Technology Corporation, is another large enterprise that shapes China's nuclear power development. State Nuclear Power Technology Corporation was established in 2007. The enterprise was assigned the task of signing contracts with foreign partners on behalf of the country, and it was tasked with conducting technology transfers of the most advanced third-generation nuclear power technology (AP1000). The company is also considered one of the main carriers and research and development platforms to upgrade its technological know-how through digestion and absorption of new technologies adapted from abroad.

In 2015, the NDRC and China Power Investment Corporation were restructured to establish the China Power Investment Corporation. At present, four units are under construction (Zhejiang Sanmen Nuclear Power Station, No. 1 and No. 2 units, and Shandong Haiyang Nuclear Power Station, No. 1 and No. 2 units), all of which are AP1000 models. One of the reasons China Power Investment Group was ordered to be restructured was the lack of competition in this field.

In 2002, China Power Investment Corporation inherited all of the nuclear power assets the former State Power Corporation had owned. It was the owner of the third domestic nuclear power operation licence, after CNNC and CGNPC. However, China Power Investment Corporation has been weaker than these two nuclear power giants in terms of nuclear power operation and performance. The State Nuclear Power Technology Corporation that merged with it had the skills of nuclear power plant design as well as research and development capabilities. Despite the lack of operating experience (it does not have a licence from the State Council) in the past, it was the lead party and recipient of the third-generation AP1000 nuclear power technology and the lead agency in implementing the demonstration project of domestic nuclear reactor technology, CAP1400/1700, which is considered 'domestic third generation'. To compete with the other two giants, the State Nuclear Power Technology Corporation and China Power Investment Group were merged together, becoming two subsidiaries of China Power Investment Corporation.

With the division of labour, China Power Investment Group is responsible for the conventional electricity sector, and the State Nuclear Power Technology Corporation took over the responsibilities of China Power Investment Group for the development of the nuclear power sector. With the restructuring completed, China Power Investment Corporation is considered a more comprehensive energy enterprise group in China that contains businesses including hydropower, thermal power, nuclear power, and renewable-energy assets. Its subsidiary, China Power Investment Corporation, is the only nuclear-powered electricity producer among the five major generational power groups that monopolise the electricity market in China.[3]

These actors' participation and the institutional changes involved in the operation process reflect to some extent the evolving trajectory of the NDRC's ability to intervene in national champions of strategic industries. In this development trajectory, we can see a type of institutional pattern that does not completely rely on the competition principle. When the policy elite decided to turn to foreign cooperation, it also implemented supplementary industrial policies, seeking to guide, integrate, and reallocate domestic industrial resources. Despite the need for policy change, the top-down mode of industrial policy also existed, seeking to interact with the key actors in the industrial structure (Pearson 2011; Zhou and Liu 2016). State managers, state-owned enterprise leaders, and foreign science and technology elites have formed a consensus-based policy to avoid social risk and encourage peacekeeping strategies (Xu 2010). The process of change during this period is gradual and slow, emphasising the protection of monopoly enterprises while cultivating its role as the industry's main development actor. This reflects the characteristics of the changes in laws and regulations governing the policy-making model of fragmentary authoritarianism (Mertha 2009).

Departmentalism inherits to some extent the principle of promoting limited competition in China's established political economic system (Yang 2017; Zang and Musheno 2017). In the case of the central state-owned enterprises involved in nuclear power generation, the NDRC does not favour a complete monopoly but emphasises the functional division of the administrative system. Some groups have deliberately been created. Sometimes they are united and occasionally compete with each other in specific areas of businesses. In addition to the already mentioned three major State Council-licenced nuclear power suppliers, China Nuclear Engineering Corporation Limited, which specialises in nuclear power plant construction, is also an important actor in the governance system of nuclear power development. The company is responsible for the construction of nuclear power engineering equipment related to reactor technology, such as Pressurised Water Reactors, experimental fast neutron reactors, and heavy-water reactors, as well as the construction of various series of units with 300 000-, 600 000-, 700 000-, and 1 million-kilowatt capacities of nuclear power plants.

In addition to being responsible for the construction of the domestic nuclear plants, such as those in Qinshan and Daya Bay, it also managed to complete the first and second phases of the Chashma nuclear power plant in Pakistan. It has the capacity to build AP1000 and EPR advanced Pressurised Water Reactors. It is noteworthy that, like the CNNC, the company also integrates military and civil engineering projects into its core business. However, it is worth noting that, in the political economy's structure, economic actors are subject to the intervention of superagencies such as the NDRC, and at the same time, they are subject to the results of fragmented and contested policies in some other policy areas (Pearson 2005). Such structural constraints lead to unintended and slow outcomes.

A significant phenomenon that can be identified in recent developments is the emphasis on the pursuit of the latest reactors designed overseas. The policy elites have also begun to consider expanding the investment of the nuclear fuel cycle hierarchically. An increasing number of international cooperation projects led by central state-owned enterprises have been launched. In the past ten years, the central state-owned enterprises have strategically invested in developing countries, including Namibia, Zimbabwe, Kazakhstan, and Mongolia. They establish subsidiaries, carrying out mergers and acquisitions of overseas uranium mines and other initiatives to secure a long-term supply of resources to meet the state's imperative of self-sufficiency in its energy supply (Zhang 2015, 61–62) because, as some believed, uranium resources are the basis of any nuclear energy development.

Mastering the access to overseas uranium mines allows China to take the initiative in completing the nuclear fuel cycle. In the 11th Five-Year Guideline, the State Council encouraged overseas trading of uranium from Canada, Australia, Africa, and Central Asia; central state-owned enterprises such as CNNC and CGNPC have taken the lead in mining activities overseas (Zhou 2011, 4364). In China, satellite imaging in Lanzhou, Emeishan, and Hanzhong also shows the expansion of the nuclear industry supply base (Stevenson 2016).

These expansions also entail the purchase of the technology for reprocessing nuclear fuel from abroad to acquire the knowledge and equipment for the treatment of spent fuel at the end of the nuclear fuel cycle. The perceived importance of the investment in these devices and know-how led to corporate strategies in cultivating the ability to reuse spent nuclear fuel and dispose of nuclear waste for new reactors. At the same time, this ability means that the need to introduce new technologies by cooperating with policy elites in advanced countries has become the mainstay of the state managers of Chinese nuclear power suppliers.

The economic actors' interests depend on the successful transfer of technology through international cooperation, enabling China to make a possible qualitative leap in manufacturing capacity. However, such a leap, in this sensitive industrial field, seems to carry a more complex social and economic burden than other centrally designed key technology industries, such as renewables. Such burdens are deeply mismatched with local grassroots groups in other developed countries and regions, making it difficult to find supporters in the localities' unplanned linear interest chains.

The coming of nuclear renaissance?

In 2011, after the Fukushima nuclear accident, the construction of the nuclear cycle showed new twists and turns. In view of the new situation, the central government tends to follow the trend of advanced economies, and it has begun to increase the cost of nuclear power construction for safety concerns. Such an initiative is also proposed against the backdrop of rising public awareness of the risks of nuclear power. After the incident, the public collectively asked relevant government authorities to issue more information about the development of nuclear power, and it requested more transparency in official decision-making processes (Thomson 2011). Not only did the State Council request that all nuclear power construction be suspended, but the central government-coordinated National Security Bureau, the National Energy Administration, and the China Earthquake

Administration jointly invited members of the expert group of the Central Academy of Sciences to conduct safety inspections for each nuclear power plant. In such a state of rising international and domestic pressure, each nuclear power plant was required to issue short-, medium-, and long-term plans after inspection to prevent nuclear accidents like Fukushima.

The new safety measures for these nuclear power plants include but are not limited to strengthening flood prevention facilities, implementing disaster emergency water-replenishment measures, increasing temporary power supply in the case of power outages, installing emergency detection devices to increase spent fuel pools, and monitoring hydrogen control (National Nuclear Security Administration 2012). The new measures were designed in response to the international regulatory agencies' requirements. Three special safety objectives have become the basic requirements after the Fukushima accident: a) accidents that cause core melting leading to early or significant radioactive leakage must be eliminated; b) accidents that may cause serious leakage from core melting should only take limited protection measures for the public in a certain area or period (no need to permanently move residents, no need for emergency evacuation, no need to limit food consumption for a long time); and c) in terms of external events, the objectives tend to take into account the deliberate impact of large aircraft (Ye 2018, 9).

Accordingly, the safety-oriented attitude is required to carry out the gradual approval of the progress of new projects; it is conceivable that under these new regulations, the cost of nuclear power will increase. From the policy documents, a change of expectation can be observed in the trajectory of nuclear development – from the optimistic attitude of the early 2000s to the new emphasis on a rather (and again) incremental development with cautiousness. This change also leads many nuclear energy experts to believe that China's policy elites and state managers are not as optimistic that nuclear power development can meet the 58 GW target by 2020 (Zhang 2015, 64). According to the data released by the China Nuclear Energy Association in June 2020, as of the end of 2019, the total capacity of China's installed nuclear power was still 48.75 GW, which still only accounts for 2.42 per cent of China's total power structure (Zhang et al. 2020). The targets of nuclear power development goals for the next five years are still under development by the time of writing. The relevant overall comprehensive goals are expected to be determined in the 14th Five-Year Guideline to be introduced after 2021. However, as indicated in Figure 5.1, with reference to the past record, one could estimate that it may not be an easy task to meet the target as scheduled by the end of 2020. That said, according to China Nuclear Society's estimate in 2019, nuclear power development in 2030 will reach 131 GW and the proportion of power generation should be able to reach 10.0 per cent of total energy consumption (China Nuclear Society 2019). A recent report introduced written by a panel associated with the Chinese government provided a relatively conservative target of installed nuclear power capacity: at the end of 2025, only the installed capacity of the nuclear power sector stays at 2.5 per cent of the total energy structure, which is far lower than wind power and solar power, which shall reach 18.2 and

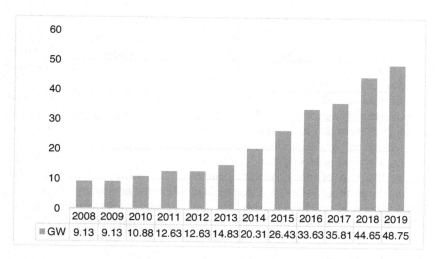

Figure 5.1 Total installed capacity of operating nuclear power plants in China, 2008–2019 (GW)

Source: Adapted from Zhang et al. (2020).

18.7 per cent of installed capacity, respectively, by the end of the planned period (GEIDCO 2020, 29).

As mentioned, a sense of obsession still exists among China's technology elites that is mixed with catching-up thinking and independent innovation in the development of nuclear technology. While they are chasing perceived national security, they are also aware of the impossibility of completely self-made innovation, especially after the Fukushima nuclear accident. The response to such a contradictory imperative has resulted in the work programme (and a series of slogans): 'Endogenous innovation is the key, but Sino-foreign cooperation is a complementary force' (*Yiwoweizhu, zhongwaihezuo*). Academician Peng Shilu proposed this initiative during his tenure as Chairman of the nuclear power Qinshan Phase II joint-venture company in the 1980s. To accomplish this task, the tendering system was introduced into China's nuclear power construction process, paving the way for the introduction of an external economic system. Since then, several consecutive rounds of external bidding have encouraged manufacturers with various types of scientific and technological specifications to invest, forming a trajectory that is actually based on an 'import-based and domestic technology-assisted' developmental pathway (Fang 2014, 48).

Paradoxically, it should be noted that after the Tiananmen Square incident in 1989, the international community imposed sanctions on China meaning that China was, in effect, encouraged to develop its own nuclear energy technology. 'Endogenous innovation' became the inevitable option for policymakers, although in 1989, China did not successfully develop large-scale operations or a successful commercial nuclear power industry. By the end of 2017, 37 nuclear power units were operating in China, and 19 were under construction (Shi 2018, 5). These projects that have been built or are under construction are Sino-foreign cooperative projects. They were also the most advanced tests in science and technology at that time. All the units in operation are built to create the most advanced second-generation technology. However, for the units under construction, the central authorities intend to demonstrate their safety by operating the best technology in the world although such ambition means more costs and operational difficulties, requires the capability to absorb new technology know-how by multinational procurement, and unifies multiple technical standards.

The policymaking process has not been smooth. China's nuclear power development, like that of many Western countries, has recently shown a trend of declining enthusiasm. After the Fukushima incident, the possibility of approving second-generation reactors designed by domestic experts was further reduced, which objectively caused the phenomenon of merely developing the AP1000, replacing the pathway that in the past had been based on domestic reactor technology.[4] For example, the National Energy Administration clearly stated in the Guiding Opinions on Energy Work in 2018 (*2018 nian nengyuan gongzuo zhidao yijian*) that in 2018, on the basis of full evaluation, a number of advanced third-generation pressurised water reactor nuclear power projects in coastal areas could be started (NEA 2018, 5).

Nevertheless, this seemingly optimistic objective has not been implemented according to the original plan. In fact, although the nuclear power production capacity of the Sanmen plant in Zhejiang Province has received much attention, the nuclear power project has been delayed and has exceeded the expected plan length of three years mainly because the security concerns regarding the AP1000 reactor have drawn the attention of high-level policy elites (Liu 2018, 82), and the Energy Bureau and the Nuclear Security Administration requested a subsequent inspection. Although CNNC held in August 2017 a high-profile inaugural launch meeting, which was the first of its kind in the world of the first stack of materials for an AP1000, the approval of No. 1 unit was still unsuccessful, resulting in delays in its construction.

With the rising risk of instability and insecurity embodied in the party state's leading economic thought, the party state's intrinsic stability belief has risen to become the politicians' primary policy choice. The pursuit of economic benefits is gradually reduced due to the change in policy preferences. The idea of economic nationalism has once again risen to dominant thinking, which implies that more top-down assessments, checks, requests for reports, and the preparation of expert committee members have been repeatedly conducted to cautiously mitigate internal doubts in the new and potentially risky technology.

Debating the risks

A key event involving disagreement within the policy elite has caused a further delay of internal policymakers' expected nuclear power revival. This incident stems from the debate between the policy and scientific elites and even the crisis of confidence derived from contradictions caused by conflicting central and local interests. The delay resulted from internal criticism from Hongjun Wen, a retired deputy chief engineer of the Planning Department of the CNNC.[5]

He published a research report questioning the absence of security control over the new reactor technology, strongly urging the inspection of shielded pumps before nuclear fuel is installed (Wen 2017). Yinan Wang, a senior researcher of the Development Research Center of the State Council, echoed Wen's views. As a government think tank scholar specialising in the development of China's new energy, in recent years, she has been one of only a few scholars to appeal publicly to the politicians to examine the issue of nuclear energy development from political and social perspectives.

Her voice echoes the public's demands albeit with an insider's perspective, as he seeks to step on the brakes of China's nuclear renaissance and economic nationalism. Her writings and speeches express views different from those of overly optimistic economic interests, especially, for example, on the issue of whether China should develop nuclear power in the inland areas by the Yangtze River. She is a scholar who strongly opposes this possible project. Unlike the optimists of the nuclear renaissance, opponents such as Yinan Wang suspect that those who are competing to construct the first inland nuclear power plant have not adopted the 'highest international standards' the State Council requires. They point out that the proposals regarding the Taohuajiang (Hunan Province), Xianning (Hubei Province), and Pengze Nuclear Power Plant (Jiangxi Province) projects are driven by local economic imperatives. Wang pointed out that whether in terms of the selection criteria or the technology itself, negligence still exists regarding safety issues, which require prudent research.

The safety requirements for the site selection for power stations involve important social and ecological factors, such as restrictions on population growth, emergency evacuation, radioactive waste liquids, and exhaust emissions. It must not, as Wang has indicated, be assumed that China should have such technology simply because of its catching-up mindset. She contends that the successful implementation of inland nuclear power plants in Europe and America does not imply that China has the same conditions, considering that the population density around the sites of nuclear power plants is four to five times that of advanced economies (Wang 2015, 43–45). In addition, she pointed out that the lack of water resources has constantly been at the core of China's energy governance debate, affecting the discussion of whether nuclear energy should be developed or how to set the priorities of energy options for development.

The risk of water pollution aggravates the many local political and economic elites' doubts regarding the issues of development of inland nuclear power plants. Such doubts have formed major controversy in the project-planning process of Hanjiang, Guangdong Province, and led to local protests against this project. The main leaders against the top-down opaque decisions are National People's Congress (NPC) deputies, not environmental organisations. In fact, the NPC deputies repeatedly asked the Nuclear Industry Group and the Guangdong Provincial

Government Development and Reform Commission to hold consultation meetings during the two sessions of the Chinese People's Congress to answer their enquiries. However, the opacity has repeatedly caused local elites to feel frustrated with the established form of political participation (Fang 2014, 107–116).

However, what may be more worrisome for some scientists is the technology of the AP1000 type of reactor the policymakers prefer. In March 2015, Zuoxiu He, an academician of the Chinese Academy of Sciences and a member of the 8th and 9th National Committees of the Chinese People's Political Consultative Conference,[6] publicly stated that some nuclear power industry advocates have been actively lobbying to relaunch inland nuclear power efforts during the 13th Five-Year Plan (2016–2020). Zuoxiu He and Yinan Wang revealed that the proposals to install AP1000 reactors in the three administrative units in Hunan, Hubei Provinces, and Chongqing city did not adopt the highest international safety standards: although the policy elites agreed to introduce the US AP1000 third-generation nuclear power technology, the standards for the construction of reactors in China and the United States are different because China's standard is based on the DCD15 version of the control documentation.

This version is limited to 'use only in China' when it is certified. However, the reactor certified in the United States is based on the DCD19 version after multiple upgrades, as the scholars indicated (He and Wang 2015, 25–26). In their article, they questioned the report's optimistic presentation of the evaluation of the possibility of developing inland nuclear power plants in the three aforementioned subnational administrative units. This article caused a heated discussion among nuclear power stakeholders. Furthermore, Yinan Wang published an article elsewhere that pointed out the contract fault in the agreement on technology transfer between the four AP1000 nuclear reactors to be installed in Sanmen and Haiyang. She denounced Westinghouse for violating its commitment to transfer 100 per cent of the technology and localisation of key equipment based on the signed contract. Westinghouse tightly holds the software design and hardware procurement of digital instrumentation of nuclear power plants, as Wang claimed, so the Chinese state is not allowed to intervene (Wang 2018, 76).

He's and Wang's criticism not only aroused strong discussions and controversy in the industry but also touched upon the vexing issues regarding how to design and implement realistic industrial policies in such a controversial industry. These policy debates raised the doubts of officials at high levels of the central state. In a move seemingly to resolve these disputes, the central government formed a special panel to visit the Sanmen site in Zhejiang Province for at least three precharge inspections in recent years. These repeated inspection activities caused the project to be temporarily delayed.

Nevertheless, the scientific community's doubts did not cease. Scholars have questioned China's lack of a regulatory environment that meets international standards. Many corresponding policies are still being worked out, as some suggest. One of the criticisms of the aforementioned nuclear renaissance plan in 2015 is not discussed in detail: the content of China's HAF102 safety regulations is outdated (He and Wang 2015, 27). Another fact affecting the overall development of nuclear power is that

China's nuclear safety regulatory agencies cannot, as some have believed, conduct independent reviews due to the historical absence of independent regulators in China (He and Wang 2015, 27). The researchers suggested that project-safety reviews should be affected by economic sectors, business interests, and local governments. They implied that the evaluation report is unrealistic in terms of safety control.

The lack of a clear and transparent regulatory framework, according to the opponents, made it impossible to start the construction of eight additional units; even in 2017, the National Energy Administration announced that the construction of the extra eight units was expected to relaunch, as was written in the *Guiding Opinions of Energy Work in 2017* (*2017 nian nengyuan gongzuo zhidao yijian*).[7] No project was finally approved at the end of 2017 (Liu 2018, 84). In the past, in the process of nuclear power project approval, as long as the Energy Bureau issued a pass (*lutiao*), the enterprise project would be approved within one month. However, many of these projects have been granted passes from the Energy Bureau, but many of them are still stalled by the State Council (Liu 2018, 84).

'Branding' and restructuring the Chinese nuclear power industry

Not until October 2012 did the State Council gradually begin reconsidering relaunching nuclear power projects and slowly incorporate nuclear energy into the policy mix of new-energy development. The relaunched policy documents, the Nuclear Power Safety Guidance (*Hedian anquan guihua*) and Nuclear Medium- and Long-Term Development Plans (*Hedian zhongchangqi fazhan guihua*), point out a new opportunity for nuclear renaissance advocates. However, the relaunch is conditional: the two major power groups must combine their latest self-developed domestic third-generation technologies.

As a unified technology brand, this relaunch marks the emergence of the so-called 'overall technical solution'. This decision is partly a new counterattack of economic nationalism in the face of globalisation, and its context, as some believe, is political: because Japanese Prime Minister Shinzo Abe has successfully sold Japanese nuclear power reactors designed by Mitsubishi to overseas buyers, policymakers seem to feel the enthusiasm and pressure to catch up. The top policymakers began to think about how to restructure scattered, polycentric (which is a long-term criticism of many observers), central state-owned enterprises in the nuclear industry.

They began to test the possibility of integrating the three major licenced groups' technological innovation capabilities. By the time they sought to restructure the nuclear power industry, three types of reactors existed, which were separately developed in three domestic independent innovation enterprise platforms: CAP1400, which the State Nuclear Power Technology Corporation developed; ACPR1000+, which CGNPC designed; and ACP1000, a type of reactor CNNC introduced. After several studies, the Energy Bureau of the NDRC led the work of technology integration. The initial goal was to integrate the latter two because their technical principles and installed capacity are similar (Han 2014a, 61).

The policy elites are thinking about how to combine the innovative advantages of the two previously mentioned organisations, CGNPC and CNNC, as a commodity to promote the export of domestically produced reactors. They expect this project's success to support the international recognition of China's manufacturing capabilities in the future (Fiori and Zhou 2015, 247). In turn, such a restructuring plan was aimed at cultivating Chinese central state-owned enterprises to create a global impact and even market their 'image projects' and then participate in bidding activities for large-scale infrastructure construction elsewhere in the world. This political responsibility for the development prospects is thus tied to a Chinese independent brand, Hualong 1, which is still in the experimental stage.

Since 2013, based on the Hualong 1 Technology Agreement (*Hualong yihao jishu xieding*), signed by CNNC and CGNPC, the two parties have jointly developed their so-called domestic third-generation nuclear reactor units, which was executed by a design company formed by each of the two nuclear power groups. The two parties own all of the shares of the design company (Han 2014a, 61). They worked together to form a new reactor unit, which was aimed at adding its own solution based on the latest Western design. In the programme, experts used the ACP1000's 1777 core technology (Han 2014b, 74).

Most of its new features are facilities to prevent an accident, such as adding a high-level exhaust system to the pressure vessel, increasing the steam generator's heat-transfer surface, using a double-layered containment structure to protect the reactor and to improve sealing, and increasing the containment's free space to 70 000 m^3 (making it more inclusive in the event of an accident), including its outer containment's ability to withstand impact from large commercial aircraft, etc. (Ye 2017, 454). Compared with the EPR large-capacity stand-alone reactor designed by AREVA, a company of the French Electric Power Group (EDF), the design of Hualong 1 is relatively simple and relatively low cost. Some consider it the new core model to solve the world's nuclear power development dilemma through the cutting of expensive costs (Wen 2015). Furthermore, as it pertains to the criticism of the complex design engineering and installation difficulties, the design of Hualong 1 is also relatively simple and relatively cheap by advanced economies' standards. It has recently passed an International Atomic Energy Agency safety review and is expected to pave the way for the possibility of internationally selling reactors made in China. In fact, as nuclear power expert Shengke Zhi said, Hualong 1 has been developed to pave the way for a future export-oriented nuclear power economy, targeting the Third World as well as filling and even becoming the primary choice for the developing world to introduce nuclear power.

Nuclear power investment has become one of the largest projects of overseas foreign-direct investment of China's Belt and Road Initiatives.[8] As the ruling party enthusiastically praised the endogenously developed third-generation reactor, Hualong 1 can be considered the direct outcome of the cooperation between the two central state-owned monopoly enterprises, which avoid the use of high-level key technologies, reducing technical and economic risks by not using shielded pumps or blasting valves in safety design (Wen 2014, 28). It seems that with the avoidance of technology emphasising higher security and technical complexity embedded in the AP1000's original design, the current Hualong 1 has become the only Chinese-made reactor that is immune from the administrative delay all other nuclear projects have suffered. It is estimated that most of the construction had encountered project delays in 2017 or had exceeded budget and financing limits due to rising costs (Ye 2017, 456). Although the CAP1400 reactor project has a net power of 1400 MW and passed the first reactor-pressure and vessel-pressure tests in Shandong Province in 2017 as a demonstration project, its large-scale commercial use still requires development, and its applicability remains to be seen.

At present, two nuclear power stations with Hualong 1 reactors under construction in China are No. 5 and No. 6 units of Fuqing Nuclear Power Plant and No. 3 and No. 4 units of Fangcheng gang Nuclear Power Plant, with estimated power ratings of 2 × 1150 MW. According to Chengkun Zhao, Executive Deputy Director of the China Nuclear Energy Industry Expert Committee,[9] the current nuclear power stations under construction in China are shown in Table 5.1.

Table 5.1 List of nuclear power plants under construction in China, as of 31 December 2018

Nuclear power plant name	Unit number	Reactor type	Start date
Hongyanhe Nuclear Power Plant	No. 5	ACPR1000	29 March 2015
	No. 6		24 July 2015
Fuqing Nuclear Power Plant	No. 5	Hualong 1	7 May 2015
	No. 6		22 December 2015
Yangjiang Nuclear Power Plant	No. 6	ACPR1000	23 December 2013
Taishan Nuclear Power Plant	No. 2	EPR	15 April 2010
Haiyang Nuclear Power Plant	No. 2	AP1000	20 June 2010
Fangcheng gang Nuclear Power Plant	No. 3	Hualong 1	24 December 2015
	No. 4		24 December 2016
Shidaowan Nuclear Power Plant	Demonstration project of high-temperature gas-cooled reactor nuclear power plant	Modular ball bed type high-temperature gas-cooled reactor	21 December 2012
Xiapu Nuclear Power Plant	Xiapu Demonstration of fast reactor	Demonstration of fast reactor	29 December 2017
Tianwan Nuclear Power Plant	No. 5	M310 improved nuclear power unit	27 December 2015
	No. 6		7 September 2016

Source: Adapted from Zhao (2019, 37–39)

Fuqing Nuclear Power Plant No. 5 unit completed dome hoisting earlier than scheduled. By 27 April 2019, the unit's primary loop hydraulic pressure test was officially launched, marking a new stage where the project moved from installation to commissioning (*tiaoshi*).

Local resistance

An important issue that seems to be embarrassing for policymakers is the rise of the anti-nuclear movement in China. Although nuclear power is usually described in the mainstream media as 'new energy', like wind energy and solar energy, and is portrayed as an important option to stabilise the effect of global warming, residents seem to have emerged as an important opposition force against the localisation of nuclear power projects. After the Fukushima incident, an important opposition force has become local regions' mainstream actors, who wish to delay or directly stall the project the top-level government officials have planned (Forrest and Braun 2017, 35).

The new nuclear project in Rongcheng, Shandong Province, contains one CAP1400 reactor unit and four AP1000 units, which the local population around the area opposed. The protests in the neighbouring city of Weihai in 2013 heightened the anti-nuclear sentiment, but the movement did not stop the policymakers' decision to implement the nuclear plan. However, the bottom-up protests in Jiangmen, Guangdong Province, in the same year directly ended a nuclear spent fuel project investment with a value of CNY 4 billion (Han 2014a, 60). In July, Jiangmen's municipal government and local media released the Public Notice of Social Stability Risk Assessment of CNNC's Longwan Industrial Park Project (*Zhonghe jituan longwan gongyeyuan xiangmu shehui wending fengxian pinggu gongshi*), which directly and unexpectedly caused the local masses to gather, march, and protest. The city government reconsidered the plan in just one week, and the proposal for this project's development was terminated one week after its introduction to the public.

Compared to the anti-nuclear history of Western countries, China, with its hierarchical system of governance, which tends toward top-down governance from leaders, may seem more likely to become a new place for a nuclear renaissance, but the politicians are sensitive to such policy issues. The lack of experience in planning and implementation of such projects often makes the policymakers overconfident, pushing forward the plans as the stakeholders' decision, but they have neglected the core users of the nuclear power policy formulation process. The bottom-up anti-nuclear movement gradually became the obstacle preventing the installation of the new nuclear projects in high-demand areas, such as the east coast. Such problems are also reflected in the problematic process of site selection for nuclear power plants caused by mass incidents in recent years, especially the nuclear cycle projects or resettlement sites for nuclear waste.

The setbacks of the central state-owned enterprises, such as CNNC, in the selection process of the spent fuel industry in recent years show that policy implementers often overestimate local people's recognition of nuclear power and overestimate the top-down oligopolistic decision-making methods. A common failure of governance often comes from the cooperation between the administrative elites of central state-owned enterprises and the local policymakers of counties and municipal governments (usually with lagging economic-performance records). To revitalise local economies and strengthen economic structures, local governments are often incentivised to promote the nuclear industrial supply chain industry. However, sometimes the local economic actors and the public's high degree of suspicion (Fang 2014, 53–54), and even the large-scale mass incidents, have stopped the nuclear power industry, even smothering it during the site selection process (Reischer 2016).

Local protests in Weihai, Rushan, Jiangmen, and Heshan[10] to some extent led to the break-up of the exclusive, narrow coalition between the local government and the nuclear power groups, withering the campaign of economic nationalism (building a 'nuclear power state'), causing nuclear projects to be put on hold or further deferred.

The recent unwarned protest in Lianyungang, Jiangsu Province, and the subsequent police-civilian conflict have sounded the alarm for this mode of governing strategy. The policy elites of the central authorities of China and France have earlier reached an agreement to build a joint-ventured nuclear recycling plant in China, which will be constructed by China Nuclear. China and France have begun negotiations on nuclear power plant projects since 2008. In June 2015, both parties signed the Statement of Intent on China's Nuclear Cycle Project, reiterating the support of the two governments for the project. Prior to this, the two countries also successively signed the Implementation Agreement of the Joint Working Group on China's Nuclear Cycle Project Cooperation, the Report of the Joint Working Group on China's Nuclear Cycle Cooperation, and the Joint Statement on China's Nuclear Cycle Project (Zhu 2015). Such a plant is a supporting project that aims to be completed in response to large-scale nuclear power plant development, seeking to provide a solution choice for solving the storage of nuclear waste with strong radiation pollution toxicity.

It is conceivable that, as one of few large-scale spent fuel treatment projects in the world that have attracted international attention, this project has received great attention from high-level officials, and the local government, as mentioned earlier, seems to actively comply with instructions given by the central government. Due to the pressure from higher-level governments – political tasks assigned from the central and provincial governments to local governments– local officials have been reluctant to consult local residents. Besides, although Lianyungang is located in a coastal province which is considered wealthier than other subnational administrative units, it is a relatively poor area in northern Jiangsu. However, the preliminary work progress of the site selection of the nuclear cycle project is not particularly optimistic.

The outbreak of the anti-nuclear mass incident in Lianyungang in August 2016 pushed this political issue to a certain extent. The protest incident originated from ordinary news: on 26 July 2016, 'Yiren Wang, Deputy Director of the National Defense Science and Industry Bureau, accompanied by Changli Yang, Deputy

General Manager of CNNC, went to Lianyungang to investigate the site of the Sino-French cooperative nuclear cycle project'. On 27 July, CNNC's WeChat account once pushed the news and then deleted it. But some other subsidiaries' websites reproduced the news, and the source is labelled 'CNNC' (Nuclear Watch 2016). Immediately afterwards, the event expanded and fermented and spread rapidly on social media.

Nearly 10 000 people gathered to protest, asking the government of Lianyungang to drive the nuclear power project out of their homes. The protests rose, leading to conflicts between the police and the people. Even the armed police stationed on the scene. On 6 August, the government issued a notice prohibiting citizens from participating the demonstration in the city centre, stating that 'the project has been established by the central government, and the provincial and municipal governments have approved it. It is a major national project that is conducive to the economic development of the city of Lianyungang' (BBC 2016).

However, this pale declaration made it difficult to calm the local residents. The masses still marched on the streets, chanting the slogan 'against nuclear waste and defending our homeland'. Demonstrations led to greater conflicts between police and civilians and nearly a hundred people have been detained. On 8 August, the Lianyungang Municipal Government issued a notice saying that 'Party members and public officials are strictly prohibited from participating in rallies, and demonstrations', and they are required to 'guide their families' and 'never act as onlookers'.

However, the situation and scale were changing too fast. On 10 August, the Lianyungang Government had to announce the suspension of the Sino-French nuclear cycle project through an official statement. Citizens saw the quashed official announcement as a temporary and successful outcome of the protests, even though the government did not affirm a full withdrawal. In retrospect, we can learn that similar incidents occurred due to the fact that governments did not provide transparent and instant communication channels for stakeholders to communicate information symmetrically. Such a short and inconspicuous style of news eventually caused serious mistrust between the government and the local residents (Ma 2017, 25–29). The protests, as mentioned earlier, are not a single incident. The (top-down) site selection process in many provinces and cities in China has been frequently opposed by local residents from the bottom up. The suitable site is said to be still being selected in the future. It is still undecided as to how this project worth more than 100 billion yuan has recently landed. 'Spent fuel', as a high concentration of unburned nuclear waste that has been replaced from a nuclear power plant, contains a large amount of radioactive elements, and it seems to have become the most difficult issue in the development of nuclear power for contemporary societies including China (Buckley 2016).

To date, the development of China's nuclear power seems to have encountered a bottleneck. Unresolved anti-nuclear pressure and economic doubts are causing nuclear abandonment in some regions (Shi 2018, 5), especially in the densely populated areas of the east coast. Such anti-nuclear movement effects seem to have forced policymakers to delay the supply of nuclear power in areas with higher electricity demand. For example, in the NEA's Guiding Opinions of Energy Work in 2018, we only saw a conservative development plan: no information was given about the development of inland nuclear power, only the preliminary evaluation of nuclear power projects with favourable site conditions and strong public support (NEA 2018, 19).

At the same time, the local anti-nuclear movement's effect also shows that the politicians seem to have started avoiding the risk of social instability; they tend to choose to move toward the sparsely populated west, and the local governments in the west have recently adapted to the demand. Moreover, the local governments have tailored their local industrial policies, attempting to benefit from this policy shift and seeking new opportunities to promote nuclear-related industries. For example, China's first National Nuclear Technology Industrial Park (*Guojiaji hejishu chanyeyuan*) was recently opened in Gansu Province. It is a deserted industrial park used to manage spent fuel. As a joint project between France and China,[11] this industrial park will be developed as a base for the treatment of reactor combustion.[12] CNNC is responsible for all of China's 'back-end-fuel-cycle' operations, and the company plans to complete the successful commercialisation of spent fuel reprocessing operations by 2030 (Forrest and Braun 2017, 34–35). CNNC and France's AREVA signed a cooperation agreement in 2007 to develop, introduce, and apply the technology of spent fuel reprocessing from France.

Currently, many spent fuels transported from other places (particularly from Guangdong Daya Bay) are stored in Gansu Province in special NAC-STC containers (Zhou 2011, 4361). Although these measures seem reasonable given the less populated areas in western China, another unexpected technical problem has impeded the opportunity for Sino-French cooperation: China does not yet have the appropriate infrastructure for transportation. The large-scale infrastructure conditions for long-distance transportation of spent fuel will inevitably increase the cost, which also includes the purchase of foreign technology (Wang 2014, 74). Considering that the issue of nuclear waste disposal has not yet entered the public agenda, the results of scientific assessment have not been disclosed to the public for a long time (Fang 2014, 59).

China and nuclear exports

That having been said, the dominant cultural biases of hierarchical political cultures seemed, to some extent, not to affect the project development of China's endogenous innovation. Hualong 1 seems to be an unhindered project beyond most of these stunted development projects. As one of the key 'going-out' projects in the Belt and Road Initiative, China's efforts to export nuclear power still face considerable challenges. First of all, it is the pressure of financing that potentially impedes long-term investment in the sector. Nuclear power export companies not only need to provide turnkey services but also need to assist in project financing. However, this is a major factor that nuclear energy projects' owners face in the developing world.

Due to high research and development costs, as well as long-term construction cycles, the process of commercialising civilian nuclear energy projects in the developing world is usually more difficult than planned. For the specific areas pertinent to nuclear power projects, going-out nuclear energy projects mainly rely on commercial loans from the Export-Import Bank of China. The source of the loans is relatively monolithic, which is different from the situation in advanced economies.

In Pakistan, starting on 20 August 2015, construction of No. 2 unit of the Hualong 1 Karachi Nuclear Power Project was started. This is the first of five Hualong 1 exports from China to Pakistan. The total amount of the Karachi Nuclear Power Project is USD 9.6 billion, of which the loan from China is USD 6.5 billion. The project is contracted by China Zhongyuan Engineering Co., Ltd., a subsidiary company of CNNC. It is expected to generate electricity in 2020. This project is the same as No. 5 and No. 6 units of China's native Fuqing Nuclear Power Plant, both of which are Hualong 1 reactors. In Karachi, in October 2019, the rotor-piercing work of the generator was successfully completed. The generator-piercing rotor is considered to be a critical process for the entire installation procedure. The hydraulic pressure test of the primary circuit of the reactor was started in December 2019, and the 'cold test' was officially launched.[13]

The successful completion of the rotor-piercing work of the generator and the start of the cold test indicate that all major equipment of the reactor unit on the conventional island is fully installed and that the construction has entered the commissioning stage (China Atomic Energy Authority 2019). Correspondingly, the No. 5 unit reactor of Fuqing Nuclear Power Plant also entered the first-stage hydraulic pressure test phase on 27 April 2019, which was earlier than the expected schedule by 50 days.

It is worth noting that the Chinese localisation rate of Pakistan's No. 2 and No. 3 units is as high as 100 per cent. Localisation has been deemed an important strategy for exporting China-made technology to the developing world (Yang 2017). Such strategy may provide an opportunity for the state to save costs for nuclear energy construction through vertical integration overseas. Hualong 1 is considered to be a Chinese brand strategy that seeks to compromise both imperatives between economic benefits and safety concerns for the development of civilian nuclear power technology. The discourse on nuclear safety seems to resonate with past discussions on the development of nuclear power in the United States. One could often find such cost-benefit economic discourses in policy documents. Hualong 1, as an alternative, has been the portrait of a specific type of reactor that may be more suitable for the developing world.

Conclusion

In this chapter, we explored China's policy paradigm of the development of nuclear power plants, its historical context, and the resulting safety regime, which we explored through the path-dependent perspective of historical institutionalism, cultural and EM theories. Policy elites are involved in nuclear power in the process of screening the policy-technology construction and the efforts to learn new knowledge. Such efforts sway the pursuit of independent innovation and international collaboration.

The scientific experiments of the third-generation nuclear-technology reactors coincided with the developmental needs for the Western firms, and they found a common interest in the political and economic contexts. The new hope of nuclear power revival nevertheless becomes the driver of domestic opponents' activism, including that of the scientific and technological elites and local people, who oppose the opaque, top-down decision-making process and institutional cultural practices. Such unexpected outcomes are emerging in the original fragmentation and fragmentation pattern of the decision-making space, leading to a slow dislocation of policy implementation.

That has been said, the safety regime can be classed as 'weak ecological modernisation' (Toke 2017) with hierarchists' mindset where the top-down mode of technocratic decision-making process can be identified. And there is emerging bottom-up anti-nuclear pressure in the localities of designated nuclear construction sites, albeit with sporadic occurrences. Some non-comprehensive technological breakthroughs have been made, but such a delay of the policy outcome seems to be contrary to the politicians' original intention, and the ruling party's expectations are increasingly overthrown by the emerging linkage of localism, which has increased political risk to some extent. The risk of instability also makes it difficult for the technology elite to implement this weak pursuit of a unilateral nuclear energy revival.

China's experience in nuclear power development shows that the development of nuclear power plants seems to have shifted from economic nationalism (focussed on self-exploratory industrial policies) to gradually enter the newly imagined competition in global nuclear power. Such imagination has prompted nuclear power policy elites – NDRC and state-owned enterprise managers – to invest in a new round of the scientific and technological arms race, which has escaped the previously cautious decision-making model and has invested heavily in the grand development process.

Nuclear power, like railway development and space exploration, has given new hopes for the country's symbolic rise. Such new hopes are necessary to absorb external experience and thereby develop a self-owned brand and strategically absorb the high cost of the development process. However, since the Fukushima incident, external security concerns have to some extent strengthened the central government's anxiety to conduct more precautionary reviews and hence repeatedly request unanticipated checks through the supranational mechanism.

The central government's expectation for the development of a new generation of nuclear power reactors is reflected in the quantity and quality of projects in catch-up mode. Therefore, the monitoring of such a request has, of course, quickly increased the delay of the completion time, and economic costs make China's nuclear power development still subject to the unresolved, indecisive policy choices and institutional practices. Plus, the lack of transparency of the systemic appearance of the policy of science and technology has led to a sharp increase in the opposition from the bottom of the economic-governance regime. These anti-nuclear forces, either online or offline, after the Fukushima incident, have to some extent caused delays in the nuclear energy revival plan in China.

Notes

1 The involvement of NDRC was partly due to the restructuring of China's political institutions. After transforming into the core unit of economic policy formulation under the State Council in 2003, it began to formulate and lead industrial policies and played a leading role in the process of economic development in China.

2 The specific requirement for the EPR reactor system in China is different from that in foreign countries due to variant national government policies. The Finnish authorities require it, but China has not required it.

3 The other 'big five' include China Huaneng Group Corporation, China Datang Corporation, China Huadian Corporation, and China Guodian Corporation.

4 The former deputy engineer of the planning department indicated that the 'second generation plus' reactor (*Er dai jia*) has a high safety standard and a price advantage, particularly for the developing world. Wen pointed out that in order to meet the requirements of the third generation, CNNC and CGNPC made new design plans based on the original second generation (ACP1000 and ACPR1000), which are much cheaper than foreign EPR and AP1000 models. See Wen (2012, 37).

5 Hongjun Wen also served as the member of the economic professional committee of Chinese Nuclear Society.

6 This is the third meeting of the 12th National People's Congress and the third meeting of the 12th National Committee of the Chinese People's Political Consultative Conference (CPPCC).

7 According to the guidelines, six of the reactors are the AP1000 model and two are the domestic CAP1400 models. The eight units, according to the guideline, are Sanmen No. 3 and No. 4 units, Ningde No. 5 and No. 6 units, Zhangzhou No. 1 and No. 2 units, Huizhou No. 1 and No. 2 units. The total project scale is approximately 9.86 million kilowatts (NEA 2017).

8 Personal communication, Zhi Shengke (Chinese nuclear industry consultant), 12 October 2018.

9 Chengkun Zhao is the former director of the National Nuclear Safety Administration.

10 Since 2010, although local protests have to a large extent been deterred by the public security agencies, the suppression of the public participation has seemed to have had no benefit to the effective promotion of related projects.

11 The Sino-French cooperation project has a rather long history, and the cooperation with France comes from the fear of unilateral dependence on the United States as a technology catch-up partnership. In order to balance political risks, high-level policymakers, after signing a cooperation agreement with the United States to introduce AP1000 units, also introduced Areva's new EPR reactor. However, in terms of technology development, the development of ERP reactor technology in China has been in a laggard state. On the one hand, its own financial crisis led to uncertainty of the firm's operation (it was on the verge of bankruptcy in 2014). On the other hand, due to the complexity of the EPR engineering itself, the construction period has been extended. The accumulated cost is considered to be difficult to anticipate by policymakers. See, for instance, Wang (2015).

12 Ironically, to a certain extent, the PRC government seems to be deliberately depoliticising the discourse on spent fuel, nuclear waste, and treating its sensitivity in a low-key manner. The sustainable use of nuclear energy, as a new emerging slogan, has become an easy-to-follow measure seeking to avoid conflict in the localities.

13 'Cold test' refers to a cold state functional test, which is a large-scale comprehensive commissioning test for nuclear power plants. Its main purpose is to verify the performance of the primary circuit system and equipment, as well as its auxiliary pipelines under high pressure.

References

BBC (2016) 'Anti-Nuclear Demonstration Broke Out in Lianyungang, Jiangsu Province, Banned by Police' (in Chinese, *Jiangsu Lianyun gang baofa fanhe shiwei zao jinfang jinzhi*), 10 August. www.bbc.com/zhongwen/simp/china/2016/08/160810_china_lianyungang_protest_nuclear_plan

Brødsgaard, K.E. (2012a) 'Politics and Business Group Formation in China: The Party in Control?', *The China Quarterly*, 211(September), 624–648. https://doi.org/10.1017/S0305741012000811

Brødsgaard, K.E. (2012b) 'Cadre and Personnel Management in the CPC', *China: An International Journal*, 10(2), 69–83.

Brødsgaard, K.E. (2017) '"Fragmented Authoritarianism" or "Integrated Fragmentation?"', in K.E. Brødsgaard (ed.) *Chinese Politics as Fragmented Authoritarianism: Earthquakes, Energy and Environment*. Abingdon: Routledge, pp. 38–55.

Buckley, C. (2016) 'Thousands in Eastern Chinese City Protest Nuclear Waste Project', *New York Times*, 8 August. www.nytimes.com/2016/08/09/world/asia/china-nuclear-waste-protest-lianyungang.html?_ga=2.156110835.97459151.1579938071-1569127560.1563587795 (accessed 18 August 2019).

Chen, Y., Guillaume, M., Chabert, C., Eschbach, R., He, H., and Ye, G. (2018) 'Prospects in China for Nuclear Development up to 2050', *Progress in Nuclear Energy*, 103(1 March), 81–90. https://doi.org/10.1016/j.pnucene.2017.11.011

China Atomic Energy Authority (2019) 'Hualong One's First Overseas Reactor Has Fully Entered the Equipment Commissioning Stage' (in Chinese, *Hualong yihao haiwai shoudui quanmian jinru shebei tiaoshi jieduan*). www.caea.gov.cn/n6758881/n6758890/c6808327/content.html (accessed 12 January 2020).

China Nuclear Society (2019) 'Prospects of China's Nuclear Power Development Strategy in 2030 and 2050', (in Chinese, *2030, 2050 nian woguo hedian fazhan zhanlue zhanwang*), 30 December. www.ns.org.cn/site/content/7339.html (accessed 30 July 2020).

Cui, H. (2009) 'Engineering Features of the Third Generation of EPR Nuclear Power Plant Construction and the Analysis of Challenges' (in Chinese, *disandai hedao tujian gongcheng tedian ji shigong nandian fenxi*), *Electric Power Construction*, 30(5) (May), pp. 97–98.

Fan, W., and Bo, Y. (2017) 'Analysis of the Difference between the Cooling System of Hualong 1 and AP1000 Passive Containment' (in Chinese, *Hualong yihao yu AP1000 feineng dong anquan kelengque xitong chayi fenxi*), *Sciences & Wealth* (in Chinese), 24, 168–169.

Fang, X. (2014) *Social Construction of Nuclear Risks in China: The Public's Participation in Civil Nuclear Issues from the Start of the 21st Century* (in Chinese, *Zhongguo hedian fengxian de shehui jiangou: 21 shiji yi lai gongzhong dui hedian shiwu de canyu*). Beijing: Social Sciences Academic Press.

Fiori, F., and Zhou, Z. (2015) 'Sustainability of the Chinese Nuclear Expansion: Natural Uranium Resources Availability, Pu Cycle, Fuel Utilization Efficiency and Spent Fuel Management', *Annals of Nuclear Energy*, 83(1 September), 246–257. https://doi.org/10.1016/j.anucene.2015.03.051

Fiori, F., and Zhou, Z. (2016) 'A Study on the Chinese Nuclear Energy Options and the Role of ADS Reactor in the Chinese Nuclear Expansion', *Progress in Nuclear Energy*, 91(1 August), 159–169. https://doi.org/10.1016/j.pnucene.2016.04.003

Forrest, R., and Braun, C. (2017) 'Managing China's Spent Nuclear Fuel: A Model Framework for Interim Storage', *The Nonproliferation Review*, 24(1–2), (January 2), 31–45. https://doi.org/10.1080/10736700.2017.1385732.

Global Energy Interconnection Development and Cooperation Organization (GEIDCO) (2020) 'Research on China's "14th Five-Year" Power Development Plan' (in Chinese, *Zhongguo "shisiwu" dianli fazhan huihua yanjiu*). www.geidco.org/html/qqnyhlw/zt20200731/index.html#research (accessed 1 August 2020).

Guan, Y., Fang, H., and Qin, O. (2012) 'Application of Passive Autocatalytic Recombiners in Tianwan Nuclear Power Station' (in Chinese), *Nuclear Power Operation*, 5(2), 154–160.

Han, S. (2014a) 'The Coming Back of Nuclear Power' (in Chinese, *Hedian huinuan*), *China Southern Power Grid*, 1, 59–63.

Han, S. (2014b) 'Fast Tracks of Domestic Third-Generation Nuclear Power Plants' (in Chinese, *Guochan sandai hedian xushi daifa*), *China Southern Power Grid*, 6, 72–75.

Hao, C., Gao, B., and Gong, D. (2019) 'Research on the Problems of Construction Quality and Measures for the Anti-Aircraft Impact Joint of Hualong 1' (in Chinese, *Hualong yihao kang feiji zhuangji jietou shigong zhiliang wenti ji duice yanjiu*), *Quality Forum*, 276.

He, Z., and Wang, Y. (2015) 'The Safety Risks of the Development Nuclear Power Plants in Hunan, Hubei, and Jiangxi Province Cannot Be Underestimated' (in Chinese, *Xian gegan san sheng fazhan hedian anquan fengxian bu rong digu*), *China Economic Weekly*, (9 March), 24–27.

Jiang, X., Wang, Z., Yang, G., and Chen, C. (2015) 'Application of Passive Hydrogen Combiner in Nuclear Power Plant' (in Chinese, *feineng dong qing fu he qi zai hedianchang de yingyong*), *Science and Technology Innovation Herald*, 25, 66.

Lampton, D.M. (2014) *Following the Leader: Ruling China, from Deng Xiaoping to Xi Jinping*. Berkeley: University of California Press.

Li, L., Pan, R., Liu, Y., and Zhan, J. (2017) 'Preliminary Study of Nuclear Power Plant Design Safety Regulations (HAF102–2016) for Concrete Structures in Nuclear Power Plants' (in Chinese), *Industrial Construction*, 47(9), 7–23.

Li, S., and Liang, W. (2019) 'Necessity Analysis of Filtered Containment Venting System of Nuclear Reactor' (in Chinese), *Hudian Technology*, 41(8), 65–73.

Liu, Y., Yang, Z., Yu, X., and Mo, S. (2012) 'Introduction of Core Catcher for Nuclear Power Plants and Installation Management of EPR Core Cather', (in Chinese, *Hedianzhan dui xinbuji qi jianjie ji EPR dui xinbu ji qian zhuang guanli*), *Theoretical Research*, 5, 35–38.

Liu, W. (2018) 'The Problems of Nuclear Power Charging in Sanmen' (in Chinese, *Sanmen hedian zhuangliao quzhe*), *China Southern Power Grid*, 2, 81–84.

Ma, Tiannan (2017) 'Risk: Accumulated "NIMBY" Mass Incidents: A Case Study of "Anti Nuclear Waste" Incident in Lianyungang' (in Chinese), *Journal of Hubei University of Arts and Science*, 38(6), 25–29.

Mertha, A. (2009) '"Fragmented Authoritarianism 2.0": Political Pluralization in the Chinese Policy Process', *The China Quarterly*, 200(1), 995–1012.

National Nuclear Security Administration (2012) *General Technical Requirements for Nuclear Power Plant Improvement Actions after the Fukushima Nuclear Accident* (*Fudao heshigu hou hedianchang gaijin xingdong tongyong jishu yaoqiu*, No. 98).

NDRC (2007) *Medium- and Long-Term Development Plan for Nuclear Power (2005– 2020)* (*Hedian zhong chang qi fazhan guihua 2005–2020 nian*), October.

NEA (2017) *The Guiding Opinions of Energy Work in 2017* (*2017 nian neng yuan gong zuo zhidao yijian*).

NEA (2018) *The Guiding Opinions of Energy Work in 2018* (*2018 nian nengyuan gongzuo zhidao yijian*).

NTI (2011) 'Guangdong Daya Bay Nuclear Power Station (GNPS)', 1 October. www.nti.org/learn/facilities/779/ (accessed 3 November 2017).

Nuclear Watch (2016) 'The "Anti-Nuclear Waste" Incident in Lianyungang' (in Chinese, *Lianyun gang "fan he fei liao" shijian shimo*). http://news.bjx.com.cn/html/20160808/759562.shtml

Pearson, M.M. (2005) 'The Business of Governing Business in China: Institutions and Norms of the Emerging Regulatory State', *World Politics*, 57(2), 296–322.

Pearson, M.M. (2011) 'Variety Within and Without: The Political Economy of Chinese Regulation', in S. Kennedy (ed.) *Beyond the Middle Kingdom: Comparative Perspectives on China's Capitalist Transformation*. Stanford, CA: Stanford University Press, pp. 25–43.

People's Daily (2019) 'Welcome the recovery nuclear power plant development' (in Chinese, *Hedian "jiedong" yingfusu*). http://energy.people.com.cn/BIG5/n1/2019/1108/c71661-31444620.html

People's Daily (2019) 'Ministry of Ecology and Environment: The interpretation of China's Nuclear Safety White Paper (in Chinese)', 9 September. http://env.people.com.cn/GB/57414/57417/429557/index.html

Reischer, R. (2016) 'NIMBYism Threatens China's Nuclear Energy Plans | GRI', *Global Risk Insights*, 26 August. https://globalriskinsights.com/2016/08/nimbyism-threatens-china-nuclear-plans/ (accessed 25 July 2019).

Shi, L. (2018) 'New Situation and New Tasks of Nuclear Energy Development' (in Chinese, *Heneng fazhanianlin de xinxingshi he xinrenwu*), in Institute of Nuclear Energy Safety Technology, Chinese Academy of Sciences (ed.) *Chinese Blue Book on Nuclear Energy Safety Technology Development*. Beijing: Chinese Academy of Sciences. pp. 3–8.

Stevenson, J. (2016) 'China's Energy Policy: New Technology and Civil Nuclear Expansion', *Strategic Comments*, 22(1), vii–viii. doi:10.1080/13567888.2016.1170408

Thomson, E. (2011) 'China's Nuclear Energy in Light of the Disaster in Japan', *Eurasian Geography and Economics*, 52(4), 464–482. https://doi.org/10.2747/1539-7216.52.4.464

Toke, D. (2017) *China's Role in Reducing Carbon Emissions: The Stabilisation of Energy Consumption and the Deployment of Renewable Energy*. Abingdon: Routledge.

Wang, Y. (2014) 'The Defaults of China's Nuclear Power Safety Requires Our Attention' (in Chinese, *Gaodu zhongshi ying xiang wo guo hedian anquan de "duanban"*), *Hongqi Wenzhai*, 10, 74.

Wang, Y. (2015) 'The Development of Chinese Nuclear Power Must Make Progress While Maintaining Stability and Ensuring the Security' (in Chinese, *woguo hedian fazhan bixu wenzhong qiujin quebao anquan*), *Review of Science and Culture* (*Kexue wenhua pinglun*), 12(4), 27–51.

Wang, Y. (2018) 'Greater Hidden Dangers of Nuclear Power Plants in China' (in Chinese, *buzhi shi xing pian, hedianzhan "kongzhi xitong shou zhi yuren" yin huangengda*), *China Economic Weekly*, 30 April, 76–77.

Wen, H. (2012) 'Looking Forward to the Rapid Development of the Chinese Third-Generation [Reactor]' (in Chinese, *Qidai "zhongguo sandai" jiasufali*), *China Nuclear Industry*, 11, 36–39.

Wen, H. (2014) 'The Market of China's Nuclear Power' (in Chinese, *cong shijie hedian Dongxiang kan zhongguo hedian de shichang kongjian*), *China Nuclear Industry*, 3, 25–28.

Wen, H. (2015) 'The Entanglement of the Advanced Nature of Nuclear Power Plants and Its Economic Effect' (in Chinese, *shijie hedian xianjin xing yu jing ji xing de jiujie*), *China Nuclear Industry*, 1, 21–24.

Wen, H. (2017) 'Analysis of the Prospect of Westinghouse on the Verge of Bankruptcy' (in Chinese, *Westinghouse binglin pochan de qianjin fengxi, woguo hedian fazhan de duice*

jianyi). www.stdaily.com/zhuanti01/dxhdz/2017-11/03/content_591451.shtml?from=
timeline&isappinstalled=1 (accessed 28 April 2019).

Xu, Y. (2010) *The Politics of Nuclear Energy in China.* Basingstoke: Palgrave Macmillan.

Yang, C. (2017) *Energy Policy in China.* Abingdon: Routledge.

Yi, F., and Gu, C. (2016) 'Introduction of the Hualong 1's Active and Passive Safety System' (in Chinese, *Hualong yihao nengdong yu feineng dong anquan xitong jieshao*),
Electromechanical Information (in Chinese, *Jidian Xinxi*), 12(474), 56–57.

Yiao, G. (2011) 'Let the People be Reassured' (in Chinese, *Rang zuguo renmin fang xin*),
China Nuclear Industry (*Zhongguo hegongye*), 33.

Ye, Q. (2017) 'Innovation Driving and Technology Leading: The Significant Implication of
Hualong One Construction' (in Chinese, *Chuangxin qudong keji yinling – "Hualong 1"
jianshe de zhongda yiyi*), *China Nuclear Power*, 10(4) (December), 454–456.

Ye, Q. (2018) 'Persist in the Self-Reliance and Develop the New Era of China Nuclear
Industry' (in Chinese, *Jianchi zizhu chuangxin, kaichuang hedian fazhan xin shidai*),
China Nuclear Power, 11(1) (March), 5–10.

Zang, X., and Musheno, M. (2017) 'Explore Frontline Work in China', *Public Administration*, 95(3), 842–855.

Zhang, H. (2015) 'Uranium Supplies: A Hitch to China's Nuclear Energy Plans? Or Not?', *Bulletin of the Atomic Scientists*, 71(3), 58–66. https://doi.org/10.1177/0096340215581358

Zhang, T., Pan, Q., Li, M., Zhang, H., Zheng, Y., Wei, S., Yu, P., Bai, Y., Wang, W., and
Gao, L. (2020) *The Report on the Development of China's Nuclear Energy 2020* (in Chinese, *Zhongguo heneng fazhan baogao 2020*). Beijing: Social Sciences Academic Press.

Zhao, C. (2018) 'The Nuclear Safety Act Protects the Safe and Efficient Development of
Nuclear Energy in China' (in Chinese), *Nuclear Power Safety*, 11–15.

Zhao, C. (2019) 'China's Nuclear Power Enters a New Era', *China Power Enterprise Management* (in Chinese), (February), 37–39.

Zhou, Y. (2011) 'China's Spent Nuclear Fuel Management: Current Practices and Future
Strategies', *Energy Policy*, 39(7) (1 July), 4360–4369. https://doi.org/10.1016/j.enpol.
2011.04.055

Zhou, Y., and Liu, X. (2016) 'Evolution of Chinese State Policies on Innovation', in Y.
Zhou, W. Lazonick, and Y. Sun (eds.) *China as an Innovation Nation.* Oxford: Oxford
University Press, pp. 33–67.

Zhu, H. (2009) *Atomic Energy and Nuclear Plants* (in Chinese). Hangzhou: Zhejiang University Press.

Zhu, X. (2015) 'Sino-French Nuclear Fuel Cycle Back-End Cooperation continues to
Upgrade' (in Chinese, *Zhongfa heranliao xunhuan houduan hezuo chixu shengji*).
www.china.areva.com/home/liblocal/docs/China%20Offer/2nd%20Back%20End%20
Seminar%20in%20Beijing%202015/%E4%B8%AD%E5%9B%BD%E8%83%BD%E
6%BA%90%E6%8A%A5%E9%87%87%E8%AE%BF%E7%A8%BF.pdf (accessed 8
January 2020).

Zhu, H., Deng, Y., Zhu, R., and He, X. (2016) 'Fear of Nuclear Power? Evidence from Fukushima Nuclear Accident and Land Markets in China', *Regional Science and Urban Economics*, 60(September), 139–154. https://doi.org/10.1016/j.regsciurbeco.2016.06.008

6 France, nuclear power, and safety policy

This chapter will examine the nature of nuclear safety regulation in France. This needs to be done by looking at a) the context in which it has been developed (which includes the influence of international factors and changing public attitudes), b) the events and institutions that have been associated with the development of nuclear energy safety policy c) whilst considering its impact on French nuclear energy outcomes.

The chapter will begin with a discussion of the history of the nuclear energy programme, and in order to understand this, a discussion of the institutional context in which this has occurred. There will then be an examination of organisation and safety philosophy and policy, and changes in interpretation of that policy which has occurred. Finally there will be a discussion of impacts of this policy and its changes on outcomes affecting existing and new nuclear power plants.

There are three key questions here of central importance to the book and the comparisons with what has happened in other countries. First is the extent to which nuclear safety policy has changed, and how it has changed in France. This is important partly because we need to know to compare it with other countries, but especially also because there may be an impression that French nuclear safety policy has been tightened, perhaps as part of an international trend. Is tightened safety a cause of the difficulties with building the new power plant at Flamanville?

A second question flows from the first in that we need to assess the extent to which any changes in safety regulations have affected the costs of building and maintaining nuclear power plants. A third question involves relating this to cultural theory in an effort to better understand the outcomes. As discussed in Chapter 2 greater egalitarian pressure may be associated with pressures for greater regulatory independence from the nuclear power industry and increased safety expectations – something that we described as 'weak' ecological modernisation given its delivery with top-down regulatory machineries. On the other hand strong individualistic pressures which balance pressure for higher safety standards with cost on a more equal level may lead to less stringent safety measures being deployed either in the case of new or existing nuclear reactors.

France is an especially important country to study in the context of nuclear power since it has the highest proportion of electricity supplied by nuclear power in the world. It is also a leading designer of nuclear power plants. What happens in France is therefore central to the world nuclear industry and its prospects.

France's nuclear development

France began its nuclear power programme in a serious fashion as a result of what was seen as setbacks in its oil security position, this being a knock-on effect of the French Colonial/independence wars in North Africa and then the oil price crisis in 1973. The government led by Charles de Gaulle started preparations for a programme of building nuclear power stations. However this did not get fully underway until a mobilisation of resources by the Messmer government from 1974. France had just 14 reactors in operation by the end of the 1970s, with the 1980s being the biggest decade in terms of commissioning reactors. Thirteen reactors had been closed by July 2020, and all but one of these were early, often small reactors that preceded the PWR programmes which comprise the current French reactor fleet (IAEA 2020).

The French nuclear programme differed from most others in its degree of centralisation. This involved not only the coordination of the nuclear power constructor Orano, formerly known as AREVA and the nationalised electricity monopoly Electricité de France and other engineering and scientific institutions (including state-owned bodies dealing with fuel preparation) but the peculiarly French system of elite administrative control. This has been done through the so-called Corps d'État which represents a carefully selected trained group of what might be called super graduates.

The corps which has, by and large, run the French electricity system is drawn from an elite university called the Corps des Mines. This has enabled joined-up thinking to deliver the French civil nuclear programme, but on the other hand it has been attacked by those not enamoured by France's nuclear policy as pretty much completely sold on the idea that nuclear power was an unquestionable good, and unable to conceive of any alternative. Latterly some of the younger members of this administrative elite have become more interested in renewables than their older counterparts (Eales and Sverrisson 2014). It should also be noted that since Chernobyl in 1986, there has been an increased emphasis on designing power plants to mitigate the worst consequences of nuclear accidents, although this is not in conflict with greater interest in renewable energy.

According to nuclear consultant Mycle Schneider:

> The elite technocrats control the Government, especially on energy and nuclear policy – these are the same in the industrial groups and the administration, the state corps [Corps d'État], an administrative elite system. They design and administer policy, they represent the interests in the companies and they control them. E.g. they hold the positions of the ministerial nuclear advisors, the CEO of AREVA [now Orano] and the Nuclear Safety Authority [ASN]. You have a very small group of elite technocrats who know everybody. You can compare them with Opus Dei in the Catholic Church. The state corps is the same thing. It is part of the organigram of the state itself. Everything in nuclear is under control of these guys, few women – only around 500

strong. You're talking less than 20 engineers from the top engineering schools per year. These guys make the rules – it's not the 'political' Government.

(interview 19/03/2019)

This centralised administrative arrangement helped organise a coherent nuclear power programme which is relatively immune from political intervention. One much prized asset of this programme was the fact that a nuclear power station design based on the American-style pressurised water reactor (PWR) was consistently used, albeit implemented in three series of slightly different designs. Other benefits include the ability to marshal the various agencies needed in a consistent way. The sheer size of the reactor programme amounted, by the time of its completion (in the 1990s), to some 58 reactors. This number of plants allowed economies of scale in terms of not just making batches of reactive parts but also importantly of marshalling the highly specialised skills, that is individual human specialist capacity that made the French nuclear programme to be the admiration of the world.

The French nuclear programme had initially in the 1970s been extremely controversial and involved many clashes with anti-nuclear campaigners (Nelkin and Pollack 1981). The opposition was effectively beaten back, although there continued to be substantial concern about nuclear safety in France compared to other EU countries (Eurobarometer 2010, 41). The nature of the centralised state run by a coherent group of non-elected elite technocrats is said to have enabled the nuclear programme and overrode the quite considerable opposition to the nuclear programme in the 1975–1977 period in particular. The lack of deliberation on the nuclear power policy issue, and the relatively closed nature of French political consultative arrangements is said to be conducive to nuclear development, in France as in elsewhere (Kitschelt 1986; Feldman 1986; Sovacool and Valentine 2010). However in France attacks by anti-nuclear campaigners on nuclear power for its potential safety implications had to be taken into account by the French planners, in theory at least.

France's nuclear programme was admired in terms of its speed of deployment and apparent cost-effectiveness. On the other hand it is difficult to make comparisons of cost-effectiveness of the French nuclear construction programme with other more privately organised nuclear programmes such as in the USA. Public ownership lends itself to greater opacity in terms of assessing economic outcomes compared to the private sector (at least when it is itself competitive rather than being a monopoly). This is because a public utility does not have to compete, or be as accountable, in cost terms as a competitive private sector. By the turn of the 21st century nuclear power supplied fully three-quarters of total French electricity needs, more than any other country.

Of course critics of the French nuclear programme say its cost-effectiveness is undermined by the need to decommission the reactors at the end of their lives, something with which the French state is now beginning to deal. However some have observed the costs of the French programme were rising in terms of construction costs even before the end of the programme. It has often been claimed that after the construction of the first reactor of a particular design, successive reactors become cheaper. This may be the case, but such cost reductions were small compared to the cost increases when new reactor designs replaced the previous ones. There were three series of reactors among France's 58 strong reactor fleet, and step-change increases in costs occurred and rose substantially compared to the previous series (MacKerron 1992; Grubler 2010).

Reactions to Chernobyl

However none of the reactor designs that featured in this programme were judged sufficiently able to deal with heightened security and safety criteria that emerged following reviews of the Chernobyl accident in 1986. Although officially played down by the French state (Liberatore 1995), this accident shook the whole of Europe including France.

On the other hand, by the 1990s nuclear power was an almost indissoluble part of the establishment. It should also be noted that as a nationalised monopoly (a position which France still largely maintains in practice), EDF and the nuclear industry was not subject to pressure to reduce costs by limiting safety improvements (perhaps unlike the USA). France involved a dominant nuclear hierarchy guided in turn by an elite administrative hierarchy. Individualist pressures favouring competition in the industry were rebuffed. It was therefore possible, operating from this position of strength, for the industry to embrace some safety improvements, thereby reducing pressures from egalitarian critics of the nuclear power industry. Certainly in the aftermath of Chernobyl, whilst the public opinion surveys continued to show support for the nuclear industry, there was a reduction in this support (Renn 1990, 157). There was a quiet debate about safety wherein, not just the Greens but the CFDT union (associated with the ruling Socialist Party) 'criticised the declarations made by the safety inspector of EDF . . . which claimed that accidents similar to that at Chernobyl could never happen in a French plant' (Liberatore 1995, 82).

The French state may have been rather more efficient in organising its own nuclear power programme compared to the United Kingdom but this was based on an implicit understanding that the technology was safe from a TMI- or Chernobyl-style disaster. The shock of such events meant that to satisfy this implicit public expectation of safety the French nuclear plant had to be seen as coping with the ramifications of severe nuclear accidents. The French state and its elite administrators wanted to ensure that anti-nuclear sentiment did not ride on the back of fears about nuclear safety. After all, the 1980s saw an increase, in Europe, of egalitarian-green concerns, and thus an incentive for dominant hierarchies to head off such challenges.

Hence not only was there was an argument to backfit existing reactors to make them less prone to Three Mile Island (TMI) or Chernobyl-type accidents, but also plans were supported whereby the next generation of reactors would be designed nearly as possible to being disaster-proof. This meant above all else that civilian society was safe even from the worst case scenario of a nuclear power accident. A related consequence of the Chernobyl accident and the increased expectation of full regulation to ensure nuclear safety was the gradual move towards greater independence for the French safety regulatory machinery.

Towards the EPR

Such had been the success in terms of deploying the 58 reactors which generated such a large proportion of French nuclear electricity that the French power system now had too much electricity. This has a lot to do with the fact that projections of future electricity demand made in the 1970s had proved to be excessive in practice. Hence it is not surprising that there was a pause in reactor construction. However the pause perhaps had a fundamental impact on the French nuclear industry because the strength of the French nuclear construction programme was particularly notable for its sheer momentum and concentrated amounts of capital of various sorts. Hence the dissolution of this programme meant that when it came to planning a more piecemeal programme of replacement of ageing reactors in the future things became more difficult.

The demand for much increased safety heralded the development of a fundamentally different design. This was still going to be a pressurised water reactor but, as mentioned earlier, designed with a central purpose of ensuring maximum safety. The development of this design, known as the European Pressurised Reactor, or EPR for short, emerged as a result of French-German industrial collaboration between Framatome and Siemens to prepare a design that could satisfy what the designers saw as advanced notions of safety. This could be deployed to meet common standards in both countries (Valkovic 2000). The French (nuclear) establishment could act proactively to improve safety, not just for its own sake, but also with an eye on selling French-designed reactors to markets overseas which were imbued with heightened demands for reactor safety.

However, the implementation of the EPR programme has not gone well. Three projects – one in Finland at Olkiluoto, one in northern France at Flamanville, and one at Taishan in China – have been terribly delayed with massive consequential financial losses. Construction of the Olkiluoto and Flamanville EPRs were started in 2005 and 2007 respectively, but at the time of writing (end 2019) are still not completed, and seems unlikely to be completed until at least 2023. The plant will cost over five times the original estimate (Wakim and Mouterde 2020). The first Taishan reactor was begun in 2009, and was completed a little over eight years later in 2017, but this took nearly twice as long as originally planned. Regardless of Flamanville's final completion date, French policy has been since 2012 to reduce rather than increase reliance on nuclear power. The Hollande Government decided in 2012 to cut the proportion of French electricity supplied by nuclear power from 75 per cent to 50 per cent by 2025, although the Macron Government has revised this target date to 2035.

In order to understand the extent to which nuclear safety may or may not have played a part in these setbacks it is first necessary to look at the safety regulatory machinery itself.

France's nuclear safety organisation and policy

In France there is a division between the body that is responsible for issuing definitive decisions on safety, the ASN ('Autorite de Surete de Nucleaire'), and a technical arm which advises the ASN, that is the IRSN ('Institut de Radioprotection et de Nucleaire'). Both these bodies are paid for by the French state, but are now (since 2006) formally independent of influence by anyone in the Government. The work on safety encompasses both existing and new plans for reactors, although in practice most of the work will be on the old reactors because of their sheer numbers. Many of the discussions are about the results of, and yardsticks applied to, safety inspections and periodic reviews of nuclear reactors applied.

According to Mycle Schneider:

> Since Chernobyl there have been several waves of revisions of the nuclear safety and radiation protection agencies. At the time there was the SCPRI, central services for the protection against ionising radiation, which was later changed into OPRI, office for the protection against ionising radiation, which then merged with IPSN and merged into the IRSN. On the safety side the main Technical Safety Organistion (TSO) was the IPSN. There were some major issues on the governance side. The IPSN was originally a department within the Atomic Energy Commission (CEA), but this was administratively separated and made independent when merged with radiation protection into the IRSN – although the staff remained the same, the building was the same, they even kept a CEA badge for a long time. So it took time until at least some independent spirit developed in these administrative entities. The same was true of the nuclear safety authority ASN. This was first a department of the Ministry of Industry before being made into a more independent nuclear safety administration. Of course, in both cases, IRSN and ASN, the elite technocrats from the Corps des Mines made sure to provide the respective bosses and keep control.
>
> (interview 19/03/2019)

According to an official of the IRSN:

> ASN will do all the control on the sites – 2000 sites. People are in the centre and also in the regions and on site. The state pays our salary. We are an independent administrative authority. There is a college of five Commissioners. Three Commissioners are named by the President of France, one by the President of the Senate and one by the Chairman of the National Assembly for six years. They are non-dismissible and for one term only. Nomination depends on competencies e.g. emergency responses, a medicine professor for radiation protection, an expert in waste management, etc.
>
> (interview 13/05/2019)

According to an IRSN official:

> The ASN and IRSN work together by ASN being clearly responsible for authorisation and IRSN is responsible for the assessment. E.g., the ASN will

get files, or safety cases, and make an initial assessment. They will decide whether they need an assessment from IRSN. IRSN has the specialists who do the technical assessments.

(interview 13/05/2019)

Hearings on particular cases are closed, and this practice of confidentiality is defended on the basis that if they are made open, as in Japan, the real discussions will merely retreat into backroom secrecy.

Safety philosophy and policy

The French safety regulators take their cue from the EU safety laws, which of course the French are influential in setting in the first place. The European Union issued a Directive on nuclear safety in 2014, this being a revision of one issued in 2009, and that being a revision of the first nuclear safety Directive issued in 2002. A crucial section is Article 8a which reads:

1   Member States shall ensure that the national nuclear safety framework requires that nuclear installations are designed, sited, constructed, commissioned, operated and decommissioned with the objective of preventing accidents and, should an accident occur, mitigating its consequences and avoiding:

    (a) early radioactive releases that would require off-site emergency measures but with insufficient time to implement them;
    (b) large radioactive releases that would require protective measures that could not be limited in area or time.

2   Member States shall ensure that the national framework requires that the objective set out in paragraph 1:

    (a) applies to nuclear installations for which a construction licence is granted for the first time after 14 August 2014;
    (b) is used as a reference for the timely implementation of reasonably practicable safety improvements to existing nuclear installations, including in the framework of the periodic safety reviews as defined in Article 8c(b).

(EUR-LEX 2014)

The safety philosophy is simple on the face of it at least, that is, if something needs to be done to assure maximum of safety then it should be done regardless of cost. However, this philosophy is hedged by practical considerations accordingly (critics would say undermined by commercial consideration). An IRSN official put it thus:

We don't take into account the cost, but there is engineering cost – there are not enough engineers to do everything. It is important to prioritise modifications, so we might say leave something until next time. ASN will define the priorities. But always there are some discussions with IRSN about this. When they don't agree it is often on the timing. The operators may try and lobby the ASN if they perceive that the IRSN is demanding too much. There are hearings which discuss these things, in a college, with EDF as the licensee.

(interview 13/05/2019)

The French nuclear power plant safety law is contained within what passes in this context a short document (Republique Francaise 2016). This relatively simple set of commitments, however, is interpreted by the ASN and IRSN in conversation with the operators (usually EDF), and the results are made in the form of case conclusions, or 'avis' (view).

Although the emphasis is on the most absolutely safe technological solution, in practice 'probabalistic' analysis takes place, with what is judged to be higher consequence accidents being treated as a risk needing abating even though it is an unlikely occurrence. Critics will argue, of course, that not only does this apparently scientific approach speak to the unknowable nature of some risks but also that some risks will remain unknown.

Critics point to problems of trust in validating safety by the operators and companies involved in the nuclear sector. Mycle Schneider cites various instances including the 'Transnuklear scandal' in the 1980s where nuclear waste was being smuggled around Europe, there were forgeries of safety documents at the Creusot Forge which makes reactor parts, and problems existed at the Cattenom site when it emerged 30 years after start-up that safety-related devices were not even installed in the cooling ponds for spent fuel. 'The Regulator and its TSO (ASN and IRSN) are worse than their reputation implies' (interview 19/03/2019).

French safety officials insist that safety regulations are not applied more strictly than during the time of the construction of the first 58 reactors. However interpretations of what is regarded as being safe seem to have changed. During the 1980s and 1990s it was decided that the existing nuclear fleet should be fitted with new devices to prevent radioactive contamination reaching the outside environment in the event of a serious nuclear accident. 'Filtered containment venting' (FCV) was fitted in all of the reactors. FCV prevents gases and particles from the reactor core escaping beyond containment. In addition to this Passive Autocatalytic Recombiners (PAR) have also been fitted to existing reactors. Periodic safety reviews are conducted every ten years and PAR devices were mandated in the 2005 review. A PAR device scoops up hydrogen that may be released following an accident and which may if unabated lead to explosive consequences. Indeed hydrogen explosions proved to be a key problem in the 2011 accident at Fukushima.

France, as well as other EU states were subject to two particular sets of EU legislation: the 2014 Directive, and also the post-Fukushima 'stress tests'. The 'stress tests' conducted by the French authorities were mandated by the EU in a 2011 decision by the European Council (EU Commission 2014).

In terms of the stress tests, the origination started in a European Commission initiative in 2011. This involved various new evaluations to examine the risks faced by nuclear plants from seismic and flooding risks and also what extra measures were needed to deal with them. Plans needed to be drawn up and implemented that would ensure that safety improvements were put in place to protect the public from such risks.

A key concept arising from the stress tests was the notion of the 'hardened safety core'. According to nuclear analyst Christof Pistner:

> The hardened safety core comprises two types of systems – additional means of electricity systems for existing systems but also there has to be extra diesel generators for each power plant for an autonomous site. Hardened safety core includes mobile diesel generator installed in a short timescale, and a bigger one that takes longer. And additional cooling systems to provide redundancy for the reactor core as well as the spent fuel pool.
>
> (interview 20/12/2018)

Pistner (ibid. interview), who is a German-based analyst, compared German and French requirements and implementation:

> Based on what we analysed we saw deficits compared to German requirements – especially with respect to implementation. Hardened safety core takes a long time to implement. [The] [f]irst phase [took] up to 2015 when small mobile equipment plus FARN (a rapid action force) was done. [The] [s]econd phase [lasted] until 2020. Additional diesel generator sets at each sites improved FARN. Only in the third phase are additional core cooling systems, additional generators etc. installed. There is no timescale on when all will be completed. The starting position was different. German plant[s][have] had additional diesel generators and additional cooling systems since 1990s. Also different generators [are] able to withstand earthquakes. French plants planned to come up to level of German plants. [The] French have been quick to implement mobile generators. There is still a difference between the French and German plants.

In Germany, also, FCV and PAR had been fitted previously.

French regulators respond that at some cases, such as the Fessenheim site, where reactors were soon to retire, the economics did not justify bringing in all of the safety upgrades.

It should be noted that this is a clearly different approach to the US safety protocols, which, as discussed in Chapter 4 merely call for 'adequate' safety in case of new reactors and say that backfitting existing reactors should only be done where there was a positive cost-benefit gain to be derived from such action. A French regulatory official commented:

> In France and in parallel with the USA we considered beyond the design accidents. In France this means a SCRAM system and also to provide backup to a failure of a safety system. In the USA this is just a SCRAM system.
>
> (interview 13/05/2019)

('SCRAM' refers to the emergency shutting down of a nuclear reactor by the immediate insertion of nuclear control rods).

Safety policy and the EPR

The design of the EPR is certainly marketed to be in line with such ideas of beyond design accidents. The EPR includes various extra safety devices on top of those included in previous (so-called Generation II) reactors. The new measures include what is called an 'advanced passive design', double containments around the reactor (that is in addition to enhanced aircraft protection), multiple redundancy in safety injection systems, and a 'core catcher'. There are four safety injection systems for both the primary and secondary systems, whereas strictly speaking only one is needed provided it works properly. The primary system involves the ability to inject material into the core to take it offline, and the secondary system is in effect a water pump to intervene in the case of a loss of coolant situation. The core catcher is a device that is aimed to prevent a core meltdown by having a shield between the reactor and the ground.

One question that emerges is the extent to which the problems associated with the construction of the EPR are to do with increased safety measures. The safety philosophy may have remained the same, but as discussed earlier, interpretations of safety have changed. Hence answering this question is more complicated than it sounds. The development of a reactor that is intended to avoid disastrous Chernobyl- or Fukushima-type outcomes has added on costs. In terms of add-on costs, one nuclear consultant I interviewed implied that the costs of a 'Generation III' reactor were increased by up to the order of 30 per cent by three features – the advanced passive design, core catcher, and aircraft protection (interview with British nuclear consultant 01/06/2018).

On the other hand it is important to say also that such plausibly safety-related cost increases (20–30 per cent), do not account for the construction delays which are the really big 'cost-killers' as far as building nuclear reactors is concerned. If a plant takes twice as long to build than projected originally, then costs are likely to more than double. Not only do staff have to be kept being paid, but interest charges accumulate on the debts that have already been accrued to finance the building of the plant. As discussed earlier the majority of such cost increases may be down to the fact that the required industrial conditions for building new reactors in the West do not (at least no longer) exist. An additional factor is that the EPR is a new design which is more complicated than previous types of reactors. This 'complexity' factor is difficult to cost, and may not be captured by accounts which focus solely on the cost of add-on features.

Certainly one argument for the much larger size of the EPR reactors (1.6 GWe each) is to try and bring down the costs of the additional safety features relative to that of the rest of the plant. This pursuit of economies of scale has been a technique of nuclear reactor designers since the 1950s, but it has not succeeded. In some ways this is only a repeat of earlier history of nuclear power in the USA in the 1960s–1970s, discussed in Chapter 4, where economies of scale in building larger reactors were cancelled out by increases in safety costs (Bupp and Derian 1978, 156–157).

Problems with the EPR construction

The construction of the first EPR began in Finland in the summer of 2005. The plan was that power station would be completed in 2009. A completion time of just four years would be one of the records of nuclear construction and with the benefit of hindsight it does seem premature to assume that it would take the short time that was projected to complete the plant. Given that construction costs are, broadly speaking, a multiple of the time it takes to build a plant (MacKerron 1992), the Finnish plant by 2019 must have been costing over three times more than originally anticipated. Yet the power station experienced increasing difficulties and delays grew. According to a report published by the World Nuclear Association detailing problems building the power plant:

> First to come to light were irregularities in foundation concrete, which caused work to slow on site for months. Later it was found that subcontractors had provided heavy forgings that were not up to project standards and which had to be re-cast. An apparent problem constructing the reactor's unique double-containment structure ha[d] also caused delays, while meeting regulators requirements for the instrumentation and control system 'may become critical for the plant time schedule', according to Silvennoinen.
>
> The latest difficulty came when Finland's nuclear safety and radiation regulator, STUK (the Finnish nuclear safety regulator), noted that 'instructions have not been observed in the welding of pipes and the supervision of welding'.
>
> (World Nuclear News 2009)

Even by the summer of 2020 the plant was still not generating electricity. A construction time of over 14 years cannot possibly be anywhere near the realm of what could be called an economically competitive project. AREVA, the state-owned French reactor constructor who were responsible for building the EPR reactor design, took most of the financial hit for the project because they had what was supposed to be a turnkey agreement with the Finnish power company OVE. There was a long legal wrangle over who should pay for cost overruns. As a result of this AREVA effectively went bankrupt, and had to be bailed out by the French Government. It was incorporated into EDF.

However back in France construction of the first EPR (at Flamanville) did not go well either. The plant began to be built at the end of 2007; yes it was continually delayed and in 2019 it emerged that the plant would not be complete until 2022 at the earliest. Again, construction costs are likely to be over three times that which was originally projected.

Of course it is hoped later projects will be much cheaper. Indeed in 2018 an EPR came online in China although this took some eight years as opposed to its expected construction time of five years, but then conditions in China are somewhat different. Mycle Schneider notes on this comparison that

> The only way to compare what is happening now with what happened in the 1970s and 1980s is to compare early construction in France in the 1980s with China in the 2010s. Like the French then, the Chinese have built up a huge skilled workforce on all levels from the project manager to the welder. They move them from construction site to construction site, so they are getting better all the time. They have a living skills workforce.
>
> That is not the case in France today. At the construction site of the EPR Olkiluoto-3 in Finland they have over 50 nationalities in the workforce; this didn't exist in the earlier French construction waves. They were all nationally built. Globalisation has brought multiple problems of communication. They run computers in India for a project in Finland. You have so many more potential possibilities for mistakes and errors in communication. But even in the 1980s there were issues; e.g. over 1000 km of rotten control-command cables in at least one dozen reactors. In one reactor that was still under construction, they replaced them, which turned out very expensive. So they have not done this at existing reactors and installed additional alarms instead.
>
> (interview with Mycle Schneider 19/03/2019)

> [A]t least one third of the workforce at Flamanville 3 is foreign. The housing and social conditions were so bad – e.g. container flats with no access to public or any other transport – that human rights organizations stepped in at some point. And, of course, globalization is not the only cause for problems (in building the reactors)!
>
> (email from Mycle Schneider 09/09/2019)

Other differences can be noted with China including less stringent health and safety rules in general, and also differences in the way that nuclear safety is organised, and such issues are discussed in Chapter 5 on China. One key difference with China is that in France, and other developed Western states, the proportion of economic activity associated with manufacturing relative to services has declined over the years. This may have reduced the availability of an industrial workforce and thus ability of Western states to deliver unique civil engineering projects at relatively low cost. Another difference with China is that in China health and safety practices will be much lower leading to lower construction costs.

One way in which the upscaling of the reactor size (to absorb costs of additional safety measures) has demonstrably backfired has been in the case of the design of the reactor lid, the forging of which caused a considerable part of the delays in the delivery of the Flamanville reactor. In 2015 it was discovered that the reactor-pressure vessel lid and base had been badly forged – and indeed that documents at AREVA's works at Creusot Forge contained 'irregularities' regarding the forging of the reactor-pressure vessel (IRSN 2017, 118). Concentrations of carbon were not constant throughout the lid.

The problem stems from the fact that previous reactors had not been so large and so there had not been such an issue of keeping the temperature of the highly specialised steel the same in all the parts of the forging. It is a classic case of how, in engineering terms, it is often very problematic to simply upscale a piece of engineering. Following lengthy negotiations between EDF, ASN, and IRSN it was agreed that if inspections warrant it, that the reactor lid may be replaced by 2024, even though the building of the plant would continue and be otherwise completed before this date. Replacement would not be possible before 2024 since it would take a long time to manufacture a new Reactor Pressure Vessel (RPV) (IRSN 2017, 132).

Alas, for the Flamanville project, another major problem emerged when inspections revealed that welding on injection pumps was judged inadequate. The problem was so fundamental that the regulators ruled that the welds had to be done again. The project's timeline had already been lengthened by successive announcements to completion in 2019, but then in 2019, it was realised that completion could not occur until 2022 if the re-welding was to be done properly.

Weldings have to be especially good on nuclear power plants because the water pressures that the steel has to withstand are many times higher than in more usual applications. A regulatory official explained the problem of inadequate weldings:

> This wasn't a problem in previous designs because welders were more competent (with a programme of nuclear power plant building). There is a problem in Europe. It is the same in UK. We don't have people who are skilled in welding as they used to be. If you don't build [nuclear] power plants people will disappear. Since the beginning of the 1990s we didn't build any nuclear power plants, and since then we have lost the competencies. The requirement in ability for welders is higher for nuclear power, and we don't have people of these competencies any more. It is difficult to find people who are sufficiently competent. . . . The control by EDF and Framatome was not adequate. They don't have this problem in China because they are building many nuclear power plants. In Normandy you need high-quality people for military naval projects as well as nuclear power. So it has been decided to create a high-level welding training group to cover these areas. It is under progress.
> (anonymous interview with ASN official 13/05/2019)

Not only did the delay have big consequences for the Flamanville project, it also created potential knock-on impacts for EDF's project to build a British EPR at Hinkley C. The British had, in the award of a contract to EDF to build Hinkley C (agreed in 2013), agreed that it would issue loan guarantees which would underpin what would amount to the majority of the investment required to build the double-EPR reactor. However this guarantee was, according to an analysis by the EU Commission (conducted whilst the project was being evaluated under the state aid rules), conditional on the timely completion of the Flamanville EPR project. The plant was supposed to be generating electricity by the end of 2020. However, after the welding judgement, this now appears impossible to fulfil. The

EU's state aid judgement says, of the contract conditions set in the contract signed by the British Government and EDF:

> The Base Case Condition is that satisfactory evidence has been provided that Flamanville 3 has completed the trial operation period and that the requirements of the Guarantor in respect of performance during such period have been met. The Guarantor has the option to extend the date for meeting the Base Case Condition into the future by increasing the amount of Base Equity and procuring that such increase benefits from the required credit support. The Base Case Condition date cannot fall later than 31 December 2020.
>
> (OJEU 2015, L109/50)

This means that either the British Government change the basis of the financial support to enable them to guarantee EDF the money or EDF find the money from elsewhere, which given the limited ability of EDF to raise such a sum from the market, will mean obtaining the money from the French Government, directly or indirectly. At the time of writing (summer 2020) there seemed no prospect of any funds being guaranteed by the British state.

Conclusion

In the introduction to the chapter, essentially three questions were posed about a) the extent of change in French nuclear safety policy, b) the extent to which such policy might have contributed to the problems with maintaining the nuclear industry and delivering the EPR programme, and c) how we can understand outcomes using cultural theory.

In the case of the first question, there have been changes in both the form and substance of nuclear safety policy. The ASN and IRSN have become more formally independent of the French state. Of course it is difficult to ascertain what difference this formal change makes, but we can say more about changes in the substance of policy. Policy has changed in that new and existing nuclear power plants are now expected to have more equipment and readiness to stop a severe nuclear accident impacting on the public and wider environment.

However, it needs also to be said that the way in which such criteria are met by new reactors is defined by the design of the only new reactor that is being deployed in France, namely the EPR. The safety features of the EPR were designed, initially, by a joint French-German industrial collaboration, and were not the product of specifications from the nuclear regulators. Hence it can be argued that increases from the 1980s onwards in the safety specifications of the French (in this case EPR) new nuclear power plants come from the nuclear industry itself rather than the nuclear safety regulators.

It is certainly not clear that nuclear safety regulatory policy changes have had a direct impact on the nuclear industry either in maintaining the fleet or in the problems that have afflicted the construction of the EPR at Flamanville. There has not been a rush to dismantle the French nuclear industry. As of the time of writing only one PWR plant, at Fessenheim (the oldest PWR in operation), had been shut down (at the end of June 2020) – that is apart from an early PWR experimental project at Chooz, which was closed in 1991 (IAEA 2020). The issues with the RPV lid and the pipe weldings at the new construction of the EPR are (according to IRSN testimony) issues that are likely to have been picked up if they had occurred in the 1970s or 1980s. The causes of these problems are problems with construction rather than an increase in the strictness of the safety rules themselves.

The problems with the weldings are attributable to a decline in the availability of welders with the required specialist skills. This is a consequence of the lack of work in building nuclear power stations. The changes in the way engineering work is organised in countries like France, with a trend towards 'globalisation' also implies that declines in the ability of now more service-oriented Western countries to deliver large, specialised, engineering projects at low cost may also be a factor.

However things may be more complex than this – complexity being the point – in that the very complexity of 'Generation III' reactors may itself be a big factor in making them more difficult to build. The Generation III reactors such as EPR – which is seen as being having around the most complex safety devices of all the designs – are designed around a (passive) safety concept rather than a simple objective of producing as much energy for the minimum of cost.

France is a country where the hierarchy that nuclear power needs is provided by the hierarchical administrative structure and the nuclear institutions that have been steered coherently from the centre. This has been relatively unthreatened in the electricity sector, at least until recent years, by individualistic concerns for competition. But now globally based competitive pressures in the sources of engineering services threaten the possibility of hierarchically based nuclear organisation. Perhaps the type of almost 'craft-based' engineering services upon which nuclear power depends are not as well served by these new conditions. On the other hand this hierarchy has felt the need to incorporate, or at least effectively deflect, egalitarian criticisms of nuclear safety by focussing on strengthening policies to improve safety. The French state has not changed its desire to have safe reactors, but in the aftermath of TMI and Chernobyl the nuclear designers, backed by the state, have altered their interpretation of how nuclear power stations and systems can deliver this safety.

Perhaps we can take this French case study and use it to form a hypothesis. Namely that countries with hierarchical systems are best placed to deliver nuclear power. In the case of egalitarian pressures, the regulatory result can be seen as 'weak' ecological modernisation, involving top-down regulatory pressure for more safety and the relative independence of the regulators from pressures from the nuclear industry to water down safety improvements.

Interviews

Mycle Schneider (nuclear policy consultant), 19/03/2019 and email communication 09/09/2019

Official (anonymous) of IRSN, 13/05/2019
Official (anonymous) of ASN, 13/05/2019
Christ of Pistner, Head of Division Nuclear Engineering and Facility Safety Office, Institute for Applied Ecology, Darmstadt, 20/12/2018
Anonymous interview with UK nuclear industry consultant, 01/06/2018

References

Bupp, I., and Derian, J.-C. (1978) *Light Water: How the Nuclear Dream Dissolved*. New York: Basic Books.

Eales, C., and Sverrisson, R. (2014) 'France's Energy Elite', *Montel Magazine*, 13(2) (May), 23–29.

EUR-LEX (2014) 'Council Directive 2014/87/Euratom of 8 July 2014 Amending Directive 2009/71/Euratom Establishing a Community Framework for the Nuclear Safety of Nuclear Installations'. https://eur-lex.europa.eu/legal-content/EN/TXT/?uri=uriserv%3AOJ.L_.2014.219.01.0042.01.ENFeldman

Eurobarometer (2010) *Europeans and Nuclear Safety*, Special Eurobarometer Report 324. https://ec.europa.eu/commfrontoffice/publicopinion/index.cfm/Survey/getSurveyDetail/search/nuclear/surveyKy/769

European Commission (2014) 'Stress Tests'. https://ec.europa.eu/energy/en/topics/nuclear-energy/nuclear-safety/stress-tests

Feldman D. (1986) 'Public Choice Theory Applied to National Energy Policy: The Case of France', *Journal of Public Policy*, 6(2), 137–158.

Grubler, A. (2010) 'The Costs of the French Nuclear Scale-Up: A Case of Negative Learning by Doing', *Energy Policy*, 38, 5174–5188.

IAEA (International Atomic Energy Agency) (2020) *France: Country Profile*. https://cnpp.iaea.org/countryprofiles/France/France.htm

IRSN (2017) 'Assessment of the Consequences of the Manufacturing Anomaly in the Closure Head and the Lower Head of the Flamanville 3 Reactor Pressure Vessel', 26 June. www.irsn.fr/EN/newsroom/News/Pages/20170628_Assessment-of-consequences-of-anomaly-in-EPR-Flamanville-reactor-pressure-vessel.aspx

Kitschelt, H. (1986) 'Political Opportunity Structures and Political Protest', *British Journal of Political Science*, 16, 57–85.

Liberatore, A. (1995) 'The Social Construction of Environmental Problems', in P. Gladbergen and A. Blowers (eds.) *Environmental Policy in an International Context: Perspectives*. London: Arnold, pp. 59–84.

MacKerron, G. (1992) 'Nuclear Costs: Why Do They Keep Rising?', *Energy Policy*, 20, 641–652.

Nelkin, D., and Pollack, M. (1981) *The Atom Besieged: Extraparliamentary Dissent in France and West Germany*. Cambridge, MA: MIT Press.

OJEU – Official Journal of the European Union (2015) 28 April. https://eur-lex.europa.eu/legal-content/EN/TXT/PDF/?uri=OJ:L:2015:109:FULL&from=EN

Renn, O. (1990) 'Public Responses to the Chernobyl Accident', *Journal of Environmental Psychology*, 10, 151–167.

Republique Francaise (2016) *Arrêté du 7 février 2012 fixant les règles générales relatives aux installations nucléaires de base*. www.legifrance.gouv.fr/affichTexte.do?cidTexte=JORFTEXT000025338573&dateTexte=20160205

Sovacool, B.K., and Valentine, S.V. (2010) 'The Socio-Political Economy of Nuclear Energy in China and India Energy', *Energy*, 35(9 September), 3803–3813.

Valkovic, V. (2000) *Radioactivity*. Amsterdam: Elsevier.

Wakim, N., and Mouterde, P. (2020) '"Echecopérationnel" et "dérive des coûts": la gestion de l'EPR, réacteurnucléaire de troisièmegénération, décriéepar la Cour de comptes', *Le Monde*, 9 July. www.lemonde.fr/economie/article/2020/07/09/nucleaire-la-cour-des-comptes-ereinte-l-epr_6045707_3234.html

World Nuclear News (unsigned) (2009) 'Olkiluoto Pipe Welding "Deficient" Says Regulator', *World Nuclear News*, 16 October. www.world-nuclear-news.org/NN-Olkiluoto_pipe_welding_deficient_says_regulator-1610095.html

7 Nuclear energy and safety in South Korea

From development to ecological modernisation

The study of nuclear energy in South Korea is important from the point of view of this book since it represents a country that has been committed to nuclear power as part of its development strategy. Until recently, indeed, it has been included in the pantheon of nations seeing nuclear power as a key part of its development strategy (Jasanoff and Kim 2009). South Korea seemed to be bucking a trend towards a slowdown in building nuclear power plants. However, in the aftermath of the Fukushima accident in 2011 a substantial anti-nuclear movement gained strength.

We need to compare Korean nuclear safety standards with those of other countries being studied in this book and examine the extent to which any changes in policies on safety are associated with changes in policy towards nuclear power. We also need to examine how any of such changes have been associated with political changes, developments, and movements.

South Korea has one of the larger nuclear fleets in the world. According to the World Nuclear Association,

- 24 reactors provide about one-third of South Korea's electricity from 23 GWe of plant.
- South Korea is among the world's most prominent nuclear energy countries, and exports its technology widely. It is currently involved in the building of four nuclear reactors in the UAE, under a $20 billion contract.
- Nuclear energy has been a strategic priority for South Korea, but the new president elected in 2017 is aiming to phase it out over some 45 years.

(WNA 2019)

All but three of the reactors are PWRs, with the other three being 'heavy-water' CANDU reactors. The two newest reactors (at the time of writing) are APR1400 reactors, known as Generation III types, although Dawson (2017) argues that these are only partly advanced given that the reactor designs build on a lot of existing features of the prior Generation II reactors.

According to the World Nuclear Industry Energy Status Report of 2019:

Nuclear power provided 127 TWh in 2018, a drop of 10 percent compared to 2017, and 19 percent below the maximum production in 2015. Nuclear power supplied 23.7 percent of the nation's electricity in 2018, less than half of the maximum of 53.3 percent in 1987.

(Schneider and Froggatt 2019, 197)

The period following the Fukushima accident in the Spring of 2011 has coincided with limitations on the South Korean nuclear power programme. At the time there were plans to build a further 13 nuclear power plants by 2024 (Squassoni 2013), but now it seems likely that no more than two will be completed by that date, the other planned power plant having being cancelled. Two power stations were closed in 2017 and 2018. In December 2019 the closure of Wolsong 1 reactor was also announced (Proctor 2020). A further four nuclear power plants are earmarked for closure by 2026. The country's nuclear development programme now looks more like a gradual closure programme.

Development of nuclear energy in South Korea exhibited the characteristics of state capitalism, perhaps typical of East Asian development, even including China (Toke 2017, 34–40). This involves decisions by the state about which industries and within that even companies, should receive special state assistance, such as cheap loans.

For many years in South Korea the dominant governmental discourse saw nuclear power 'as a symbol of the power of science and technology that Korea should actively seek to acquire in order to develop into a strong, modern nation' (Jasanoff and Kim 2009, 131). Indeed there has been an intermittent interest in developing a nuclear military capability as well as a civil one (Jasanoff and Kim 2009, 132). More recently South Korea has maintained an interest in developing techniques for reprocessing spent nuclear fuels, some products of which could be used in bomb-making (Lim 2019).

For many years following World War 2 South Korea was ruled by authoritarian regimes, sometimes backed up by military force. In one notorious incident in 1980 (the Gwangju uprising) up to 2000 protestors were killed by the police and military. The regimes were notable for favouring an elite hierarchy of industrial corporations whose interests were promoted by the state. Democracy emerged in 1987, initially under conservative leadership (Ku et al. 2017).

The electricity industry in South Korea was, and still is, state owned, through the agency of the Korea Electric Power Corporation (KEPCO). A complex of inter-acting nuclear industry organisations was established which coordinated nuclear development (Jasanoff and Kim 2009, 132–136). The coordinated and centrally directed nature of Korean nuclear power, which emphasised achieving self-sufficiency in as many engineering aspects of the industry as possible, led to what was widely perceived as being an effective, well-organised and cost-effective path of nuclear power development. This type of hierarchical approach not only mirrored the dominant nature of the cultural basis of the South Korean regime, but seems to suit the deployment of nuclear power. This hierarchical cultural facet is said to have been missing in the nuclear industry in states such as the UK (Toke and Baker 2016).

The post-Fukushima period has been associated with a turnaround in the position of the nuclear energy industry compared with the trajectory beforehand. The conduct of nuclear safety activity came under intense scrutiny with cover-ups and failure to observe safety regulations being discovered (World Nuclear Association 2019). The country's hitherto apparently consensus objectives in favour of continued nuclear power development have fractured.

President Moon Jae-in was elected in 2017 on a platform of phasing out nuclear power in South Korea, a policy to which he committed himself on taking office. However, following a deliberative discussion (involving appointment of a body of citizens to conduct a deliberative poll to make policy recommendations) this policy was tempered to the extent that the two power plants under construction were allowed to complete. On the other hand the deliberative poll said that after this the reliance on nuclear power should be reduced. President Moon accepted these judgements.

Hence the Government's policy is that the reliance on nuclear is to be reduced, and the emphasis on renewable energy increased, up from 7.6 per cent in 2017 (WNA 2019; Xinhua 2019). According to a draft of the ninth national energy plan issued by the Government in May 2020, the plan aimed to take the

> total renewable capacity to around 79GW, which the government expects to represent around 40pc of the country's installed capacity, compared with 15pc now. The ninth plan sees coal, nuclear and gas-fired capacity accounting for 14.9pc, 9.9pc and 31pc, respectively, by 2034.
>
> (Lee and Horslen 2020)

A major factor associated with the change in South Korea's policies on nuclear power is the arousal of an anti-nuclear movement in the shadow of Fukushima. Hence there is a need to study this.

Nuclear protest and debate

According to Jasanoff and Kim (2009, 134), prior to the 1980s:

> The failure to escape from underdevelopment and to catch up with advanced industrial nations, economically and militarily, was perceived as one of the most serious risks for the nation. In this atmosphere, nuclear safety was relegated to secondary importance.

However, in the 1980s and 1990s concern about nuclear safety gradually developed, driven partly by concern over the political economy and opacity of the regime itself (which was not democratic), but also whether the trend towards Korean designs for nuclear power included enough concern for safety. Protests increased in the 1990s, focussing on disposal of nuclear waste (Jasanoff and Kim 2009, 134–138). Initially this involved localised action, and successful opposition was mounted to proposed nuclear waste sites, with less success in derailing the nuclear power construction programme (Richardson 2017). Nevertheless, the policy domain of nuclear power in South Korea was still being characterised (along with Japan) by the end of the first decade of the 21st century as involving 'low levels of civic activism' (Valentine and Sovacool 2010).

However things changed after the Fukushima accident. According to Richardson (2017, 134) 'the South Korean anti-nuclear movement expanded to unprecedented proportions in the aftermath of Fukushima'. According to Kim and Chung (2018, 112):

> Rallies demanding exit-from-nuclear were attended not only by the usual activists but also by housewives, intellectuals, students and middle-class workers. They were joined by anti-nuclear weapons activists who had been mostly silent on the nuclear power issue for decades. This represented a new convergence of Japanese civil activists.

'Since Fukushima, Korean civil activism has ridden a tide of rising public awareness of nuclear safety and an increasing unwillingness to accept the construction of nuclear plants and waste storage facilities on their doorstep' (Kim and Chung 2018, 117).

The anti-nuclear movement developed international links and became a more credible opponent of the country's nuclear programme, focussing both on opposing new constructions and calling for the closure of older plants. Yet, the anti-nuclear movement was still not able to achieve their objectives in these cases.

A so-called 'energy citizenship' movement emerged, with local cooperatives formed to deploy renewable energy schemes, helped by a Feed-in Tariff introduced in 2002 (Park 2018). Some of this was directly associated with anti-nuclear actions, for example the activities promoted by the Seoul Metropolitan Government (SMG) which established a framework for participative energy governance. This involved what was called the 'One Less Nuclear Power Plant Citizens Council' and the parallel 'One Less Nuclear Power Plant Implementation Council'. These involved debates and discussions, and alongside this went various practical initiatives such as groups organising energy saving and promotion of solar PV installations (Yun 2018).

Increasing focus was centred on nuclear safety issues and perceived weaknesses of regulation. Then candidates in elections standing on the basis of ending the nuclear power construction programme were elected. This culminated in the election of President Moon-Jae-in, who took office in May 2017 who fought, and after taking office, pledged to implement a programme of ending construction of nuclear power plants.

Moon set in motion a public debate on the future of nuclear power in South Korea. The public debate was structured along textbook 'deliberative' lines. In fact, the South Korean 'deliberative turn' emerged in a context of local citizen's group initiatives, including organising local 'voluntary' referenda on a proposal for a nuclear waste dump in Buan and later in 2014 a proposal to build a new nuclear power plant at Samcheok (Ku 2018, 35–38).

A major focus of contention in the debate was whether the construction of reactors Shin Kori 5 and 6 near the city of Uslan in the South East of Korea should be completed. There was local opposition to the schemes, with fears existing about whether the number of nuclear power stations should be increased in an area that had been subject to significant earthquakes in the past. According to Se (2017) the deliberative design was chosen according to the theory set out by James Fishkin (Fishkin 1995), and coordinated by a committee:

> The committee conducted four rounds of surveys in total, including initial phone interviews of about 20,000 people . . . the committee randomly selected 500 people, considering demographics in South Korea, and invited them for deliberation. The participants were provided with briefing materials prepared by both pro- and anti-nuclear energy organizations. Lectures were also offered by competing experts followed by Q&A sessions, and then the participants were given opportunities to discuss the issue face-to-face in small groups.
>
> (Se 2017)

President Moon did not insist that Korean export of nuclear technology be ended and his anti-nuclear programme was prefaced on a process of public consultation which was undertaken soon after he gained office. The deliberative process just described formed the central part of this consultation. The debates attracted international attention, and some leading scientists and engineers wrote in to defend the nuclear power programme.

The deliberation had mixed results, with two plant constructions (which had been started shortly beforehand) left to continue, while plans for further plants were cancelled. The ultimate aim of phasing out nuclear power was agreed. In this presidency, at least, a shift towards seeing renewable energy rather than nuclear power as providing the main alternative to fossil fuels has been established as state policy. The prospect of extensions to the operating lives of existing reactors has been much reduced and old reactors are being closed down (World Nuclear News 2013; Se 2017; Lim 2019; WNA 2019).

It should be noted that this upsurge in concern for nuclear safety occurs in a period where there has been a high level of concern for environmental problems in general, and energy-related issues in particular. Indeed South Korea has been rated as being the most concerned, or among the most concerned in a survey of 24 nations covering environmental, climate, and energy issues (IPSOS Global Study 2020).

There has also been opposition to the efforts to undertake a form of reprocessing called 'pyro processing' which generates a form of plutonium. Some argue that this process, which could lead to plutonium being burned in a fast breeder reactor, could be a response to the country's growing problem of what to do with the country's used nuclear fuel rods (Park 2009). However, others argue that this would greatly add to the expense of the nuclear industry, and that a much cheaper method of dealing with nuclear waste would simply be to store the used fuel rods in dry conditions until a disposal site can be agreed. In any case fast breeder reactors have never been commercialised successfully (Kang and von Hippel 2017). Nevertheless the Korean Atomic Energy Research Institute has continued to develop plans for this strategy. Support for the path comes partly from those wanting to see South Korea have a plutonium-based nuclear weapons capability (Lim 2019).

Nordhaus and Wang (2020) argue that

> The nuclear industries of Taiwan, South Korea, and Japan are . . . the product of authoritarian or de facto one-party states, where the ruling party passed control over the energy sector (and many other parts of the economy) to state-owned corporations, government-issued monopolies, or quasi-cartels of favoured companies . . . just as the nuclear establishment was part and parcel of post-war economic planning by what were effectively one-party states, opposition to that establishment has become a cause for those who demand political and economic reform.

Under this explanation anti-nuclear opposition in South Korea was often identified with opposition to what became widely seen as a corrupt industrial hierarchy. Energy democracy became part of a counterposed democracy. The post-Fukushima upsurge in opposition to nuclear power and emergence of 'energy citizenship' can be said to be part of this opposition to the industrial hierarchy. Given that it seems plausible to link the egalitarian opposition to nuclear power as an allegedly unsafe centralising force with the egalitarian opposition to the post-WW2 military-industrial hierarchy.

Nuclear safety regulation

Although coherent legislation on the nuclear power industry dates back to 1958 it was only in 1996 that a separate nuclear safety regulatory agency was established in the form of the Atomic Energy Safety Commission. Even then the body appeared to be almost directly integrated into the Government since its Chairman was the Minister for Education, Science, and Technology (OECD 2009, 17). It was not until 2011, that, according to the present nuclear regulators: 'The Nuclear Safety and Security Commission (NSCC) was launched after the accident at Fukushima Daiichi nuclear power station as people longed for a safer community' (NSSC 2019, 2).

This body has greater independence in the sense that rather than being chaired by a member of the Government, the Chair is appointed by the President, and members of the Nuclear Safety and Security Commission are appointed for their expertise in technical areas. According to the law on nuclear regulation, 'Commission members shall be evenly from relevant fields, such as nuclear power, the environment, public health, medicine, science, technology, public safety, law, humanities, and social science, who are able to contribute to the safety of nuclear power' (Nuclear Laws of the Republic of Korea 2019). There is a combination of regulation through the issue of technical standards and also specific enforcement decrees and regulations.

Following a review the NSSC announced it was taking the following action:

> To prepare against possible earthquakes and tsunamis, the NSSC has improved the safety of nuclear power plants by requiring enhanced anti-seismic design, installing automatic shutdown systems and flood gates, and extending flood barriers. In case of loss of power or flooding of nuclear power plants, the NSSC requires preparations to prevent the situation from advancing into a severe accident by providing mobile EDGs (Emergency Diesel Generators) and extra storage batteries, and installing outside injection channels for emergency cooling water. In case of a damage to nuclear fuel, the NSSC requires measures to prevent massive release of radioactive materials including the installation of extra hydrogen elimination devices and CFVS (Containment Filtered Venting System). To establish a firm legal basis for regulatory control of severe accident, the NSSC revised the NSA (the Nuclear Safety Act) and carried out subsequent rule-making process to stipulate all the necessary matters on regulatory control of severe accident.
>
> (NSSC, 8)

The reference to 'extra hydrogen mitigation' includes fitting of Passive Autocatalytic Recombiner technology (PAR) to all existing reactors (Kim et al. 2015). It was reported, in 2014, that FCVS equipment would be fitted to all of South Korea's reactors (OECD-NEA 2014), and a contract was issued to a French company to fit some of them (Framatome 2017), although it seems that problems have occurred with fitting FCVS in some cases (personal communication with Yang Yi Wonyoung, 19/03/2020). This does not necessarily mean that the nuclear safety standards have reached European levels, partly because they are playing catch-up from a much lower baseline. Some steps, including examining the seismic vulnerability of existing reactors, are not scheduled to be completed until some time ahead (Kim 2019).

Recent reactors under construction are 'Generation III' reactors (APR1400) designed by KEPCO, the state-owned Korean Electric Power Company. It seems that such reactors have been said to lack some of the features of the French EPR, including a core catcher and full aircraft protection (Green 2017). This general conclusion concurs with an analysis by Dawson (2017) who argues that, if the APR1400 was to be approved by the British nuclear safety system, then substantial upgrades would be needed, including enhanced aircraft protection, enhanced containment, enhanced system blackout operational (SBO) capability (involving provision for mobile generators and improved water supply), and perhaps greater redundancy.

According to a UK-based nuclear consultant three innovations inherent in 'Modern Western European Generation III+ PWRs' (which includes the EPR) make such reactors (that would comply with UK standards) 'probably 20%–30% more expensive than Asian Generation II PWRs'. These three innovations are an

'Advanced passive cooling design', a 'Fuel melt core catcher', and '9/11 aircraft protection' (anonymous interview with nuclear industry consultant 01/06/2018, and email communication 09/07/2018).

However Dawson (2017) comments that the next reactors to be deployed by South Korea would have more safety features, including better aircraft protection and more 'safety train' redundancy. These would be the AP1550 MWe version (called APR +).

However, it is likely that Korean nuclear designs are less likely to incur issues with the US nuclear safety rules, (given adequate aircraft protection) since there are less stringencies at least on system blackout capability and hydrogen mitigation (where PAR is not required). The Korean AP series includes Passive Auto-catalytic Recombiners which are not required under US regulations. The APR + design also includes Filtered Containment Venting Systems (IAEA 2013), again which is something not required by the US NRC (or even by the UK's ONR) for new plants.

Nuclear safety has become embroiled in a big public scandal. In the political context following the Fukushima accident the work of the nuclear safety administration came under greater focus, something which may have contributed to the emergence of a scandal involving falsification of regulatory documents. According to the World Nuclear News (2013):

> The scandal of the forged quality control certificates hit the news in November 2012, when South Korea's Ministry of Knowledge Economy announced that state-owned KHNP had allegedly been supplied with falsely-certified parts for at least five of its 23 nuclear reactors. The two most affected units, Yonggwang 5 and 6 (since renamed Hanbit 5 and 6), were taken off line for the parts to be replaced. Officials of leading electricity companies were indicted as a result of the affair.

Bribery was said to have taken place involving ensuring that components, including cables, were given the requisite safety certificates. One hundred people were indicted, including leading officials of the biggest Korean electricity companies, Korean Electric Power Corporation KEPCO and Korea Hydro and Nuclear Power Company. The operation of six reactors were initially suspended and the building of new reactors was slowed down as cables needed to be checked (Park 2013).

The scandal could be part of a process by which the safety regulatory process was able to at least temper the culture of impunity with which a nuclear establishment had existed. It could be viewed as part of a transition from what was much earlier an overtly military-influenced developmentalist strategy to one where an engaged citizenry has increased the power of a more independent nuclear safety regulatory regime.

This scandal coincided with heightened concern about the nuclear power risks associated with earthquakes. In this context completion of the most recently ordered reactors has been slowed. This includes the Generation III reactors.

Construction used to take as little as four years, but the most recent reactors are taking at least eight years to construct (IAEA 2020).

Nuclear exporting

KEPCO has been keen to export its designs for nuclear power plants. This rested on Korea's claims to be efficient and low-cost deliverers of nuclear power plants in Korea. Indeed it is generally agreed that this has been the case. However, as discussed earlier, the extent to which this translates into delivery of the more complex (more safety-oriented) newer designs remains to be seen. However, as discussed earlier, the APR1400 could be said to be a 'stripped down' version of Generation III nuclear designs. The big export project so far has been the (now partly completed) Barakah complex of four reactors in the United Arab Emirates.
According to Dorfman (2019, 1):

> The Barakah nuclear plant is being built by the South Korean reactor supplier Korea Electric Power Corporation (KEPCO) and the Emirates Nuclear Energy Corporation (ENEC), in a consortium with Korea Hydro & Nuclear Power (KHNP), Hyundai Engineering & Construction, Samsung C&T, and Doosan Heavy Industries & Construction, with the UAE's Federal Authority for Nuclear Regulation providing regulation. The South Korean government has a majority financial holding in KEPCO/KHNPC, and has provided loan guarantees for the Barakah project. Yet less than a decade after Barakah broke ground, the UAE contract remains South Korea's one and only export order – with KEPCO and its subsidiary KHNP unable to replicate the Abu Dhabi contract elsewhere, despite major initiatives in Lithuania, Turkey, Vietnam and the UK.

Certainly South Korea's pitch to the United Arab Emirates, who asked for tenders for a nuclear power complex in the first decade of the century, was based on its nuclear delivery record. Indeed KEPCO, which led a consortium to bid for the contract to build the power plant at Barakah in Abu Dhabi, won the tender competition, and beat the French offer to build the EPR.
One of the ways in which KEPCO's own (third-generation) reactor design was able to come in at a lower price (compared to the EPR) has been, it has been alleged, because the EPR contains more safety features compared to the Korean APR1400 design. Such features (which the APR1400 lacks) includes, a 'core catcher', more extensive containment features, greater redundancy, more extensive 'system blackout' measures, and enhanced aircraft protection. On the other hand, other factors may (also) have been in play. According to Kim (2019),

> [R]umors started swirling that the UAE deal had come with a number of compromising provisions. The most serious allegation was that Lee had secured the project by secretly promising armed support to Abu Dhabi in the event of a military conflict. In 2011, South Korea did begin deploying special forces to the UAE, but Lee denied any connection.

However, despite construction being started in 2012, the complex remains incomplete, behind schedule, and the first of the four units only came online in August 2020, although it was supposed to be generating in 2017 (NEI 2018), with the final unit unlikely to be operational before 2023. In 2012 the World Nuclear Association said that 'All four units planned for Barakah, close to the border with Saudi Arabia, should be in operation by 2020' (World Nuclear News 2012).

Fears have been expressed that the construction of nuclear power plants in the Middle East may lead to nuclear proliferation in that area. Dorfman (2019, 19) commented that

> The tense geopolitical environment in the Gulf makes nuclear a more contro-versial issue in this region than elsewhere, as new nuclear power provides the capability to develop and make nuclear weapons. It's worth noting that emer-gent back-channels exist which may facilitate Gulf states obtaining advanced nuclear fuel cycle enrichment technologies if the decision is made to pursue a military proliferation option. Hence, due to risk of regional nuclear prolifera-tion, it may be prudent for international nuclear suppliers to commit not to supply Gulf states with enrichment capabilities.

Conclusion

At the start of this chapter we stated the need to examine the nature of South Korean nuclear safety standards in the context of studying nuclear power devel-opments and also political developments, and examining associations between these different streams.

For much of the period in between the end of WW2 and the end of the 20th-century South Korea was dominated by a military-influenced regime and nuclear policy agenda. Such an agenda was governed by a hierarchical set of institutional biases which involved not merely top-down economic development but also some orientation towards seeing nuclear power development as both a civil and a mili-tary objective. The military side of the regime atrophied and was blown away, and the nuclear weapons overtones of the nuclear power sector have become less pronounced, although they have not, so far, been completely extinguished.

The military-developmentalist tradition may have lived on to an extent in the drive to export nuclear reactors. However, as discussed in the later section of this chapter this has petered out, with one (very large) project in the UAE being its only apparent outcome. This result may be a consequence of a combination of the depressed world nuclear reactor market, but also of pressure to increase the safety and complexity of nuclear power designs.

Latterly (certainly in the 21st century) economic development has brought forth a very consumer-oriented society. Alongside this has been an increasing concern among the citizenry for environmental considerations. This combination is a cornerstone of the concept of ecological modernisation in Europe.

Anti-nuclear activism had begun to increase since the 1990s, and devel-oped a deliberative tradition featuring local referenda. Then, in the wake of the

Fukushima accident in March 2011, this activism became mainstream. The other face of nuclear activism was support for local energy projects and 'energy democracy' movements. This has some resemblance with what had happened in Germany many years earlier, and a deliberative turn grew.

This deliberative approach reached its zenith following the 2017 Presidential election which resulted in a Government committed to phasing out nuclear power. Citizen deliberation was adopted as the method by which Government policy on the nuclear phase-out was tested and delivered. Although in the end the Government's policy was tailored to allow two reactors whose construction was well advanced to be completed, this process is particularly notable because a deliberative method was given authority by the Korean Government to make a definitive policy decision.

Hence the public context in South Korea as concerns the nuclear power policy could be said to be closer to the 'strong' end of ecological modernisation compared to 'weak' ecological modernisation. Egalitarian influences seem very strong, exhibited by strong 'bottom-up' mobilisations and also by heightened support for environmentalist objectives. The emergence of a stronger form of ecological modernisation in the area of nuclear policy may be associated with opposition to the centralised political and economic industrial hierarchy that dominates South Korea.

The nuclear safety institutions themselves have evolved considerably away from the situation of nuclear industry capture that was evident until well into the 1990s. The safety rules have taken into account the recommendation by the nuclear safety agency for new measures to mitigate accidents in both new and old reactors. These safety rules have developed faster than those existing in the US, incorporating (in the case of South Korea) techniques such as PAR and FCVS. In that sense they are closer to European provisions than those of the USA. Despite some ambiguities, the formal policy position of the South Korean Government is one of phasing out nuclear power, at least in the long term, a policy position that is certainly less pro-nuclear than Western states such as the UK and the USA.

References

Dawson, A. (2017) 'An Overview of the KEPCO APR1400', *Energy Matters (Euan Mearns)*, 18 December. http://euanmearns.com/an-overview-of-the-kepco-apr1400/

Dorfman, P. (2019) *Gulf Nuclear Ambition: New Reactors in the United Arab Emirates.* Paris: Nuclear Consulting Group.

Fishkin, J. (1995) *Voice of the People: Public Opinion and Democracy.* New Haven, CT: Yale University Press.

Framatome (2017) *South Korea: AREVA NP Awarded Contract for Safety Upgrades in Seven Reactors*, 16 October. www.framatome.com/EN/businessnews-837/south-korea-areva-np-awarded-contract-for-safety-upgrades-in-seven-reactors.html

Green, J. (2017) 'Is South Korea's Nuclear Industry a Model for Others to Follow?', *Nuclear Monitor*. www.wiseinternational.org/nuclear-monitor/844/south-koreas-nuclear-industry-model-others-follow

IAEA (2013) 'APR + (Advanced Power Reactor Plus) Korea Hydro and Nuclear Power Company', *Republic of Korea*. https://aris.iaea.org/sites/..%5CPDF%5CAPR.pdf

IAEA (Intern Fational Atomic Energy Agency) (2020) *Republic of Korea: Country Profile, Republic of Korea*. https://cnpp.iaea.org/countryprofiles/KoreaRepublicof/Korea Republicof.htm

Jasanoff, S., and Kim, S. (2009) 'Containing the Atom: Sociotechnical Imaginaries and Nuclear Power in the United States and South Korea', *Minerva*, 47, 119–146.

Kang, J., and von Hippel, F. (2017) 'Reprocessing Policy and South Korea's New Government', *Bulletin of the Atomic Scientists*, 15 May. https://thebulletin.org/2017/05/reprocessing-policy-and-south-koreas-new-government/

Kim, C., Sung, J., Ha, S., and Yeo, S. (2015) 'Implementation of Passive Autocatalytic Recombiner System as a Hydrogen Mitigation System in Korean Nuclear Power Plants', *Internationale Zeitschriftfuer Kernenergie*, 60(8–9), 512–516.

Kim, M. (2019) 'How Greed and Corruption Blew Up South Korea's Nuclear Industry', *MIT Technology Review*, April.

Kim, S.C., and Chung, Y. (2018) 'Dynamics of Nuclear Power Policy in the Post-Fukushima Era: Interest Structure and Politicisation in Japan, Taiwan and Korea', *Asian Studies Review*, 42(1), 107–124.

Ku, D. (2018) 'The Anti-Nuclear Movement and Ecological Democracy in South Korea', in K.-T. Chou (ed.) *Energy Transition in East Asia*. London: Routledge, pp. 28–44.

Ku, Y., Lee, I., and Woo, J. (2017) *Politics in North and South Korea*. Abingdon: Routledge.

Lim, E. (2019) 'South Korea's Nuclear Dilemmas', *Journal of Peace and Disarmament*, 2(1), 297–318.

NEI (Nuclear Engineering Information) (2018) *More Delays for UAE's Barakah Project*, 6 July. www.neimagazine.com/news/newsmore-delays-for-uaes-barakah-project-6233083

Nordhaus, T., and Wang, S. (2020) 'It's Not Techno-Angst That's Driving East Asia to Abandon Nuclear Power', *Foreign Policy*, 17 June. https://foreignpolicy.com/2020/06/17/nuclear-power-japan-south-korea-japan-fukushima-disaster/

NSSC (Nuclear Safety and Security Commission) (2019) 'Nuclear Safety and Security, Our Top Priority', *NSSC*. www.nssc.go.kr/attach/namo/files/000001/20191205184646909_UCG2AKZH.pdf

Nuclear Laws of the Republic of Korea (2019) 'Act on the Establishment and Operation of the Nuclear Safety and Security Commission'. www.kins.re.kr/en/img/global/pdf/Act%20on%20Establishment%20and%20Operation%20of%20the%20Nuclear%20Safety%20and%20Security%20Commission.pdf

OECD (2009) *Nuclear Legislation in OECD and NEA Countries: Republic of Korea*. www.oecd-nea.org/law/legislation/korea.pdf

OECD-NEA (2014) 'Status Report on Filtered Containment Venting', *Nuclear Safety*.

Park, Jin-Hee (2018) 'The Grassroots Movement for Energy Transition in Korean Society', in K.-T. Chou (ed.) *Energy Transition in East Asia*. London: Routledge, pp. 125–141.

Park, Ju-Min (2013) 'South Korea Charges 100 with Corruption over Nuclear Scandal', *Reuters*, 10 October.

Park, S. (2009) 'Why South Korea Needs Pyroprocessing', *Bulletin of the Atomic Scientists*, 26 October. https://thebulletin.org/2009/10/why-south-korea-needs-pyroprocessing/

Proctor, D. (2020) 'South Korea Continues Nuclear Phase-Out', *Power*, 3 February. www.powermag.com/south-korea-continues-nuclear-phase-out/

Richardson, L. (2017) 'Protesting Policy and Practice in South Korea's Nuclear Energy Industry', in P. Van Ness and M. Gurtov (eds.) *Learning from Fukushima Nuclear Power*

    in East Asia. Acton, ACT: Australian National University Press. http://library.oapen.org/
        bitstream/id/a50d42c6-022d-47f8-b4d8-12312446b623/639354.pdf#page=159
Schneider, M., and Froggatt, A. (2019) *WNISR (World Nuclear Industry Status Report)
        2019*. Budapest: Mycle Schneider Consulting Project. file:///C:/Users/Toke/Dropbox/
        nuclear%20power%20book/Korea/wnisr2019-v2-hr.pdf
Se, Young Yang (2017) 'South Korea's Nuclear Energy Debate', *The Diplomat*, 26 Octo-
        ber. https://thediplomat.com/2017/10/south-koreas-nuclear-energy-debate/
Squassoni, S. (2013) 'South Korea's Prospects for Nuclear Energy at Home and Abroad',
        Presentation to EUCI 4th Annual Nuclear Export Control Symposium, 11–12 February,
        Washington, DC.
Toke, D. (2017) *China's Role in Curbing Carbon Emissions*. Abingdon: Routledge.
Toke, D., and Baker, K. (2016) 'Electricity Market Reform: So What's New?', *Policy &
        Politics*, 44(4), 445–461.
Valentine, S., and Sovacool, B. (2010) 'The Socio-Political Economy of Nuclear Power
        Development in Japan and South Korea', *Energy Policy*, 38, 7971–7979. www.world-
        nuclear.org/information-library/country-profiles/countries-o-s/south-korea.aspx
WNA (World Nuclear Association) (2019) 'Nuclear Power in South Korea'. www.world-
        nuclear.org/information-library/country-profiles/countries-o-s/south-korea.aspx
World Nuclear News (2012) 'Construction Underway at Barakah', 19 July. www.world-
        nuclear-news.org/NN-Construction_under_way_at_Barakah-1907124.html
World Nuclear News (2013) 'Indictments for South Korea Forgery Scandal', 10 October. www.
        world-nuclear-news.org/RS-Indictments_for_South_Korea_forgery_scandal-1010137.html
Xinhua (2019) 'South Korea to Permanently Shut Second Reactor', *Xinhuanet*, 24 Decem-
        ber. www.xinhuanet.com/english/2019-12/24/c_138654998.htm
Yang, Yi (2020) Wonyoung, Korean Federation for Environmental Movement, email com-
        munication 19 March.
Yun, S.-J. (2018) 'Citizen Participation-Based Energy Transition Experiments in a Megac-
        ity: The Case of the One Less Nuclear Power Plant in Seoul, South Korea', in K.-T.
        Chou (ed.) *Energy Transition in East Asia*. London: Routledge, pp. 77–103.

8   Nuclear safety politics in the UK

This chapter seeks to understand the interaction between discussions of cost and safety and nuclear power. A particular purpose of this chapter is to examine the debates about the costs and Government policies underpinning the construction of new nuclear power plants. This will be done to establish whether high costs of nuclear are a recently occurring phenomenon, or merely part of the usual practice of developing nuclear power. This will help us understand the politics of nuclear safety, in order to understand the extent that recent safety changes in regulations have affected nuclear costs.

In order to achieve this there will first be a historical discussion of relevant history of nuclear power in the UK. This is important since in order to examine the hypothesis that nuclear power construction costs have been increased because of safety reasons, we need to examine how such costs have changed, if at all, over time as safety demands may have increased.

This will be followed by a discussion of the nuclear safety regime and philosophy. There will be special attention paid to the issues of aircraft protection and post-Fukushima safety measures. There will then be a discussion of factors that contribute to the costs of building nuclear power stations in the UK. Finally, in the conclusion there will be an assessment of how the UK nuclear regime can be categorised using cultural and ecological modernisation theory.

A U-turn in British nuclear power policy?

In January 2019 Business Secretary Greg Clark announced that the plans for a nuclear power plant at Wylfa in Wales, organised by Hitachi, were being deferred. He said that given the fall in costs of offshore wind power in particular,

> renewable energy may now not just be cheap, but also readily available. . . .
> . . . this positive trend has not been true when it comes to new nuclear. Across the world a combination of factors including tighter safety regulations, have seen the cost of most new nuclear projects increase, as the cost of alternatives has fallen and the cost of construction has risen.
>
> (Clark 2019)

This was a turnaround given earlier Government policy, since 2005, which emphasised the importance of a revival in building nuclear power plants. Privatisation of the electricity industry in 1990 brought greater transparency to the issue of costs. This is because the new competitive nature of industry now led to an emphasis on justifying each project in terms of costs rather than cross-subsidising the costs of more expensive plants through consumer bills levied by the previous monopoly electricity suppliers, the Central Electricity Generating Board.

From privatisation to Greg Clark

At the time of writing (early 2020) the UK had 15 nuclear power stations operating on eight sites around the UK. In 2018 British nuclear power produced 22 per cent of UK electricity generation (DUKES 2019, chapter 5 Table 5.6).

I shall focus on two periods. The first period is a brief one, at the end of the 1980s at a moment when nuclear power construction was halted in the context of the privatisation of the electricity industry. This is important, for the inability of the British state to continue this programme may help us understand what has happened more recently in its difficulties in expediting a nuclear construction programme.

Despite being the first to supply power to the public network from a nuclear power station (in 1956), Britain's nuclear power programme suffered construction delays and lagged behind other Western countries such as the USA and France, leading to the abandonment of efforts to continue building nuclear power plants with British designs. Adoption of an American-based design led to just one power plant, Sizewell B, being completed for generation in 1995. Plans for other plants were cut short by the impact of privatisation and market liberalisation.

In 1988–1990 the Government under Mrs Thatcher set about privatising the electricity industry. The nationalised monopoly, the Central Electricity Generating Board (CEGB) was broken up into competing companies. At the same time, the Government continued to promote nuclear power. Nevertheless, nuclear power proved difficult to fit into the structure of electricity privatisation and the programme of building Pressurised Water Reactors (PWRs) was discontinued.

It emerged that the costs of the PWR programme, under privatisation, were much higher than generally realised. Prior to this costs of the nuclear power building programme were relatively opaque in the sense that the Central Electricity Generating Board (CEGB) could select their own criteria to justify their decisions to go ahead with building new power plants. They then made consumers pay for whatever expenditure the nationalised industry decided was necessary to spend. Descriptions of costs were made by the developers, effectively the CEGB themselves. However, privatisation meant that the costs had to be subjected to specific, market-based criteria and judgements.

In a detailed paper prepared by National Power (set up provisionally to take on nuclear power from the CEGB) the costs of electricity from new nuclear power was estimated to be around £62.50 per MWh in 1989 prices, at a 10 per cent discount rate using a 20-year contract length (Baker 1989). This is equivalent to £131.60 per MWh in 2012 prices.

Using the detail given by National Power it is possible to compare this price to the one given to Hinkley C (which was given a 35-year contract). When account is taken of such factors, this figure (i.e. for a post-privatisation PWR programme) works out to be almost exactly the same as the price of electricity in the contract awarded to EDF for Hinkley C, that is circa £92.50 per MWh in 2012 prices.

To summarise, the PWR programme could only have continued under the privatised regime if the Government issued guarantees to underwrite money borrowed to finance the developments, and on top of this ensured that somebody had an obligation to buy all of the electricity generated at a high price over a very long-term contractual basis. Yet this was contradictory to the notion of competition between different technologies that underpinned electricity privatisation. As can be seen in the foregoing discussion the Government seemed to forget these issues when the new nuclear power programme was prepared from 2006 onwards.

Policy-based evidence

In the 1990s, in the context of an abundance of British natural gas supplies and falling energy prices, the Government eschewed any propensity to promote the construction of nuclear power plants.

However, after the turn of the century Britain became a net importer of natural gas and, from 2004 onwards, world energy prices rose as oil prices increased. The Labour Government (in a White Paper published in 2003) initially deferred calls for a new programme of nuclear, relying on advice from a number of academics and others who pointed out the evidence suggesting nuclear power was not economic. However then, in 2006, the Government, led by Tony Blair, mounted a review which called for the nuclear option to be revisited to close what seemed to be a likely generation gap as ageing nuclear and coal plants were closed down.

The Government seemed to be over-optimistic about the costs of nuclear power compared to earlier advice. In 2006, the Government's energy review contained a call for a new generation of nuclear build (Department of Trade and Industry 2006). The Government's central estimate of cost of new nuclear power was £38 per MWh (Department of Trade and Industry 2006, 114). At the time there seemed to be little appetite (in Government) for giving nuclear power any major financial incentives, although the planning procedure for nuclear power plants was reformed.

This financial estimate seemed to be way out of line with experience gained during electricity privatisation. This (£38 per MWh figure) is, uprated to take account of inflation, equivalent to £46.55 in 2012 prices. 2012 is the year used here as a comparison because 2012 is used as the base year for the price of Hinkley Point C at £92.50. In other words the first nuclear power station ordered under the new nuclear build policy turned out to be almost exactly twice as expensive as thought just six years previously. This was a crucial problem since the apparent low prices assigned to future nuclear power plants strengthened plans to build new nuclear projects, leading to plans being made for specific projects which were able to gain political momentum. How did this apparent oversight occur?

A key factor is that little weight appears to have been placed on the figures for Pressurised Water Reactors produced by the Government in 1989. Rather, the White Paper seemed to place faith in the estimates of costs made for so-called 'third-generation' nuclear technologies produced by companies such as EDF. EDF, in a submission to the review, asserted that 'We would estimate the generation cost of a limited series [e.g. 4 units including the first-of-a-kind] in the same context as in France, would be around £27/MWh' (EDF 2006). In fact, at that point there was no completed or even near completed 'third-generation' reactor. Hence the estimates for costs appear to be based on little more than hope.

In fact, it was left up to groups such as Greenpeace to argue that the UK Government's initial optimism about nuclear power economics was misplaced and that renewable energy was a better bet for the future. Greenpeace published arguments and evidence suggesting that construction costs and also delivery times for nuclear power were increasing, whilst costs for renewable energy sources such as wind and solar power were falling (Thomas et al. 2007).

The judicial review case led the Government to issue a new consultation specifically on the topic of nuclear power. This found that new nuclear power was economic compared to other means of reducing carbon emissions (BERR 2007). However, 'some respondents' (such as the Science Policy Research Unit) were noted as saying that

> nuclear generation costs are typically underestimated and the assumptions on discount rates and financing period for nuclear are too optimistic while the discount rate for appraising wind generation costs is too high. A further point was raised (by critics such as SPRU) that the only new nuclear power station being built (in Finland) is behind schedule and over budget.
>
> (BERR 2007, 59)

The authors of the White Paper responded to such criticisms stating that 'While there have been cost overruns and delays in constructing nuclear power stations, such as at Olkiluoto in Finland, experience elsewhere in Europe is different. For example, plants have been built to schedule in France and Romania' (BERR 2007, 61). It worth reflecting upon this Government response since this illustrates how the Government was willing, apparently, to use challengeable justifications for its defence of new nuclear economics. At that time the construction of the plant in France had only just begun (two months before the White Paper was published), so this could hardly be cited as good evidence that this project was on course – in fact, since then the plant has experienced very long delays in construction. It is true that a nuclear power plant had just been completed in Romania, but that plant had taken 35 years to build.

In short, whilst it is the case that that there were uncertainties in what might happen, nevertheless the apparent zeal with which the evidence was ignored and/ or forgotten, or simply misstated makes the Government's evidence look like evidence found to support a policy rather than policy being based on evidence. However, despite all of this, the policy began to be embedded. Sites were identified, consortia formed, work preparing planning cases began, and industrial and local political lobbies hoping for and then expecting jobs and business developed.

In 2008 a Climate Change Act was adopted by the UK Parliament which established a target of reducing 1990 levels of greenhouse gas emissions by 80 per cent by the year 2050. The Committee on Climate Change was established to advise the Government on progress towards meeting this target. This heralded a drive to give incentives for nuclear power on the basis of it being a low carbon source. David McKay, who emphasised the need for a large amount of nuclear power to meet climate change targets, was appointed Chief Scientist at the Department for Energy and Climate Change in 2009.

Indeed, things seemed to be looking up for nuclear power when, in 2010, the new coalition government announced a consultation on proposals for a 'low carbon' oriented 'Electricity Market Reform' (EMR). This promised to assure long-term premium price contracts for the supply of nuclear power as well as renewable energy and carbon capture and storage. In doing so, the Government claimed that subsidies were not being given to nuclear power, but rather low carbon energy sources in general were being incentivised. It was initially anticipated that these technologies would compete with each other to secure the long-term contracts. Cost estimates for new nuclear power rose compared to the White Papers of 2006 and 2008, but it was still projected as having the lowest price of all the low carbon technologies in the medium term. Up to 18 GW of nuclear power were projected in the Government's National Policy Statement for Energy (Department of Energy and Climate Change 2011, 22). By comparison the 3.2 GW of the Hinkley C project representing 7 per cent of UK electricity supply is the only plant being built at the moment.

However, soon after the Government finally published its White Paper proposals to implement EMR, two out of three of the consortia formed to implement the schemes collapsed. E.ON and RWE, who owned the Horizon consortium which involved developing a site at Wylfa and Oldbury, and Iberdrola, SSE, and GDF-Suez, who owned the Nugen consortium for nuclear development at Moorside, gave up their options. Only one set of proposals for projects at Hinkley C and Sizewell C, led by the French (mainly state-owned) company EDF, remained in the picture. Even EDF suffered a setback when Centrica withdrew from its minority stake in their nuclear consortium, and a Chinese nuclear company CGNPC was later brought in to provide around one-third of the equity capital in the project. However the UK Government managed to sell off the rights to the abandoned Horizon and Nugen projects respectively to Hitachi and Toshiba.

It should be noted that the power companies that had quit the scene, such as E.ON, RWE, Iberdrola, and SSE, were companies that were not closely associated with reactor designs, whereas the only companies remaining interested in the nuclear build options, that is Toshiba, Hitachi, and EDF were closely associated with reactor designs. EDF was well placed in the sense that it was owned by a state, that is France, which was better equipped to take long-term risks than private companies. EDF promotes the 'third-generation' 'European Pressurised Reactor' (EPR). This is the model being built at Hinkley C in the UK.

This left EDF with the most well-prepared set of proposals for a plant, and what turned out to be protracted negotiations opened with the Government giving a contract to EDF to build a nuclear power plant at Hinkley C.

Even EDF struggled to maintain necessary investment in the first proposed scheme, at Hinkley Point C in Somerset. It only managed to keep the scheme afloat by a) raising a third of the equity capital from the Chinese state-owned nuclear power company CGNPC who in turn were offered the opportunity to develop their own nuclear power plant at Bradwell, b) gaining in principle approval for the Treasury to lend the scheme many billions of pounds worth of money, and c) after protracted painful negotiations gaining government agreement for a 35-year-long premium price for electricity generated at a level that was controversially high.

CGNPC is keen on deploying the Hualong 1 reactor type, another 'third-generation' design which China wants to demonstrate in hope of selling overseas. Negotiations between the Office for Nuclear Regulation (ONR) and CGNPC have continued, with ONR requiring extensive safety-related design changes. It remains to be seen what the financial requirements will be for this project, or indeed whether geopolitical security issues will affect this project in the future.

EDF's contract for £92.50 per MWh for electricity generated (2012 prices) for 35 years following commissioning, together with loan guarantees for the debt element, was cleared by the European Commission under state aid rules in late 2013. Eventually, following arguments over the security implications of Chinese investment in the project, the deal was finally signed off with the British Government in 2016. However, by then there were increasing problems with mobilising other projects.

Finally, negotiations between Hitachi and the UK Government over the proposed nuclear project at Wylfa were suspended in early 2019. As indicated in the earlier quote by Greg Clark, the Government could not secure an agreement with the developers to proceed at a low enough price.

It should be noted that the British Government has, latterly, replicated some of the conditions that used to exist in the nationalised electricity industry before 1990. In the context of the Hinkley C deal the developers now have a guaranteed market for their electricity at a premium price and also they had an offer of Government guarantees for the debt part of the investment. This fell short of underwriting the costs of the project, but in an important sense EDF has state underwriting of its debts through the aegis of the French Government. Faith in the nuclear build programme has faltered in Government circles even before the Wylfa announcement in early 2019. The National Infrastructure report issued on the summer of 2018 emphasised building up renewable energy, especially offshore wind power, and stated that 'Government should not agree support for more than one nuclear power station beyond Hinkley Point C before 2025'.[1]

This opinion followed on from the previous autumn where wind power prices continued to fall. Onshore wind had already been granted contracts for a lower price than Hinkley C in 2015, but by 2019 contracts for large-scale offshore wind farms were being awarded for rather less than half the price of the Hinkley C project (Gov.UK 2019). Also, the contract lengths are much shorter – 15 years for the wind farms as opposed to 35 years for Hinkley C.

In an effort to reduce the headline price for the next EPR that EDF wants to build (Sizewell C), the Government considered a different funding model for the nuclear plant. This is the 'Regulated Asset Base' (RAB) model which uses government guarantees to reduce the cost of capital for the construction. It also comes at the potential cost of the Government having to pay for cost overruns. Given the history of nuclear power construction, this acceptance of construction risk is a difficult pill for the Government to swallow.

However, a point to take from this earlier discussion is that in the UK, nuclear power, at least since the end of the 1980s, has never been cheap. This is demonstrated by the comparison between the costs produced for nuclear power at the time of privatisation (at the end of the 1980s) and the costs of Hinkley C as discussed earlier.

Having discussed this history, we are now in a better place to discuss the question whether, in the case of the UK, is safety to blame for the high cost of nuclear power? To help us do that we should look next at the UK's nuclear safety apparatus.

UK regulatory philosophy

The Office for Nuclear Regulation (ONR) emerged in its present form only in 2011, although the nuclear regulatory capacity had existed within the ambit of the Health and Safety Executive (HSE) machinery since the 1960s. References to ONR activities prior to 2011 imply the 'HSE Nuclear Directorate'.

The philosophy underpinning the ONR follows on from that of the HSE and emphasises that the cost of protection against risk can exceed expected benefits if this reduces risks to a level that is 'ALARP' (as low as reasonably practicable). Demeritt et al. (2015, 377) explain this British health and safety philosophy as a 'principles-based' approach that requires employers to ensure the health and safety of their employees only so far as is reasonably practicable ('SFAIRP'). The term reasonably practicable was already established in mining case law (following a miners' accident compensation case in 1949): the cost and effort required to reduce risk should not be 'grossly disproportionate' to the benefit gained.

The ONR's application of this British health and safety theory was elaborated by consultants conducting a review of the safety philosophy (NERA Consulting 2017). ONR guidance explains how licensees should follow established good practice and states that

> the onus is on the licensee to implement measures to the point where the costs of any additional measures (in terms of money, time or trouble – the sacrifice) would be grossly disproportionate to the further risk reduction that would be achieved (the safety benefit).
>
> (ONR 2018b, para 1.3, 2)

Indeed, the ONR quotes a statement by the chief inspector at the Sizewell B Enquiry: 'for risks to the public, . . . where the risks were low (consequence and likelihood) a factor of about 2 was suggested, whereas for higher risks the factor should be about 10' (ONR 2018b, para 5.4.8 (i)). In fact, NERA Consulting (2017) appeared to criticise the ONR's reliance on the principle of 'gross disproportion'. However, this was rejected by the ONR, who said that 'we remain confident that ONR and HSE are using the appropriate legal precedent, as recommended by HSE solicitors' (ONR 2018d, 16).

The published ONR safety guidance represents a much thinner corpus of documents compared to the US NRC. Overall safety policy objectives are contained in a 'Safety Assessment Principles' (SAPs) document, the first of which was published in 1979 and the current iteration of which was published in 2014 (ONR 2014). Underpinning this however is a series of 'Technical Advice Guides' (TAGs), covering a range of issues, and which go into considerably more detail than the SAPs. It has not proved possible to compare the evolution of these documents from previous versions because they are not publicly available and a FOI request for them to be retrieved and supplied to the author was refused on account that it would take too much time to retrieve the documents.

Nevertheless, despite (or perhaps because of) the paucity of documentation compared to the US NRC, the British system has the potential to have stricter implicit standards.

A key facet of the ONR system (and one that distinguishes itself from other nuclear safety regulatory regimes) is that the SAPs and TAGs constitute a system whereby developers and operators are set 'objectives' to meet. This is opposed to specifying precise means of meeting them, as is more the style of the US NRC.

The problem, as discussed by the then Chairman of the UK Atomic Energy Authority, Walter Marshall (who later became Chairman of the CEGB), was put thus:

> We rely on regulations in the aircraft industry, the chemical industry and in many other areas. We feel that formulating a regulation may not guarantee safety, but gets very close to it; however, in a highly technical area like nuclear power, formulating regulations like that is very difficult.
>
> (Marshall 1982, 371)

He went onto discuss the example of a loss of coolant accident (LOCA) – the type that happened at Three Mile Island – and the problems with trying to define a regulation that covered it given that even relatively small LOCA event could have very serious consequences (maybe much more than a large one), so a level of loss of coolant could not adequately define safety.

Marshall backed the approach of the US Kemeny Report, established in the wake of the Three Mile Island accident, of which Marshall said 'the excessive attention to regulation does not have a positive effect on safety' (Marshall 1982, ibid.). The Kemeny approach was not adopted in the USA; otherwise it would have moved closer to the British system according to Marshall and would have involved the utilities taking more responsibility for assuring safety rather than offloading this onto a system of rules (Marshall 1982, ibid.). One could also add that the British system, which concerned judgements being made by the nuclear regulators about whether a system is safe, as opposed to whether it met a series of regulations, was also closer to other Western European systems, such as the French (discussed in Chapter 6) than the USA's approach.

The UK ONR system operates through expert judgements being made on subjects such as designs for nuclear reactors or licences being awarded for specific sites. The Wood Engineering Group provides technical advice to the ONR. The details of specific licences awarded to nuclear developers are not published by the ONR, with only generative versions put on the ONR website.

Under the ONR's rubric, developers and operators of nuclear power plants are required to conduct 'Probabilistic Safety Analysis' (analogous to the 'Probabilistic Risk Analysis' used by the USA's NRC). In the case of a 'high consequence event of low frequency beyond the design basis', PSA analyses are expected to look at low frequency events.

> In judging the adequacy of safety cases, inspectors should especially consider the effects of very low frequency events from non-discrete hazards, e.g. seismic events in the exceedance frequency range $1.0 \times 10^{-5}/\text{yr}$–$1.0 \times 10^{-7}/\text{yr}$. If these can credibly lead to severe accident plant states, they should be considered as part of the SAA (Severe Accident Analysis).
>
> (ONR 2018c, para 138, 38)

Further guidance is stated in ONR (2018a, 8):

> Where a potential condition depends upon human activity (e.g. probability of an operator being present in a cell at the time of the IE[Initiating Event]), or upon some other aspect that might vary over time or with changing operating circumstances, then a generous level of conservatism should be made in the allowance since such variations or changes will occur without triggering a revised safety analysis.

The implication of this is that the ONR expects to guard against rather more unlikely events (up to $1.0 \times 10^{-7}/\text{yr}$) than the aforementioned PRA guideline set by the NRC (up to $1.0 \times 10^{-5}/\text{yr}$). However, critics of PSA/PRA may still complain that there are unknowns which will not be foreseen and which will only be learned through experience (Downer 2017).

A summative comparison of philosophies

The US nuclear regulatory system appears to be much more transparent than that of the UK. The UK system can also be said to be much more elitist, in that judgements are made by experts with no direct political accountability, as appears in the case of the US NRC, which is run by publicly appointed Commissioners.

However, the UK's system works according to what seems to be an avowedly precautionary philosophy, where safety improvements are supported unless they incur costs that are a great deal higher than expected benefits. By contrast, the

US system emphasises that safety protection should be 'adequate', a term whose meaning is not specified, but is open to political interpretation. On the other hand, safety improvements can be subject to the Cost Benefit Analysis (CBA), meaning that such improvements should not be more costly than the benefits that improvements will bring about. Hence, if the NRC is not minded to give priority to a safety measure under the 'adequate protection' rule, it can subject the measure to CBA.

Such a strategy would be much more circumscribed in the UK, owing to its more precautionary attitude. This means that the ONR cannot rule out a safety measure simply by saying that the costs exceed the benefits, at least in the instance of high consequence risks. The costs could be several times more than the benefit but still the measure would be approved. In contrast, the UK system of risk assessment requires (in the case of high consequence events) assessment of risk according to a higher level of unlikelihood compared to that of the USA. In short, the UK system appears to have a stricter safety philosophy and appears to have greater clarity than that of the US.

Aircraft protection in the UK nuclear safety system

The 9/11 attack on the Twin Towers increased calls for nuclear power stations to be fitted with containment to resist deliberate impacts by large aircraft. The UK's nuclear safety regulator (now called the ONR) had already included a general objective in the 1992 edition of its Safety Assessment Principles (SAP) that stated that 'the predicted frequency of aircraft and helicopter crash on or near safety-related plant at the nuclear site should be determined'(ONR 1992, 18), although there was no reference to deliberate impacts. In addition to this, the UK's safety guidance, previously quoted, was inherently biased towards 'conservatism' in requiring safety measures to be considered.

An ONR official stated that the

> ONR recognised in late 2001 that there was a need to consider the effects of malicious aircraft crash on proposed new facilities. GDA Requesting parties were advised of this requirement in the early stages of planning for GDA entry. ONR's expectations were further amplified during the GDA process.
>
> (anonymous interview and email communication
> with ONR officials, 14/08/2014 and 03/10/2018)

The next SAP (ONR 2006) made full reference to the need to deal with malicious impacts by aircraft.

GDA refers to the 'Generic Design Assessment' with which, for all practical purposes, all nuclear power plants of a new design have to engage under the British nuclear regulatory system. The licencing of a site-specific plant occurs after this process. This GDA procedure was introduced as part of an effort to speed up the planning and regulatory system for civil nuclear power (BERR 2007, 34). The UK's last completed nuclear power station, Sizewell B, went through a lengthy, five-year Public Enquiry, which included public deliberations about safety issues.

Under the new system, the safety assessment is carried out by the ONR and residual non-technical planning issues are dealt with through the planning system.

Britain's first nuclear reactor in the 21st century is to be the French European Pressurised Reactor (EPR). An ONR report (under the aegis of its HSE Nuclear Directorate predecessor) talking about the design proposed for the new EPR noted 'claims that the design has been modified since the events of 9/11 and that the design "takes into consideration all of the direct, indirect and potential consequences" of a commercial airliner impacting the Nuclear Island' (HSE 2007, 7). However the same report commented that 'a more considered view . . . will be required' of 'hazards' such as 'such as flood, wind and seismic' (HSE 2007, 6). It could therefore be argued that the ONR were, in effect, urging a conservative approach that presaged the ONR's precautionary judgements in its post-Fukushima study.

Fukushima

Following the Fukushima accident in March 2011, the UK Government asked the ONR to come up with measures that would ensure the safety of UK reactors in light of lessons learned (ONR 2011). According to Chris Huhne, who was Secretary of State for Energy and Climate Change at the time of the Fukushima accident:

> We asked Dr Weightman, a former nuclear regulator who was familiar with all of the issues and above suspicion, to make recommendations. I thought that the key thing in terms of the public, particularly given what was going on in Germany, was that the public knew they were going to be dealing with a family of low carbon energy that was absolutely safe. I think that if there had been a public debate about a trade off between safety and cost we could have had been in a German situation of people saying well we don't want to take that sort of risk. Nuclear safety is like a hygiene factor, in that you do not eat in a restaurant that you think is dirty. It needs to be absolutely established, even if it slightly increases the cost.
>
> (interview with Chris Huhne, 20/06/2018)

The post-Fukushima report contained a number of recommendations (ONR 2011), with the main contestations appearing to come mainly from anti-nuclear groups such as Greenpeace, at least judging by the responses to the consultation which (unusually for the ONR) was organised on this issue. Critics of the nuclear industry might argue that efforts such as the post-Fukushima report on nuclear safety may be part of a process to 'frame it [the Fukushima accident] in ways that allow risk-assessment experts to "disown" it' (Downer 2014, 287).

Three key issues may be worthy of attention, since they are central to perceived inadequacies of Fukushima safety systems: first, the lack of a sufficiently long-lasting 'back-up' generating facility to allow for the cooling of the reactor and spent fuel rods; second, the build-up of hydrogen associated with the 'loss of coolant' episode that led to explosions at the plant; third the issue of evaluating threats from floods and earthquakes.

On the first issue, of providing back-up power and water to avoid a loss-of-coolant accident, The ONR recommended that 'The UK nuclear industry should review any need for the provision of additional, diverse means of providing robust sufficiently long-term independent electrical supplies on sites, reflecting the loss of availability of off-site electrical supplies under severe conditions' (ONR 2011, IR-18, xiii). According to the ONR:

> EDF NGL has reviewed the on-site diesel generator or gas turbine power supplies and confirmed that all are capable of a minimum of 72 hours of operation. EDF NGL has now demonstrated the deployment of backup generators should an event result in all on-site and off-site power supplies becoming unavailable. Suitable electrical connection points are installed at each site. . . .
> . . . Wider arrangements for storage and deployment of equipment have been developed, which include the provision of fuel supplies. All sites currently have at least 72 hours of fuel and water supplies. After this, back-up equipment will be able to provide supplies via reverse osmosis and fuel delivery should this be required.
>
> (ONR 2017, 18–19)

A second key issue was that the ONR was concerned that the (one, Sizewell B) existing Pressurised Water Reactor system (which was vulnerable to hydrogen build-up, unlike the other gas-cooled reactors in the UK) should be protected against the hydrogen build-up experienced in Fukushima. Hydrogen mitigation measures were to be fitted. In order to deal with this (that is, absorb excess hydrogen) it was recommended that Passive Autocatalytic Recombiners (PARs) be backfitted into the existing PWR, as well as included in future light water reactors. It was also recommended that a filtered containment venting system (FCV) be fitted, which is aimed at reducing pressure in case of an accident. The PARs have been fitted (ONR 2015a, 7), although not (as yet) the FCV (ONR 2015a, 7).

A third issue was whether enough consideration was being given to flood and earthquake risks. Indeed, a key recommendation in respect to both existing and planned reactors was that the ONR ask the nuclear operator (EDF NGL) to

> provide further details of the beyond design basis margins available for seismic, flooding and meteorological hazards together with evidence to support any judgments made. EDF NGL should also demonstrate that the resultant risks are as low as reasonably practicable (ALARP).
>
> (ONR 2011, 12)

Later, the ONR said; 'EDF NGL is undertaking significant flood modelling improvements and has submitted summary coastal flood information sufficient to close PARR-2 (the relevant recommendations of the review)' (ONR 2017, 13)

UK safety regulations, new designs and costs

A further issue is to examine evidence of the relationship between safety considerations and the recent redesigning of reactors and costs, using recent British examples as a case study. So far, the ONR has issued three completed GDAs for new reactors, the AREVA/EDF EPR, Hitachi's Advanced ABWR, and the Westinghouse APR 1000. There are only (currently) plans to develop the EPR and the ABWR.

A (UK-based) nuclear consultant said that three innovations inherent in 'Modern Western European Generation III+ PWRs' (which includes the EPR) make such reactors 'probably 20%–30% more expensive than Asian Generation II PWRs'. These three innovations are an 'Advanced passive cooling design', a 'Fuel melt core catcher', and '9/11 aircraft protection' (anonymous interview with nuclear industry consultant 01/06/2018, and email communication 09/07/2018). In the case of the EPR, two of these innovations were present in the original design, with aircraft protection increased later, as discussed earlier. The ONR does not give a discrete list of changes made as a result of the EPR GDA. However, it does do so in the case of the Hitachi ABWR. This is set out in ONR 2015b, (16–17). The list of changes involves a number of substantial alterations including aircraft protection, changes to the chemistry and chemical operation of the plant, extensive changes to the system of control and instrumentation and how it is housed and backed up, more complex building work to increase safety criteria, more redundancy to cooling apparatus and heat controlling machinery, changes to the way hydrogen is controlled (including fitting of PAR systems), and various other matters.

Reported costs of the proposal to build two reactors at Wylfa using the ABWR design increased from £14 billion to £20 billion pounds after the completion of the GDA, and costs increases were linked in newspaper reporting with the need for safety improvements (Twidale 2018, and a comparison between earlier and later costs reported in Barry 2015; BBC 2015; Nikkei Staff Writers 2018). It is impossible to analyse such claims (of links between cost increases and safety improvements) without access to internal nuclear industry documents.

A (UK-based) nuclear consultant commented that 'It is not the case' that

> regulators are responsible for cost increases for reactor designs. . . . [Y]ou need a mature finalised design ideally with a reference plant before you start building. . . . [W]here things go wrong is if you have a partially designed nuclear reactor and you are building it on the fly, as you are designing it, that is when cost delays come in . . . the point at which you do the first concrete pour, the organisation starts haemorrhaging money. That is when you have to build as rapidly as possible with minimum delays and commission as quick as you can.
>
> (anonymous interview with nuclear consultant, 01/06/2018)

If delays occur once the construction programme has started, then the workers and operational costs of keeping the programme going still have to be funded.

Added to this, interest charges accrue on the money borrowed to finance the project until such time as the project is completed and commissioned and energy generation has begun. Hence, if the plant is projected to be finished in seven years, a delay of five years will double the costs of building the plant. This trend is shown in Figure 8.1.

In fact, nuclear power plants are often projected to be completed in five years, which in the West, given the recent record, would seem to be heroic. If they are completed, and are generating electricity in 'just' eight years then the cost overruns would amount to approaching an extra two-thirds of the initially estimated cost. If it takes ten years then the costs will more than double.

Of course reactor construction times seem to be shorter in China compared to that of the UK. However, it may not be possible to replicate the Chinese experience in building nuclear plants in the context of British health and safety policies. Commenting on this difference a nuclear consultant said:

> The Chinese EPR as you probably know is half the cost of the UK version but the Chinese deploy a 12,000 workforce on it. They throw lots of man hours on it, there are not many westerners involved in site construction. I have visited Chinese nuclear fabrication plants and some of the equipment, things were not guarded, there were open forgings without protective heat shields in place. Just by walking through factories you get a sense of the safety culture. Walking through any kind of modern facility you will get a sense of are they comparable with western standards, beyond western standards, how do they compare? My sense was that they are a good way behind. They know

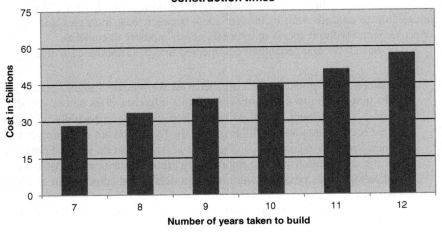

Figure 8.1 Variations of costs of nuclear power plants according to different construction times (7–12 years)

that. Most of their interactions with the UK or at least with me were around nuclear safety issues and construction issues.

(anonymous interview with UK nuclear industry
consultant 01/06/2018)

Conclusion

There is a clear difference between the underlying institutional norms of the UK's Office for Nuclear Regulation (ONR) and that of the US Nuclear Regulatory Commission (NRC). The emphasis on looking to see what is the safe design rather than (allegedly) relying on cost-benefit criteria (as in the USA) puts the British safety approach much closer to that existing in France rather than the USA. In the case of the US system there are a series of precisely expressed engineering rules. On the other hand in the French and British systems safety judgements are determined according to whether the design solutions are safe according to proba-bilistic criteria, with severe accident avoidance being a key criterion.

The ONR's culture (as well as that of the French nuclear safety agencies, as seen earlier) is based on a more precautionary attitude to risk that will require safety improvements, even if the costs outweigh the benefits, especially for security threats of high consequence. By contrast, the criteria for taking safety measures in the case of the NRC, with its injunction to take 'adequate' safety measures, is less clear. Moreover, the application of safety improvements is subject to cost-benefit analysis, wherein costs exceeding benefits are enough to render the improvement inappropriate.

Despite the NRC being more transparent and more open to direct public influ-ence, through the rule-making process, in practice the ONR appears to be rela-tively more sensitive to public pressures for greater safety. Perhaps paradoxically, the 'elite' expert-driven approach of the UK's ONR appears to rest on a stricter normative interpretation of nuclear safety. In this, again, it is like that of France.

This difference in normative philosophies is borne out in practice in the exam-ples of the biggest (nuclear power) security challenges arising this century: the responses to 9/11 and Fukushima. The ONR had decided more or less immedi-ately after 9/11 that future new nuclear power plants would have to have aircraft protection sufficient to withstand a strike by a large commercial aircraft. By con-trast, it was only after several years of argument (and campaigns by anti-nuclear groups) that a similar rule was established in 2009 in the US.

A similar pattern (of comparison) can be seen in the case of the post-Fukushima safety improvements in that the UK's ONR has been stricter in its application of safety rules compared to the US's NRC. The British and the American task forces established broadly similar types of task forces to investigate lessons and make safety recommendations. However, the outcome of the regulatory actions were different. The UK's safety requirements are stronger in that they required the nuclear operators to put in place measures to ensure independent provision of power and water for at least 72 hours beyond a post-accident blackout, they required hydrogen mitigation to be fitted to the UK's PWR, and they required all nuclear power plants to undertake seismic and flooding risk analysis for beyond design-based threats. However, despite initial recommendations in support of these objectives, the NRC gave way to nuclear industry lobbies so that all three of these objectives were neither recommended nor implemented.

British safety policies can be traced back to traditional safety institutions of 'proportionality' in dealing with safety, that is it is incumbent on the authorities to ensure that safety is achieved unless 'grossly disproportional' costs are involved. The British hierarchy, then, it can be said is oriented towards managing risk with an eye on a precautionary approach. It is a hierarchy which is grounded in egalitarian norms. The original case law acted as a 'bottom-up' influence which represents a cultural disposition towards safety precaution – at least in stated intention (although anti-nuclear quarters would dispute the substance of this commitment). The hierarchy as represented by the ONR seeks to make itself the manager of this cultural tradition. It is contained within the concept of 'weak' ecological modernisation which has been described in Chapter 2.

The problem of high costs in the nuclear industry's construction programme has been a long-standing one. Unlike the French programme of the 1970s/1980s the British nuclear construction programme has never had the size needed to assure the existence of a big enough cadre of engineering specialists. A clue to explain how China's construction costs may be lower compared to those in the UK (and by implication other Western states) is given by reports of less stringent health and safety and work practices, as well as the sheer volume of relevant workers available in China compared to countries like the UK.

Interviews quoted in the text

Anonymous interview and email communication with ONR officials, 14/08/ 2014 and 03/10/2018

Anonymous interview with UK nuclear industry consultant 01/06/2018, and email communication 09/07/2018

Interview with Chris Huhne, former Secretary of State for Energy and Climate Change, 20/06/2018

Note

1 National Infrastructure Assessment (2018) 'Low Cost Carbon', Chapter No. 2, www.nic. org.uk/assessment/national-infrastructure-assessment/low-cost-low-carbon/

References

Baker, J. (1989) Letter to the Department of Energy, from John Baker, CEO National Power, 11th October 1989, 'AGR and PWR Indicative Prices', see Appendix II, file C.194 (see also file D.17) GB 0014 MRSL (Papers of Walter Marshall), Churchill Archives Centre, Churchill College, Cambridge (UK).

Barry, S. (2015) *Once in a Lifetime £5.7bn Boost for Welsh Economy from New Nuclear Power at Wylfa, 07/04, Wales*. www.walesonline.co.uk/business/business-news/once-lifetime-57bn-boost-welsh-8989250 (accessed 15 November 2018).

BBC (2015) 'Wylfa Newydd "Once in Generation Opportunity" Worth £5.7bn', *BBC Wales News*, 7 April. www.bbc.co.uk/news/uk-wales-32161817 (accessed 15 November 2018).

BERR (2007) 'The Future of Nuclear Power: Consultation May 2007', *Department of Business Energy and Regulatory Reform*. http://webarchive.nationalarchives.gov.uk/+/http:/www.berr.gov.uk/files/file39197.pdf (accessed 15 November 2018).

Clark, G. (2019) 'Statement on Suspension of Work on the Wylfa Newydd Nuclear Project', *Department of Business Energy and Industrial Strategy*. www.gov.uk/government/speeches/statement-on-suspension-of-work-on-thewylfa-newyddnuclear-project

Demeritt, D., Rothstein, H., Beaussier, A.-L., and Howard, M. (2015) 'Mobilizing Risk: Explaining Policy Transfer in Food and Occupational Safety Regulation in the UK', *Environment and Planning*, A47, 373–391.

Department of Energy and Climate Change (2011) *Overarching National Policy Statement for Energy (EN-1)*. London: Stationery Office.

Department of Trade and Industry (2006) 'The Energy Challenge: The Energy Review', *Cm* 6887

Digest of United Kingdom Energy Statistics (2019) 'Gov.UK', Chapter No. 5, www.gov.uk/government/statistics/electricity-chapter-5-digest-of-united-kingdom-energy-statistics-dukes

Downer J. (2014) 'Disowning Fukushima: Managing the Credibility of Nuclear Reliability Assessment in the Wake of Disaster', *Regulation and Governance*, 8, 287–309.

Downer, J. (2017)'The Aviation Paradox: Why We Can 'Know' Jetliners But Not Reactors', *Minerva*, 55, 229–248.

EDF Energy (2006) *Summary of EDF Energy's Response to Key Questions for the Review*. London: EDF Energy.

EU Commission (2014) *Commission Decision (EU) 2015/658 of 8 October 2014 on Hinkley Point C*. https://eur-lex.europa.eu/legal-content/EN/TXT/?uri=uriserv:OJ.L_.2015.109.01.0044.01.ENG&toc=OJ:L:2015:109:FULL (accessed 15 November 2018).

Gov.UK (2019) 'Contracts for Difference Round 3 Allocation'. https://assets.publishing.service.gov.uk/government/uploads/system/uploads/attachment_data/file/838914/cfd-ar3-results-corrected-111019.pdf

HSE (2007) 'Health & Safety Executive Nuclear Directorate Assessment Report – New Build Step 2 EPR Civil Engineering and External Hazard Assessment'. Bootle: HM Nuclear Installations Inspectorate. http://www.onr.org.uk/new-reactors/reports/eprcivil.pdf (accessed 15 November 2018).

Marshall, W. (1982) 'Problems of Introducing New Technology: Lecture at the University of Birmingham 24th March 1982', *Nuclear Energy*, 21(6) (December), 371–376. From archives of Walter Marshall held at Churchill College, Cambridge, holding H.90-H.93, see www.chu.cam.ac.uk/media/uploads/files/MRSL_sMDtBKW.pdf

National Infrastructure Assessment (2018) 'Low Cost Carbon', Chapter No 2. www.nic.org.uk/assessment/national-infrastructure-assessment/low-cost-low-carbon/

NERA Consulting (2017) 'The Economic Impact of ONR Safety Regulation: Final Report', Bootle: Office for Nuclear Regulation. http://www.onr.org.uk/documents/2018/nera-report-the-economic-impact-of-onr-safety-regulation.pdf

Nikkei Staff Writers (2018) 'Hitachi Seeks Assurance from UK's May on Shared Stake in Nuclear Project', *Nikkei Asian Review*, 29 March. https://asia.nikkei.com/Business/

Companies/Hitachi-seeks-assurance-from-UK-s-May-on-shared-stake-in-nuclear-project (accessed 15 November 2018).

ONR (1992) *Safety Assessment Principles for Nuclear Facilities*. Bootle: Office for Nuclear Regulation.

ONR (2011) *Japanese Earthquake and Tsunami: Implications for the UK Nuclear Industry*. Bootle: Office for Nuclear Regulation. www.onr.org.uk/fukushima/final-report.pdf (accessed 15 November 2018).

ONR (2014) *Safety Assessment Principles for Nuclear Facilities*. Bootle: Office for Nuclear Regulation.

ONR (2015a) *Fukushima Recommendations and Stress Test Findings: Overall Review of EDF Energy Nuclear Generation Limited Responses*. Bootle: Office for Nuclear Regulation. www.onr.org.uk/pars/2015/edf-14-031.pdf (accessed 15 November 2018).

ONR (2015b) *Summary Report of the Step 3 Generic Design Assessment (GDA) of Hitachi-GE Nuclear Energy's UK Advanced Boiling Water Reactor (UK ABWR)*. Bootle: Office for Nuclear Regulation. www.onr.org.uk/new-reactors/uk-abwr/reports/step3/uk-abwr-step-3-summary-report.pdf (accessed 15 November 2018).

ONR (2017) *Japanese Earthquake and Tsunami: Update on UK 'National Action Plan' – 2nd Updated Progress Report*. Bootle: Office for Nuclear Regulation. www.onr.org.uk/fukushima/ensreg-report-2017.pdf (accessed 15 November 2018).

ONR (2018a) *Safety Systems, Nuclear Safety Technical Assessment Guide, NS-TAST-GD-003 Revision 8*. Bootle: ONR. www.onr.org.uk/operational/tech_asst_guides/ns-tast-gd-003.pdf (accessed 15 November 2018).

ONR (2018b) *Guidance on the Demonstration of ALARP (As Low as Reasonably Practicable), Technical Advice Guidance 5, (NS-TAST-GD-005 Revision 9)*. Bootle: ONR. www.onr.org.uk/operational/tech_asst_guides/ns-tast-gd-005.pdf (accessed 15 November 2018).

ONR (2018c) *ONR Guide External Hazards, Technical Advice Guidance 13, NS-TAST-GD-013 Revision 7*. Bootle: ONR. www.onr.org.uk/operational/tech_asst_guides/ns-tast-gd-013.pdf (accessed 15 November 2018).

ONR (2018d) *ONR Response to the NERA Report 'the Economic Impact of Safety Regulation'*. Bootle: ONR. www.onr.org.uk/documents/2018/onr-response-to-the-nera-report.pdf (accessed 15 November 2018).

Thomas, S., Bradford, P., Frogatt, A., and Milborrow, D. (2007) *The Economics of Nuclear Power*. Amsterdam, The Netherlands: Greenpeace.

Twidale, S. (2018) 'Hitachi's Nuclear Project to Get Guarantees from Government', *Reuters*. https://uk.reuters.com/article/uk-britain-nuclear-hitachi/hitachis-u-k-nuclear-project-to-get-guarantees-from-government-media-idUKKBN1IA0IV?rpc=401& (accessed 15 November 2018).

9 Nuclear power and safety policy in Russia

In this chapter, we examine the nuclear power industry in Russia. Specifically, we examine the evolution of nuclear safety regulation in Russia and the influence that this exerted over the evolution of the nuclear power industry in Russia. Russia is an especially important country to study in the context of nuclear power since it has one of the highest proportions of electricity supplied by nuclear power in the world (nearly 20 per cent in 2019), was the fourth-largest generator of nuclear power in the world in 2019, and had the fifth-largest installed nuclear capacity.

It is also the leading designer of nuclear power plants (NPPs) in the world, with established and proven designs such as VVER-1000 and VVER-1200 installed in Russia and abroad. It is also at the forefront of developing new models, such as Generation III+ VVER-TOI and fast neutron reactors. It is especially important because Rosatom, the state corporation in charge of Russia's nuclear industry, is exporting reactors. Deals have been signed for the construction of many reactors to be exported although plans and deals do not always lead to completed projects. Thomas (2018) has cast doubt on the ability of Russia to complete many of the deals. According to Thomas (2018, 236) 'Russia was claiming firm orders for about 35 reactors in 10 countries with advanced negotiations in several other countries'. As such, the evolution of the Russian nuclear industry is of crucial importance to the future of the global nuclear industry.

We begin with a brief outline of the history of the nuclear energy programme and its organisational structure, first in the Soviet Union, and then, after 1991, in the Russian Federation. This is followed by an examination of the evolution of nuclear safety policy. Here, we show how considerable progress was made in the aftermath of both the Chernobyl accident and the collapse of the Soviet Union. Finally, we explore the impact that nuclear safety policy has exerted over both existing NPPs, and on the construction and development of new NPPs in Russia.

We show how the nuclear power industry occupied a leading role in the Soviet economy, both because it represented a high-technology solution to the country's energy supply challenges, and also because it was closely linked to the country's nuclear weapons programme. The latter provided the basis for the Soviet Union's claim to superpower status. Today, the nuclear power industry plays an important role in the country's domestic energy strategy. It is also an important component of Russia's foreign economic policy.

Nuclear power in Russia: history and organisation

The modern Russian nuclear power industry has its roots in the Soviet nuclear programme (Holloway 1994; Josephson 2000). Sporadic attempts at conducting nuclear research were interrupted by the outbreak of World War 2. However, after the US nuclear attacks on Hiroshima and Nagasaki in 1945, a crash programme – based on both domestic research and espionage abroad – to develop an indigenous nuclear weapons capability was launched, resulting in the successful testing of the first Soviet atomic device in 1949, and the first Soviet hydrogen bomb in 1953 (Holloway 1994).

The Soviet civilian nuclear programme emerged alongside, and in many ways as a by-product of, the military programme (Simonov 2000). While work was underway on developing the first atomic bomb, the Council of Ministers adopted a resolution in 1946 'On the development of research on the study of the atomic nucleus and the use of nuclear energy in technology, chemistry, medicine and biology'. This envisaged a wide range of civilian applications of nuclear technology, including nuclear power to produce electricity. With strong support from the highest levels of power, including Joseph Stalin and Lavrenti Beria, rapid progress was made. By 1954, the Soviet Union commissioned the world's first atomic power station – the 5 MWe *Atom Mirnyi* (peaceful atom) – in Obninsk, in Kaluga *oblast'* (region), south-west of Moscow (Josephson 2000).

By 1953, both the civilian and military nuclear programmes were organised under the innocuously titled Ministry of Medium Machine Building (*Ministerstvo srednego mashinostroyeniya*), which was the authority charged with coordinating and managing nuclear science and technology in the Soviet Union until 1989, when it was reorganised and renamed the Ministry of Atomic Energy and Industry of the USSR (*Ministerstvo Atom Noy Energetik Ii Promyshlennost I*). The Ministry of Medium Machine Building grew to become one of the Soviet Union's leading industries. Because it was a crucial part of the Soviet military effort, it enjoyed privileged access to the country's brightest people and its most advanced machinery. These strong links with the military resulted in it rising to become powerful but immensely secretive. By the 1960s, a vast network of closed cities spread across the Soviet Union, with each containing research institutes and production facilities required for both military and civilian purposes. Such was its power, influence, and relative autonomy that it was described as a 'state within a state' (Cooper 2000, 148). The designation given to closed cities was 'closed administrative territorial units' (*zakrytye administrativno-territorial 'nye obrazovaniya'* or ZATO).

The Ministry of Medium Machine Building developed a range of products. Two main reactor types were employed in NPPs across the Soviet Union. The first and most widely produced type was the water-cooled, graphite-moderated reactor, known as high-power channel reactors (*reaktor bolshoy moshchnosti kanalnyy*), or to use the Russian acronym, RBMK reactors. A total of 15 different versions of the RBMK reactor were installed between 1971 and 1987, including the reactor at the centre of the accident at the Chernobyl NPP in 1986. The second type of reactor was the pressurised water reactor (PWR), or to use the Russian abbreviation – VVER (*vodo-vodyanoi energetiche sky reactor*).

Between 1964 and 1985 a total of eight reactors were installed at NPPs within Russia. Further VVER reactors were commissioned after 1985 and they were also exported to socialist satellite states and Finland. In addition, two fast breeder reactors (FBR) were also installed, first in Kazakhstan in 1969 (the first-generation BN-350) and the second in Beloyarsk in Russia in 1980 (the second-generation BN-600).

Over time, atomic energy grew steadily to occupy an increasingly important role in the Soviet economy (Campbell 1980). To be sure, it did not grow as quickly as some expected. However, after a period of rapid expansion in the late 1970s, installed capacity doubled between 1977 and 1980. Nuclear power plants accounted for 5.6 per cent of all electricity produced in 1980 (Office of Technology Assessment 1982, 113). It was a source of national pride, employing a large number of highly educated and trained scientists, engineers, and workers. There were very few high-technology industries in which the Soviet Union could claim to be as advanced as its Western and Japanese competitors. But the atomic energy industry was one of few in which this claim was not hollow.

By 1985 – the year before the accident at the Chernobyl NPP in Ukraine – the Soviet Union operated 25 nuclear reactors across the country, with 28.1 GEEE installed capacity (Unsigned, *Narodnoekhoziastvo SSSR* 1987, 161). Nearly all these reactors were located west of the Ural Mountains, in the European part of the Soviet Union. The exceptions were the Bilibino NPP in Chukotka in the far north-east of the Soviet Union and the Shevchenko NPP (now Aktau) on the Caspian Sea coast in Kazakhstan.

NPPs were located in the republics of Armenia, Kazakhstan, Lithuania, Russia, and Ukraine. Soviet planners formulated ambitious plans that targeted increasing installed capacity to nearly 100 GWe by 1990 (Office of Technology Assessment 1982, 121). These plans, however, were interrupted by the accident at Chernobyl in 1986. The vast majority of new NPPs either under construction or planned were temporarily abandoned. This was soon followed by the collapse of the Soviet Union in 1991.

The collapse of the Soviet Union undermined plans for the continued rapid expansion of nuclear power. Russia found itself in what would become a decade of political and economic disarray, which resulted in a near-decade long period of economic depression. Nevertheless, the nuclear industry did not perform as badly as other parts of the economy. It was organised under the newly established Ministry of Atomic Energy (Minatom). Minatom inherited ten NPPs (comprising 31 reactor units) with a total installed capacity of over 23 GWe. Most importantly, those within Minatom were able to preserve their elite bureaucratic structure and integrity, as well as its access to political power (Cooper 2000, 160).

These important legacies of the Soviet period enabled Minatom to avoid the disarray experienced by other Soviet-era structures forced to adapt to the nascent market economy. Even as electricity output shrank over the course of the 1990s (due to the severe economic situation), the share of nuclear power in electricity output rose from 11 per cent in 1990 to 14 per cent in 1999. Nevertheless, with the procurement of nuclear weapons drastically reduced, and with investment in large-scale nuclear power projects shelved, the nuclear industry did not significantly expand installed capacity, even if it did perform better than most other industries in the 1990s (Cooper 2000, 156). Between 1986 and the mid-1990s, only one NPP was commissioned in Russia: the four-unit Balakovo NPP in Saratov *oblast'*. A further reactor (Unit 3) was added to Smolensk NPP.

In the early 2000s, Russia gradually recovered from the financial and economic chaos that followed the disintegration of the Soviet Union. This coincided with the revival of NPP construction in Russia. Construction on the first reactor of the Rostov NPP – which had started in 1981 but was halted due to a lack of financial resources – resumed in 1999. It was commissioned at the end of 2001. Export sales also enabled the industry to generate much-needed revenues, with lucrative deals to export NPPs to China, India, and Iran signed in the late 1990s and early 2000s. Export sales from the nuclear industry rose from $500 million in 1991 to nearly $2 billion in 1998 (Cooper 2000, 155).

As the state regained the administrative capacity that was so absent during the 1990s, and as it enjoyed rapid growth in tax revenues from a growing economy, greater efforts were made to reinvigorate the nuclear complex. The appointment of former prime minister, Sergei Kiriyenko, in 2005 to the position of general director of the Federal Atomic Energy Agency signalled the beginning of what would become a major restructuring effort. A period of rapid reorganisation followed, ultimately resulting in the consolidation of control over the nuclear industry by the newly created State Corporation, Rosatom, in 2006. Under the aegis of Rosatom, and with the full support of an active state, the civilian nuclear industry enjoyed a renaissance. Ambitious plans were formulated for the expansion of nuclear power, both in Russia and abroad. And, as one of Russia's few high-technology industries, the nuclear industry also played a key role in the leadership's plans to diversify the country's largely resource-based economy (Cooper 2006; Connolly 2008, 2012).

The organisation of the nuclear power industry in Russia today

The law abolishing the Federal Atomic Energy Agency was signed by President Vladimir Putin on 1 December 2007. Its assets and competencies were transferred to 'State Atomic Energy Corporation Rosatom'. Rosatom is a vertically integrated and fully state-owned company that manages the assets of the Russian nuclear industry – both civilian and military – throughout all stages of the nuclear production cycle. In total, Rosatom comprises nearly 350 enterprises and organisations, and in 2018 employed 255,400 people (Rosatom 2018a). Of this number, around 100,000 are estimated to work in the Nuclear Weapons Directorate (Cooper 2018, 2).

Rosatom presides over a virtually closed production cycle, beginning with uranium mining, its subsequent enrichment and conversion for use as a nuclear fuel for use in power generation, and, after further enrichment, to produce nuclear weapons. Rosatom also manages the decommissioning of obsolete nuclear facilities and the disposal of spent nuclear fuel (Frolov 2014, 531). This is a legacy of the Soviet period, when the industry exhibited an exceptionally high degree of self-reliance from other branches of industry. Research and manufacturing took place within the nuclear complex, with little in the way of input from outside agencies and suppliers.

The legacy of self-reliance is even more evident when we consider that Rosatom is engaged in far more than the production and management of nuclear fuels for military and civilian purposes. Its place as perhaps the country's leading high-technology manufacturer grants it additional strategic importance. The NPPs operated under Rosatom are designed and built by subsidiaries and affiliates of JSC Atomenergoprom – the organisation managing Rosatom's civilian assets – and are operated using equipment produced by machine-building enterprises within Atomenergomash, another subsidiary of Rosatom. This marks Rosatom out among most other Russian industrial enterprises, which to some degree rely on imported components or technology. By contrast, Rosatom relies overwhelmingly on the internal manufacturing capabilities managed within its own structures. This indigenous manufacturing prowess enabled Rosatom to engage in other high-technology industrial activities, including nuclear medicine, robotics, supercomputers, and wind turbine production. In this respect, Rosatom is a source of technologies that can be diffused across the economy (Frolov 2014).

Rosatom also plays a strategically important role in the Russian Government's emerging Arctic policy, a large part of which is based on the development of the Northern Sea Route (NSR). The NSR is expected to reduce transit time between Asia and Europe to half that of existing routes. According to deputy Prime Minister, Yuri Trutnev, annual shipments passing through the NSR should reach 80 million tonnes by 2025 (Staalesen 2020). To this end, the recently signed Arctic policy targets a significant expansion of the nuclear icebreaker fleet over the next 15 years to ensure that year-round navigation of the NSR is possible (*Ukaz Prezidenta Rossiyskoy Federatsii* 2020). Rosatom currently manages the world's only nuclear-powered icebreaker fleet through its subsidiary, Rosatomflot (FSUE Atomflot). The current nuclear fleet consists of four icebreakers and one container ship. All eight new icebreakers – including the *Arktika*, the world's largest and most powerful icebreaker – are expected to be operational by the early 2030s (*Sudostroenie.info* 2019).

Rosatom's leading role in the Arctic encompasses more than operating the nuclear icebreaker fleet. A law signed by President Putin at the end of 2018 granted Rosatom responsibility for the construction and maintenance of NSR infrastructure, including ports (Rosatom 2018b). Another important component of Rosatom's maritime role is the construction and operation of floating nuclear power plants (FNPPs). To date, only one FNPP has been built – the *Akademik Lomonosov* – although the construction of further units is envisaged (Soldatkin 2019).

In addition to Rosatom's many functions within the domestic economy, it is also extremely active abroad. According to Rosatom's Development Strategy, published in 2012, the corporation should rank in the top three enterprises in every segment of the global nuclear market – from uranium extraction through to the disposal or reprocessing of spent fuel – by 2030 (Rosatom 2012). The document stated the objective of increasing the share of revenues from foreign sales from around a third in 2011 to over 50 per cent of total revenues by 2030. This target was subsequently revised upward to 'over two thirds' by 2016 due to export revenues already approximating half of all revenues (Mehdiyeva 2019).

The focus on external activities is not only motivated by commercial considerations. By virtue of its role as a state corporation, Rosatom also serves to maximise Russian political influence abroad. It is able to sign agreements with foreign states. Unlike its international competitors, it presents itself as a 'one-stop shop' that is able to offer a comprehensive package of goods and services that solve many of the complex problems associated with the production and operation of NPPs. These include the provision of attractive finance, construction, training and development of staff, and solutions to addressing safety, security, and export control requirements. The provision of these services is only possible because of Rosatom's privileged place within the Russian system of political economy. Financing, for example, is sometimes provided by Russia's state-owned development bank, VEB (Aris 2019). Access to state-backed finance enables Rosatom to offer what is effectively 'vendor financing' facilities, where it extends credit to customers so that they can place orders for NPPs.

The construction and operation of NPPs – with all the attendant complexities at each stage of the fuel cycle, as well as operating cycles that can last for well over half a century – can lead to the development of dense links between supplier and consumer. The precise nature of these ties will vary according to the provisions of each contract and are likely to contain long-term financing conditions and all stages of the fuel cycle.

The close linkages that can emerge from the sale of NPPs have the potential to help foster closer relations between Russia and client states in a number of areas, including providing Russia with greater access to and influence over leaders and elites in recipient states; symbolising Russia's commitment to the recipient's energy security against perceived or real internal or external threats; creating opportunities for the enrichment of local elites in recipient countries; creating or maintaining Russian prestige as the supplier of advanced technologies; and providing access to scarce, expensive, or strategic resources (Minin and Vlcek 2017, 41–42). Indeed, Rosatom's export success tends to occur alongside other arms and energy deals, with Bangladesh, China, India, Iran, and Turkey all serving as cases in point (Connolly and Senstad 2017; Connolly 2018).

Nuclear power plants in Russia today

At the beginning of the century, the Russian state harboured grand ambitions for the expansion of nuclear power in Russia. In 2007, Rosatom envisaged nuclear power providing 23 per cent of Russia's electricity by 2020, rising to 25 per cent by 2030 (Oxenstierna 2010, 25). It was assumed that 24 reactors distributed around 15 sites (including the floating NPP, the *Akademik Lomonosov*) would need to be built by 2020 to meet these objectives. These plans were further refined to correspond with the objectives contained within the Energy Strategy to 2030 (ES-2030), published at the end of 2009 (Government of the Russian Federation 2009). This document was published alongside a raft of other strategic planning documents that collectively laid out plans for a period of broad-based economic growth and modernisation within Russia (Connolly 2013).

Based on an optimistic scenario of economic growth for Russia over the same period, the ES-2030 envisaged electricity consumption rising sharply. It also projected an increase in the proportion of electricity generated by nuclear power (replacing older coal- and oil-fuelled power stations). The share of nuclear power in a much larger supply of electricity was, it was hoped, to rise from 16 per cent in 2008 to 20 per cent in 2030. In absolute terms, this required an increase in installed capacity of 4–9 GWe by 2015 (depending on the economic growth scenario), and of 28–38 by 2030. Given that, in 2010, Rosatom operated 32 reactors with an aggregate installed capacity of 23 GWe, these were extremely lofty ambitions. Energoatom, the subsidiary of JSC Atomenergoprom that operates Russia's NPPs, would need to more than double its installed capacity by 2030, even in the less optimistic economic growth scenario. Moreover, older reactors and NPPs would need to be replaced over that period, as well. This would require an enormous expansion in both human and physical capital (Oxenstierna 2010, 37–40).

The assumptions regarding the rate of economic growth contained within ES-2030, and with it, growth in electricity consumption and in nuclear power generation capacity, proved to be wildly optimistic. Through Energoatom, electricity generation from nuclear power plants grew from just under 100 terawatt-hours (TWh) in 1995 to 208.7 TWh in 2019 (TASS 2020). This allowed Rosatom to provide over 40 per cent of the electricity produced in the European part of Russia in 2019, and to supply 19.7 per cent of the total electricity produced in Russia (ibid.). The fact that nuclear power generation more than doubled in just under 25 years meant that Russia was the third fastest growing country by electricity generated by nuclear power, behind China (nuclear-powered electricity generation increased by 281 KWh over the same period) and the USA (140 TWh increase). This trend stands in sharp contrast to the stagnation seen in France and the decline observed in Japan, Germany, and the UK.

This expansion of installed capacity was facilitated by a steady rate of construction of NPPs, although the pace of this construction was slower than was envisaged in the ES-2030 produced in 2010. Between 2010 and 2019, eight new reactor units were installed with a combined installed capacity of 8 GWe (IAEA 2020). As a result, there were, at the end of 2019, a total of ten NPPs in Russia operating 36 reactor units with a total capacity of almost 29 GWe. Whilst this was an increase in nuclear power generation capacity from the 2010 level, it was significantly below the level envisaged in ES-2030. This was true of nearly all the projections contained within ES-2030. In short, nuclear power was advancing, but not as fast as many Russian officials would have liked.

To sum up so far. The nuclear power industry emerged from the end of the 1940s to become an extremely important part of the Soviet economy. Because of its central role in the Soviet military effort, it enjoyed privileged access to the country's brightest people and its most advanced machinery. These strong links with the military resulted in the nuclear sector rising to become powerful but immensely secretive. Due to its power, influence, and relative autonomy, it was described as a virtual 'state within a state'. It remains a politically and economically important part of the Russian system of political economy today. Organised under the aegis of the state corporation, Rosatom, the nuclear industry remains at the forefront of high-technology and knowledge-based activity in Russia. It is also a strategically important industry, with Rosatom playing a crucial role in ensuring domestic energy security and in advancing Russia's economic and political interests abroad. It has also been assigned responsibility for harnessing the economic and geostrategic potential of the Arctic.

Because of the important role that Rosatom plays within Russia, and because of its place as a powerful instrument of the state, it enjoys advantages that most other firms – within Russia or abroad – do not. It possesses access to significant diplomatic, financial, and institutional resources that enable it to carry out its operations without being forced to abide by the same commercial considerations that constrain other firms in the industry. As we will show, Rosatom's privileged place within the Russian economy and the advantages conferred upon it have exerted a strong influence over the expansion of nuclear power in Russia and abroad.

Nuclear safety in Russia

The Soviet legacy

As the Soviet Union expanded the nuclear power sector, state organisations tasked with supervising nuclear safety were developed. By 1983 the primary organisation fulfilling this role was the State Committee for the Supervision of Nuclear Power Safety, or Gosatomenergonadzor (Potter 1991). However, Gosatomenergonadzor was not an independent organisation. Instead, it was placed under the authority of existing Soviet bureaucratic structures responsible for power production. These were, in turn, responsible to the State Committee for Planning (*Gosplan*), which guided economic activity in the Soviet Union's planned economy and took its instructions from the senior leadership of the ruling Communist Party of the Soviet Union (CPSU). This meant that, in effect, the regulating authority was subordinated to political and economic considerations of the country's ruling elite.

In addition to the obvious weakness of the regulating authority vis-à-vis the Soviet Union's planning structures, Soviet safety practices prior to the Chernobyl accident were also considered by many to be considerably less demanding than those prevalent in Western countries at the time. Philosophically, Soviet safety policies were based on the assumption that, when determining the Maximum Design Accident (MDA) of a reactor (i.e. the most extreme failure a reactor should be designed to cope with) only credible scenarios should be taken into account, rather than less plausible but more catastrophic scenarios (Pryde and Pryde 1974; Debardeleben 1985). This philosophical approach to reactor design meant that Soviet NPPs were less able to deal with catastrophic events than NPPs produced elsewhere in the world at that time.

The existence of a more lenient attitude towards safety in reactor design was exacerbated by the absence of transparency throughout Soviet society. Information about accidents and other reactor failure incidents was not shared, either with outside observers and authorities, or with others within the Soviet system. This suppression of information prevented the other parts of the nuclear industry from being able to learn from failures elsewhere.

Thus, despite the Soviet Union being one of the world's leading nuclear powers, the combination of regulatory weakness, a relaxed attitude towards reactor safety, and a general absence of transparency within the nuclear industry and Soviet society more widely, created a permissive environment for the accident that took place at Chernobyl in 1986. These weaknesses were further compounded by a number of other deficiencies (Aleksashin et al. 2006). The existence of multiple structural failures and deficiencies were at least tacitly acknowledged by the Soviet authorities who, in the aftermath of the accident, radically restructured the regulatory framework governing nuclear power plant safety. By 1989, Gosatomenergonadzor was replaced by Gospromatomnadzor (the State Committee for the Supervision of Safety in Industry and Nuclear Power), which was genuinely independent and modelled on the US Nuclear Regulatory Commission (Potter 1991).

Nuclear safety in Russia today

Contemporary Russia has a considerably more robust framework for ensuring nuclear safety than the Soviet Union. In some ways, this is a result of lessons learned from the Chernobyl disaster, including the need for a genuinely independent regulatory authority as well as a more robust approach to safety (Aleksashin et al. 2006). Russia today benefits from a sophisticated legislative and regulatory framework, which is in turn embedded within a dense patchwork of international obligations. The culture and philosophy of reactor safety is also much improved. Russian designs are considered by many specialists to incorporate among the most stringent design requirements in the world. Furthermore, the creation of a market-based economy in the 1990s also reduces the extent to which the political considerations of the ruling elite can supersede regulatory activities, as they did during the Soviet period.

Nevertheless, the strategically important role assigned to Rosatom – and the nuclear industry more widely – in the Russian system of political economy does raise questions as to how much authority Russia's regulatory system exerts over its activities. A pervasive culture of secrecy also continues to blight many aspects of Russian society, especially in areas close to the defence and military sphere, such as the nuclear industry (Golts 2013).

Legislative and regulatory framework

The Federal Service for Ecological, Technological, and Nuclear Supervision (*Federal'nayasluzhba po ekologicheskomu, tekhnologicheskomuiatomnomunadzoru*), or Rostekhnadzor (previously Gosatomnadzor) as it is more commonly known, is charged with the regulation of the construction, operation, and decommissioning of civilian NPPs and of all other civilian applications of nuclear technologies.

It exists within a sophisticated legislative and regulatory framework. Rostekhnadzor exercises the state-level regulation of safety in the use of atomic energy, reports to the government, and is independent of the state bodies for control over the use of atomic energy.[1]

The application of nuclear technologies in the military sphere, including in the production of nuclear weapons and in power units for naval vessels, is regulated by the Department of State Oversight over Nuclear and Radiation Safety and Security of the Russian Ministry of Defence (in Russian, the *Upravleniyegosudarstvennogonadzora za yadernoyiradiatsionnoybezopasnost'yuMinisterstvao boronyRossiyskoyFederatsii*). It is more commonly known by its Russian acronym, UGN. As pointed out by Bunn and Kovchegin (2018, 536), '[t]here is some uncertainty about the exact point at which nuclear material crosses the "border" between these two regulatory domains, and some facilities operate under both civilian and defence licenses'.

The regulatory basis for the security of nuclear activities in the civilian domain is based on several layers of legislation. In broad terms, they include:

- An overarching law ('On the Utilisation of Atomic Energy', first issued in 1995);[2]
- Presidential decrees (*ukazy*), including 'About the operating of nuclear power plants of the Russian Federation', 7 September 1992 No. 1055;
- Government decisions and orders (*postanovleniyairasporyazheniya*), outlining general approaches to construction, operation, and maintenance of NPPs, as well as all other aspects of civilian nuclear power application. Notable and relevant examples include 'On the federal executive bodies and authorized organisations implementing state management of the use of atomic energy and state regulation of safety in the use of atomic energy', 3 July 2006 No. 412, and 'On state construction supervision of the Russian Federation', 1 February 2006 No. 54;
- Federal norms and rules in the field of the use of atomic energy (*Federal'nyyenormyipravila v oblastiispol'zovaniyaatomnoyenergii*), more commonly known by their Russian acronym, FNP, and issued by Rostekhnadzor, which set out more detailed requirements;
- And agency-level rules, providing more specific requirements, as well as several technical and administrative regulations. Notable and relevant examples include the 'Technical regulation on the safety of machinery and equipment'(TR TS 010/2011), decision of the Commission of the Customs Union of 18 October 2011 No. 823; and 'Technical regulation on the safety of buildings and structures', Federal Law of 30 December 2009 No. 384-F3.[3]

Licencing process

Before issuing a licence to build and operate NPPs, Rostekhnadzor is required to conduct a review of a detailed justification from the applicant describing how it will ensure safe and secure operation. This is known as a 'licence demand'. Rostekhnadzor also carries out inspections to verify the applicant's information and to validate that the safety and security measures contained in its justification are sufficient.

Recent changes to the regulatory framework

During the course of preparing the 'Seventh National Report of the Russian Federation on the Fulfillment of Commitments Resulting from the Convention on Nuclear Safety for the Period from August 2013 to July 2016', prepared in compliance with Article 5 of the Convention on Nuclear Safety, Rostekhnadzor approved a number of measures to enhance the legal and regulatory framework covering nuclear energy (Rostekhnadzor 2017).

Most notably, a decision was made in 2015 to revise the federal standards and regulations 'General Safety Provisions of Nuclear Power Plants'(NP-001–15). This followed a comparative analysis of the requirements of corresponding Russian regulations with the provisions of the IAEA safety standards SSR-2/1 and SSR-2/2. While this analysis demonstrated that Russian NPP safety requirements corresponded with IAEA requirements in general, several areas were identified as requiring greater harmonisation with the IAEA safety standards. As a result, in the revised version:

- The meaning of 'nuclear power plant safety' has been changed to meet the upper level IAEA safety standard SF-1;
- The requirements in relation to the procedures to be used in the analysis of design basis accidents and beyond design basis accident were reformulated;
- The rules of classification of NPP systems and components were revised to conform with IAEA safety standards SSR-2/1; and
- The formulation of NPP safety target probabilistic indicators was changed.

Regulation of NPP exports

Because of the importance of NPP exports to Rosatom, it is also worth considering the role of safety regulations governing the export of NPPs. Russia, like other international exporters of NPPs (the USA, France, China, Japan, and South Korea), is a signatory to international nuclear safety and security conventions, such as the Convention on Nuclear Safety (CNS).[4] Russia encourages its export clients to do the same (Schepers 2019, 7). However, framework agreements of the sort signed by Rosatom with a range of customers from across the world do not require customer countries to be a signatory to any treaty or convention beyond the Non-Proliferation Treaty (NPT). Customers are also required to have a Comprehensive Safeguards Agreement with the IAEA.

Safety concerns and NPP design

There are currently a wide range of different reactors under development in Russia today. Since the mid-1990s, most of the NPPs built in Russia and for export have been of the AES-91 and AES-92 designs, making use of the third-generation VVER-1000 pressurised water reactor, or, more recently, of the AES-2006 design, based on the VVER-1200 pressurised water reactor. The latter is essentially an incremental improvement on the VVER-1000, which was designed by OKB Gidropress (Experimental Design Bureau Hydropress) in the 1980s. The VVER-1000 and 1200 reactors have equipped nearly all NPPs built in Russia since the collapse of the Soviet Union, as well as NPPs exported to China, India, and Iran. The VVER-1000 received a certificate of compliance with the requirements of European Utility Requirement (EUR) in April 2007, with the VVER-1200 incorporating further features designed to increase the safety of the reactor.

Most of the new reactors currently under construction within Russia are of the 'third-generation+' VVER-TOI model (VVER-1300/510). Again, in line with many forms of high-technology equipment in Russia, it represents the next stage in the evolutionary of an existing design, in this case the VVER-1000 and VVER-1200 series. It is designed to incorporate a wide range of safety design features that are compliant with IAEA safety standards. Incorporating these design features delayed the development of the reactor, which was initially intended to be ready for construction in 2012. As a result, construction of the first VVER-TOI reactor at Unit 1 of the Kursk II NPP did not begin until May 2018 (Atomstroyeksport 2018). Nevertheless, the reactor design received a certificate of compliance with the requirements of European Utility Requirement (EUR) in June 2019 (World Nuclear News 2019). The VVER-TOI reactor will form the basis of the vast majority of planned NPP construction projects in Russia and is being marketed abroad.

The only other commercially active reactors in Russia that do not make use of the VVER-1000/1200 reactors are either of the much older (updated) RBMK design, the BN-800 sodium-cooled fast breeder reactor at the Beloyarsk NPP, or the two KLT-40S small modular naval reactors used on the *Akademik Lomonosov* floating nuclear power plant, which became operational in December 2019 when it was deployed off Russia's north-eastern Arctic coast, near the town of Pevek in Chukotka (Vavina 2019). While the latter in particular has been the subject of intense international (and domestic) criticism, Glavgosexpertiza (the State Expert Examination Board), the body responsible for appraising design documentation on behalf of the Ministry of Construction, stated that the design documentation and the results of engineering surveys on the facility comply with IAEA technical regulations (Neftegaz.ru 2018; Rosatom 2018c).

Rosatom and nuclear safety regulations

The regulatory framework governing the safety of nuclear power in Russia improved tremendously in the post-Soviet period, especially after 2000, when greater financial resources were made available to both the relevant state authorities and organisations within the nuclear industry. The IAEA's last two peer review missions in Russia noted a number of instances of good practice which were worthy of replication outside Russia. The two missions also noted improvements in the country's legislative framework, Rostekhnadzor's 'authority' and capacity to act as 'an effective independent regulator with a professional staff', and the regulator's ability to work effectively with other parts of the nuclear industry in Russia (IAEA 2013, 2018). Echoing the views of the IAEA, two specialists observed that Russian nuclear security standards – including the safety of civilian nuclear facilities – had been on a trajectory of 'continuous improvement' since the end of the 1990s (Bunn and Kovchegin 2018, 544).

While a desire to reduce the shadow cast by the Chernobyl accident has been important, Rosatom's reorientation towards export markets has also played an important role in driving safety standards up. As Bunn and Kovchegin (p. 545) argue, exporters of NPPs have 'long understood that their reactors' reputation for safety is crucial to their ability to make sales abroad'. As Rosatom was given a leading role in 'increasing Russia's strategic presence in the markets of high-tech products and intellectual services in the global energy sector', the imperative to ensure that Russian reactors were considered by prospective customers to be safe as well as financially accessible became much stronger (Government of the Russian Federation 2009, 124). In short, a strong reputation for safety serves to support Rosatom's export ambitions. There are, nevertheless, two principal sources of concern in relation to the strength of existing safety practices and culture in Russia today.

First, Rosatom is considered to be one of the most strategically important parts of the Russian economy. It has been assigned ambitious commercial and political objectives at home and abroad. Its scientific and industrial capabilities are among the most advanced in Russia and represent areas the Russian state wishes to husband and nurture further. Rosatom is also an important component of the defence-industrial complex (*oboronno-promyshlennyikompleks*, or OPK) and its activities are crucial to the maintenance of Russia's parity with the US in strategic nuclear weapons. As a result, it is plausible to suggest that, in certain circumstances, safety concerns might be subordinated to security concerns. Security concerns have historically been prioritised over other considerations in Russia (Connolly 2020). This means that there are grounds for caution when assessing the relative importance of, for example, Rostekhnadzor's concerns, on the one hand, and Rosatom's pursuit of strategically important objectives, on the other.

One area of international concern is the controversy over three recent episodes of radiation leakages measured in neighbouring countries that were not, initially at least, explained by the Russian authorities. Under IAEA protocols it is a requirement that information concerning significant radioactive events are notified to the IAEA.

One leak was registered in neighbouring countries in September 2017. According to a paper by Masson et al. (2019) there was 'A massive atmospheric release of radioactive ^{106}Ru'. This paper discussed a likely connection with the reprocessing facility at Mayak which had a contract to supply nuclear materials to a research organisation in Italy.

In August 2019 and June 2020 there were further spikes in radiation recorded outside Russia, and again the Russian authorities did not initially notify the IAEA. The sources of these radiation spikes are unclear although there have been reports from defence sources that one of these leaks was related to military activities (Nilsen 2019).

Whether or not these incidents presented serious international (or local) threats, the fact that there was limited transparency about these cases from the Russian authorities does raise questions concerning the credibility of what the Russian nuclear safety regimes actually say and do. It may be that the fusion of military and civilian nuclear institutions leads to problems when it comes to the lack of release of information – information releases that may actually produce less damage than the damage to credibility caused by the appearance of secrecy. It may be that the hope that greater transparency would be the case since the Chernobyl disaster has not been completely fulfilled.

Second, a number of financial challenges remain. The first set of challenges relates to the financial resources available to regulatory authorities. This, of course, is a concern for regulators all over the world and in different sectors. How can relatively under-resourced regulatory authorities regulate comparatively better funded and more prestigious counterparts? This problem was especially acute in Russia in the first decade of the millennium (Aleksashin et al. 2006). There is every reason to think that it remains a concern, especially after three recessions – in 2009, 2015, and 2020 – have subsequently reduced the funds available to the public sector.

Relatively poor pay for Rostekhnadzor employees was highlighted in the 2013 Peer Review Mission carried out by the IAEA (2013). The second set of problems is related to the need to make NPP construction projects commercially viable while satisfying onerous safety requirements. Again, this is a problem faced by all producers in the industry. However, a large part of the narrative from Rosatom in support of its export drive is that it can act as a 'one-stop shop' for the country's wishing to access nuclear power, and that it can do so at a competitive price. Providing such a comprehensive package at a comparatively low price inevitably raises the question of how Rosatom is able to square the circle in a way that has so far eluded its competitors.

One issue here that acts as a constraint on export opportunities are the terms of the loans for the importing country. Details of the loan arrangements tend to be opaque, but it has emerged that, at least in the case of Hungary, the size of loans to the host Hungarian Government is capped at a maximum (IAEA 2019a). Given that Russia is only committed to lending (in this case) 80 per cent of a stated 'turnkey' price, it seems that Hungary is liable to pay for cost overruns.

Hence the problem of risking liability for paying for cost overruns (a notorious hazard in building nuclear power plants) can potentially put prospective importers off making final commitments to building power plants. As a result the degree to which Russia can export its reactors to the countries with whom initial agreements have been signed hinges heavily on the perceived financial sustainability of Russia's system of financing its nuclear exports. This is yet to be fully tested.

A further issue is the extent to which Russia can itself have the resources to complete a high proportion of its deals to export nuclear reactors. According to Thomas (2018, 246):

One issue is the extent to which the market that Russia has, was created by Russia itself through promises on prices and finance that it cannot fulfil. For example, in 2009 in Bangladesh, two Russian reactors were forecast to cost US$1.5bn but by 2015, the estimate had increased 9-fold. The outcome may be that many of the orders will be abandoned. Where firm orders have been placed and it is the customer that abandons the order, this could result in significant direct costs. For example, Bulgaria has been required to pay Rosatom about €600 m in compensation for the equipment produced for the cancelled Belene project.

Impact of safety and anti-nuclear criticism on NPP construction

While incorporating enhanced safety features into new reactors delayed the introduction of new reactors and NPPs in the 2010s, these concerns have not prevented Russia from setting ambitious targets for the construction of NPPs in Russia and abroad.

One important dimension of the context in which nuclear power is organised in Russia is the relative muted nature of anti-nuclear opinion in that country. Although anti-nuclear opposition was substantial in the aftermath of the Chernobyl accident, it dissipated in the emergent post-Soviet nationalisms and economic dislocations of the 1990s. More recently civil society groups have claimed that environmental NGOs have been actively suppressed (Newell and Henry 2016). 'The Putin administration has labeled many environmental groups "anti-Russian" and used aggressive tactics such as raiding NGO offices, intimidating journalists, and instituting severe legislative measures to quash advocacy and dissent' (Newell and Henry 2016, 779). Anti-nuclear activities have included protests against plant lifetime extensions, nuclear waste arrangements, and nuclear pollution associated with reprocessing facilities. It is alleged that a number of incidents of 'inspections' arrests and prosecutions of organisers of protest against various aspects of nuclear power have been made, according to the anti-nuclear organisation 'Beyond Nuclear International'. It has been claimed that Rosatom is an active party in action taken against anti-nuclear activists (Beyond Nuclear International 2020).

Russia's current construction strategy is based on raising the share of nuclear-powered electricity in total electricity generation from just under 20 per cent at the end of 2019 to 45–50 per cent by 2050 and to 70–80 per cent by the end of the century. However, with constructions taking longer than in the past, this remains to be seen.

Most of the new planned construction will make use of established or recently developed technologies, such as the VVER-1200 and VVER-TOI reactors. If the Kursk II 1 and 2 projects proceed according to schedule – and thus show that new manufacturing and construction processes have been mastered – the likelihood of Rosatom being able to meet government targets will be much increased. Indeed, one of the reported advantages of the VVER-TOI model is that it will benefit from a standardised design and construction process that will reduce costs and construction times.

However, the prospects for Russia's plans to expand nuclear energy will be heavily influenced by whether these claims prove to be true. It is worth noting that a total of eight terrestrially based reactors were built between 2010 and 2019. A significant increase in the rate of construction will be needed for these plans to come to fruition. In addition, a reduction in construction times would also seem to be necessary for a successful programme. The average construction time for the last five reactors brought into commercial operation was over eight years (IAEA 2019b), with one plant, Leningrad 2–2 still not generating (at the time of writing) over ten years after construction started.

Although the Russian Government gives projects a much larger share of electricity generation from nuclear energy compared to renewable energy within Russia, construction times as long as this will make the Russian nuclear technology less competitive in (most) world markets where competition with renewables is much more of an issue. This is because the cost of a nuclear power station will be largely proportional to the time it takes to build them. A given workforce (which makes up much of the cost) needs to be employed and is more expensive the longer it is needed. Additionally interest on loans needed to pay for the construction builds up until income can be derived from sale of energy generation.

From a technological point of view, claims are made that there are several more innovative and potentially even more promising projects planned, including several fast neutron reactors. Russian authorities set much store on the BREST-OD-300 lead-cooled fast neutron reactor facility at the Seversk site. Named the *Proryv* (Breakthrough) project, it is intended to result in a closed nuclear fuel cycle. The 300 MWe unit will represent the key component of the Pilot Demonstration Energy Complex (PDEC). Construction at the Siberian Chemical Plant site was originally expected to be completed in 2020. It is hoped that development of this technology can achieve the full recycling of fuel, from balancing thermal and fast reactors, so that for example, 100 GWe of total capacity would require only about 100 tonnes per year from enrichment of tails and natural uranium, with minor actinides being burned. However, to achieve this the Russian programme will have to do better than the research and demonstration into fast reactors that has been conducted over several decades in numerous countries.

The commissioning of a major fast neutron power plant in Russia (the BN 1200) has been put back to 2036 (Diakov and Podvig 2019). It has been argued that, because of the relative expense of fast reactors compared to conventional reactors, it seems unlikely that this technology will have a large market unless the price of uranium supplies increases substantially (Cochran et al. 2010).

Because export contracts form such an important role in Rosatom's Development Strategy (2014), it is no surprise that work outside Russia forms a large and growing share of Rosatom's activities. As of 2020, Russia was the world leader in the number of NPPs being built abroad, with Rosatom building over 20 per cent of all the world's NPP gross generating capacity under construction. This comprises work on eight reactors at five different sites, with concrete having been poured at Bangladesh (Rooppur 1 and 2), Belarus (1 and 2), India (Kudankulam 3 and 4), Iran (Bushehr 2), and Turkey (Akkuyu 1).

A large number of other construction deals were signed with a growing number of countries (Rosatom 2018a, 54–55). These were in addition to a range of other agreements on nuclear power cooperation with states in Africa, Asia, and Latin America. It appears that on paper that demand for Rosatom's products is extremely high and constitutes by far the largest of any country in export terms.

It is unclear how many reactors will in fact be built in practice. Indicative agreements may not lead to actual constructions. Factors that have led to much less nuclear build in the past in different countries have included declines in earlier projections of increased energy demand (leading to cancellation of projects), cheaper energy alternatives emerging, and poor financial outcomes associated with building a nuclear power plant.

Perhaps the more important question relates to Rosatom's capacity to supply this high volume of demand. One clear issue is the time it takes to build the nuclear power plant themselves. For example the PAKS nuclear power plant in Hungary is scheduled to be completed in six years (initially with a 2018 start) (World Nuclear Association 2020). However if, following first pouring of concrete, this takes rather longer than six years and the Hungarian Government racks up considerable debts, this may not encourage other countries with indicative agreements with Rosatom to carry through with them. Similarly, with other plans, for example Akkuyu in Turkey which is scheduled to be finished in just five years. Indeed the fact that the recent average construction time for reactors in Russia itself is longer than eight years does question the certainty of Rosatom's future plans.

Conclusion

Nuclear power is a politically and economically crucial component of the modern Russian system of political economy. In this respect, it is a cultural legacy of the elevated place that the industry occupied within the Soviet system. It is a highly centralised system which fits in with a cultural bias towards hierarchy. The system of hierarchy is emphasised and reinforced by the fusion of civilian and military nuclear activities under Rosatom. Arguably nuclear power can be organised most effectively in a highly centralised system where one dominant body can marshal the highly specialised skills needed to develop nuclear power. However, in the process this hierarchy has repressed egalitarian pressures in the form of grass roots anti-nuclear opposition.

Organised under the aegis of the state corporation, Rosatom, the nuclear industry is situated at the forefront of high-technology and knowledge-based activity in Russia. It is one of the few areas in which Russia can legitimately claim to be a world leader, a fact appreciated by the country's political leadership. Nuclear power is considered to be of central importance to the country's national security, energy security, and, ultimately, the country's status as a so-called 'Great Power'. Concerns from other countries and quarters that nuclear power might be dangerous have not prevented Rosatom and its political supporters from pressing on with ambitious expansion plans.

As a result, it is considered a strategically important industry, with Rosatom playing a crucial role in ensuring domestic energy security and in advancing Russia's economic and political interests abroad. It has also been assigned responsibility for harnessing the economic and geostrategic potential of the Arctic. Together, these responsibilities mean that nuclear power enjoys support from the highest levels of Russia's political system.

Because of the important role that Rosatom plays within Russia, and because of its place as a powerful instrument of the state, it is afforded advantages that most other firms – within Russia or abroad – do not possess. It enjoys access to significant diplomatic, financial, and institutional resources that enable it to carry out its operations without being forced to abide by the same commercial considerations that constrain other firms in the industry. Rosatom's privileged place within the Russian economy and the advantages conferred upon it have exerted a strong influence over the expansion of nuclear power in Russia and abroad.

Safety policy is taken more seriously in Russia today compared to the Soviet period, a particular driver being the need to offer credibly safe reactors to sell on the world market. Following Fukushima an effort was made to bring the safety standards up to IAEA levels. The nuclear power industry in Russia today is governed by a rich framework of regulations, an experienced regulator, and a concern to show customers within Russia and abroad that safety concerns are taken seriously. Nevertheless, there remain two principal sources of concern in relation to the strength of existing safety practices and culture.

First, Rosatom is considered to be one of the most strategically important parts of the Russian economy. It has been assigned ambitious commercial and political objectives at home and abroad. Its scientific and industrial capabilities are among the most advanced in Russia and represent areas the Russian state wishes to husband and nurture further. As a result, we should be cautious when assessing the relative importance of regulatory concerns and Rosatom's pursuit of strategically important objectives. The very centralised military-industrial complex that gives Rosatom organisational importance also brings with it habits of secrecy, and when radiation leaks occur, a lack of transparency may reduce its international credibility.

Second, a number of financial challenges remain. The first set of challenges relates to the financial resources available to regulatory authorities. This problem was especially acute in Russia in the first decade of the millennium. There is every reason to think that it remains a concern, especially after three recessions – in 2009, 2015, and 2020 – have subsequently reduced the funds available to the public sector. The second set of problems is related to the need to make NPP construction projects commercially viable while satisfying onerous safety requirements.

Incorporating enhanced safety features into new designs delayed the introduction of new reactors and NPPs in the 2010s. However, these delays have not prevented Russia from setting ambitious targets for the construction of NPPs in Russia and abroad. Rapid and continuous expansion of nuclear power within Russia is envisaged to take place alongside unprecedented construction abroad.

Perhaps the most important question facing Rosatom today is whether it has the industrial and financial capacity and also ability to meet and deliver a huge volume of demand for timely NPP construction.

Encouragement for Rosatom's (and the Russian state's) position is provided by the large number of low- and middle-income countries outside North America and Europe that have expressed interest in acquiring NPPs from Russia. This demand has found fertile ground in Russia's security-oriented ruling elite. The constraints on such ambitions include a) whether there is a continuation of anticipated increases in demand for energy and the degree of competition from other sources and also b) from domestic industrial constraints that might hamper Rosatom's ability to deliver on the large number of deals it has signed over the past decade, and c) the ability to deliver projects on time and therefore on cost.

However, in the out-turn so far, recent construction times for its own reactors have been longer than hoped. If this performance is replicated abroad, the Russian nuclear programme, though much acclaimed for its reach in its own plans, may fall far short of its expectations. A key test for the Russian nuclear export programme will be the sustainability of its system of financing the reactors in host countries, and the extent to which the host countries are saddled with large debts. Another test will be the extent to which Russia itself will be able to sustain the financing of these reactor export plans. In reality, the Russian export programme may pass neither of these tests.

Notes

1 A comprehensive description of the history and current functions of Rostekhnadzor can be found (in Russian) at: https://atomaudit.ru/atomnyj-nadzor-fsetan.html
2 Federal Law of 21 November 1995 No. 170-F3 'On the Utilisation of Atomic Energy'. There are a range of other relevant federal laws. They and all regulations summarised here are accessible at: http://gosnadzor.ru/nuclear/app/acts/
3 For example, see technical regulation 'On the safety of machinery and equipment' (TR TS 010/2011), decision of the Commission of the Customs Union of 18 October 2011 No. 823; and 'Technical regulation on the safety of buildings and structures', Federal Law of 30 December 2009 No. 384-F3.
4 Convention on Nuclear Safety, 17 June 1994, at: www.iaea.org/topics/nuclear-safety-conventions/convention-nuclear-safety

References

Aleksashin, P.P., Bukrinskii, A.M., and Gordon, B.G. (2006) 'Safety Regulation: 20 Years after the Chernobyl Accident', *Atomic Energy*, 100(4), 271–282.
Aris, B. (2019) 'Russia's Nuclear Power Exports Are Booming', *Moscow Times*, 9 May. www.themoscowtimes.com/2019/05/09/russias-nuclear-power-exports-are-booming-a65533
Atomstroyeksport (2018) 'Na ploshchadkeKurskoy AES-2 nachalos' sooruzheniye-novykhatomnykhenergoblokov' [Construction Began on Site of Kursk NPP-2], *Atomstroyeksport Press Centre*, 3 May. https://ase-ec.ru/
Beyond Nuclear International (2020) 'Standing Up to Rosatom'. https://beyondnuclearinternational.org/2020/06/21/standing-up-to-rosatom/

Bunn, M., and Kovchegin, D. (2018) 'Nuclear Security in Russia: Can Progress Be Sustained?', *The Nonproliferation Review*, 24(5–6), 527–551.

Campbell, R.W. (1980) *Soviet Energy Technologies: Planning, Policy, Research and Development*. Bloomington: Indiana University Press.

Cochran, T., Feiveson, H., Patterson, W., Pshakin, G., Ramana, M., Schneider, M., Suzuki, T., and von Hippel, F. (2010) *Fast Breeder Reactor Programs: History and Status*, International Panel on Fissile Materials. http://fissilematerials.org/library/rr08.pdf

Connolly, R. (2008) 'The Structure of Russian Industrial Exports in Comparative Perspective', *Eurasian Geography and Economics*, 49(5), 586–603.

Connolly, R. (2012) 'Climbing the Ladder? High-Technology Industrial Exports in Emerging Europe', *Eurasian Geography and Economics*, 53(3), 356–379.

Connolly, R. (2013) 'Strategies for Economic Development in Russia', in *Russian Analytical Digest*, July, No.133. Zurich: Centre for Security Studies.

Connolly, R. (2018) *Russia's Response to Sanctions*. Cambridge and New York: Cambridge University Press.

Connolly, R. (2020) *The Russian Economy: A Very Short Introduction*. Oxford and New York: Oxford University Press.

Connolly, R., and Sendstad, C. (2017) 'Russia's Role as an Arms Exporter: The Strategic and Economic Importance of Arms Exports for Russia', *Russia and Eurasia Programme Research Paper*, March. www.chathamhouse.org/sites/default/files/publications/research/2017-03-20-russia-arms-exporter-connolly-sendstad.pdf

Cooper, J. (2000) 'Minatom: The Last Soviet Industrial Ministry', in G. Easter and S. Harter (eds.) *Shaping the Economic Space In Russia: Decision Making Processes, Institutions and Adjustment to Change in the El'tsin Era*. Aldershot: Ashgate.

Cooper, J. (2006) 'Can Russia Compete in the Global Economy?', *Eurasian Geography and Economics*, 47(4), 407–425.

Cooper, J. (2018) *The Funding of Nuclear Weapons in the Russian Federation*. Oxford: Changing Character of War Programme, Pembroke College. https://static1.squarespace.com/static/55faab67e4b0914105347194/t/5bb1ea3ee4966b5320fa197c/1538386496442/The+funding+of+nuclear+weapons+in+the+Russian+Federation.pdf

Debardeleben, J.T. (1985) 'Esoteric Policy Debate: Nuclear Safety Issues in the Soviet Union and German Democratic Republic', *British Journal of Political Science*, 15(2), 227–253.

Diakov, A., and Podvig, P. (2019) 'Construction of Russia's BN 1200 Fast Neutron Reactor Put Back Until 2030s', *International Panel on Fissile Materials*, 20 August. http://fissilematerials.org/blog/2019/08/the_construction_of_the_b.html

Frolov, I. (2014) 'Nuclear Industry in Russia: Results of Reform, Politics, and Development Problems', *Studies on Russian Economic Development*, 25(6), 529–538.

Golts, A. (2013) 'Secrecy, the Last Refuge', *The Bulletin of Atomic Scientists*, 10 January. https://thebulletin.org/roundtable_entry/secrecy-the-last-refuge/#

Government of the Russian Federation (2009) *Energeticheskayastrategiya do 2030 godu* [Energy Strategy for the Period Up to 2030]. Moscow: Ministry of Energy. https://minenergo.gov.ru/activity/energostrategy/Strategiya/Energostrategiya-2030.doc

Holloway, S. (1994) *The Soviet Union and Atomic Energy, 1939–1956*. New Haven, CT: Yale University Press.

International Atomic Energy Association (2013) 'IAEA Mission Concludes Peer Review of the Russian Federation's Nuclear Regulatory Framework', *IAEA*, 19 November. www.iaea.org/newscenter/pressreleases/iaea-mission-concludes-peer-review-russian-federations-nuclear-regulatory-framework

International Atomic Energy Association (2018) 'IAEA Mission Sees Safety Commitment by Russia's Rosenergoatom, Encourages Continued Improvement', *IAEA*, 29 November. www.iaea.org/newscenter/pressreleases/iaea-mission-sees-safety-commitment-by-russias-rosenergoatom-encourages-continued-improvement

IAEA (International Atomic Energy Agency) (2019a) *Hungary Country Profile*. https://cnpp.iaea.org/countryprofiles/Hungary/Hungary.htm

IAEA (International Atomic Energy Agency) (2019b) *Russian Federation Country Profile*. https://cnpp.iaea.org/countryprofiles/Russia/Russia.htm

Josephson, P. (2000) *Red Atom: Russia's Nuclear Power Program from Stalin to Today*. Pittsburgh: Pittsburgh University Press.

Masson, O., et al. (2019) 'Airborne Concentrations and Chemical Considerations of Radioactive Ruthenium from an Undeclared Major Nuclear Release in 2017', *Proceedings of the National Academy of Sciences of the United States of America, PNAS*, 20 August, 116(34), 16750–16759. https://doi.org/10.1073/pnas.1907571116

Mehdiyeva, N. (2019) *Review of the Document Development Strategy of State Corporation Rosatom to 2030 [Strategiyarazvitiya "GK" Rosatom do 2030 goda], June 2014, Russian Studies Series* 3/19. Rome: NATO Defence College. www.ndc.nato.int/research/research.php?icode=584

Minin, N., and Vlcek, T. (2017) 'Determinants and Considerations of Rosatom's External Strategy', *Energy Strategy Reviews*, 17, 37–44.

Neftegaz (2018) 'PATES "Akademik Lomonosov" planiruyutvvesti v ekspluatatsiyu k 2019 g. Glavgosekspertizaodobrila' [Glavgosekspertiza Approved Plans to Put the FNPP 'Academic Lomonosov' into Operation in 2019], *Neftegaz.ru*, 9 January. https://neftegaz.ru/news/nuclear/204262-pates-akademik-lomonosov-planiruyut-vvesti-v-eksplua-tatsiyu-k-2019-g-glavgosekspertiza-odobrila/

Newell, J., and Henry, L. (2016) 'The State of Environmental Protection in the Russian Federation: A Review of the Post-Soviet Era', *Eurasian Geography and Economics*, 57(6), 779–801.

Nilsen, T. (2019) 'Casualties after Missile Engine Explosion Near Severodvinsk', *The Barents Observer*, 8 August. https://thebarentsobserver.com/en/security/2019/08/casualties-after-missile-jet-engine-explosion-near-severodivnsk

Office of Technology Assessment (1982) *Technology and Soviet Energy Availability*. Boulder, CO: Westview Press.

Oxenstierna, S. (2010) *Russia's Nuclear Energy Expansion*. Stockholm: Swedish Defence Research Agency, Department for Security Policies and Strategic Studies.

Potter, W.C. (1991) 'The Impact of Chernobyl on Nuclear Power Safety in the Soviet Union', *Studies in Comparative Communism*, 24(2), 191–210.

Pryde, P.R., and Pryde, L.T. (1974) 'Soviet Nuclear Power: A Different Approach to Nuclear Safety', *Environment: Science and Policy for Sustainable Development*, 16(3), 26–34.

Rosatom (2014) 'Strategiyarazvitiya "GK" Rosatom do 2030 goda' [Development Strategy of State Corporation Rosatom to 2030]. Moscow: Rosatom, June 2012. http://2012.atomexpo.ru/mediafiles/u/files/Present2012/Karavaev.pdf

Rosatom (2018a) 'Itogideyatel'nosti za 2018 god' [Performance Results for 2018]. Moscow: Rosatom. www.rosatom.ru/upload/iblock/fa7/fa759a96c90510116b0b0632519522cb.pdf

Rosatom (2018b) www.rosatom.ru/en/press-centre/news/vladimir-putin-singed-a-law-on-rosatom-s-powers-in-northern-sea-route-development/

Rosatom (2018c) 'Rosenergoatom: plavuchiyenergoblok "Akademik Lomonosov" dlyazagruzkiyadernogotopliva v Murmanske' [Rosenergoatom: The Floating Nuclear Power

Plant 'Academic Lomonosov Has Arrived in Murmansk to Be Loaded with Nuclear Fuel'], *Rosatom.ru*, 19 May. https://rosatom.ru/journalist/news/rosenergoatom-plavuchiy-energoblok-akademik-lomonosov-pribyl-dlya-zagruzki-yadernym-toplivom-v-murma/

Rostekhnadzor (2017) *The Seventh National Report of the Russian Federation on the Ful- fillment of Commitments Resulting from the Convention on Nuclear Safety.* Moscow: Rostekhnadzor. www-ns.iaea.org/downloads/ni/safety_convention/7th-review-meeting/ russia-national-report-7th-rm-cns_en.pdf

Schepers, N. (2019) 'Russia's Nuclear Energy Exports: Status, Prospects and Implications', in *Non-Proliferation and Disarmament Papers, No.61.* Brussels: EU Non-Proliferation and Disarmament Consortium. www.sipri.org/sites/default/files/2019-02/eunpdc_no_61_ final.pdf

Simonov, N.S. (2000) 'New Postwar Branches: The Nuclear Industry', in J. Barber and M. Harrison (eds.) *The Soviet Defence Industry Complex from Stalin to Khrushchev.* Houndmills: Macmillan Press.

Staalesen, A. (2020) 'Putin Signs Arctic Master Plan', *The Barents Observer*, 6 March. https://thebarentsobserver.com/en/arctic/2020/03/putin-signs-arctic-master-plan

Soldatkin (2019) *Russia's First Sea-Borne Nuclear Power Plant Arrives to Its Base.* www. reuters.com/article/us-russia-nuclear-floating-idUSKBN1VZ0CY

Sudostroenie.info (2019) 'Nachalas' rezka metalla dlya ocherednogo ledokola proyekta 22220' (Metal Cutting for the Next Project 22220 Icebreaker Has Begun), *Sudostroenie. info*, 11 December. https://sudostroenie.info/mobver/novosti/28878.html

TASS (2020) 'Rossiyskiye AES v 2019 goduvyshlinanovyyrekord po vyrabotkeelektroen- ergii' [Russian Nuclear Power Plants Reached a New Record for Electricity Generation in 2019], *TASS*, 1 January. https://tass.ru/ekonomika/7457365

Thomas, S. (2018) 'Russia's Nuclear Export Programme', *Energy Policy*, (121), 236–247.

UkazprezidentaRossiyskoyFederatsii [Decree of the President of the Russian Federation]. (2020) 'Ob OsnovakhgosurdarstvennoypolitikiRossiyskoyFederatsii v Arktikena period do 2035 goda' [On the Fundamentals of the State Policy of the Russian Federation in the Arctic for the Period Until 2035], *Kremlin.ru*, 5 March. http://static.kremlin.ru/media/ events/files/ru/f8ZpjhpAaQ0WB1zjywN04OgKil1mAvaM.pdf

Unsigned, NarodnoekhoziastvoSSSR za 70 let (1987). Moscow: Finansystatistika.

Vavina, E. (2019) 'V Rossiizarabotalapervaya v mire plavuchayaatomnayastantsiya' [The World's First Floating Nuclear Power Plant Has Been Launched in Russia], *Vedomosti*, 19 December. www.vedomosti.ru/business/articles/2019/12/19/819169-rossii-zarabotala- plavuchaya-stantsiya

World Nuclear Association (2020) *Nuclear Power in Hungary.* www.world-nuclear.org/ information-library/country-profiles/countries-g-n/hungary.aspx

World Nuclear News (2019) 'Russia's VVER-TOI Reactor Certified by European Utilities', *World Nuclear News*, 14 June. https://world-nuclear-news.org/Articles/Russia-s-VVER- VOI-reactor-certified-by-European-ut

10 Conclusion

In the introduction chapter we set out an overall research question: what is the role of nuclear safety in the lack of expansion of nuclear throughout the world? This overarching question was then resolved into some sub-questions:

1   What role, in general, does safety play in increasing nuclear costs?
2   Specifically, what is the relative role of different nuclear regulatory systems and their safety rules in the non-expansion of nuclear power?
3   Leading on from point 2, is there evidence that national safety systems which impose less costly rules on nuclear power are associated with easier paths towards maintaining and expanding nuclear power in such countries?
4   How can we explain, in political terms, the differences between the strictness of different nuclear safety regimes?

Let us answer these questions.

Safety and nuclear costs

First as regards the issue of what role safety plays in nuclear safety costs, one can say that in general safety is fundamental, although this issue can often be obscured by a lack of attention to the very nature of nuclear engineering. It would be wrong to cost the safety features of nuclear power simply by looking at the back-up features of nuclear power plant, although these in themselves tend to be costly. A more general point is that the very nature of a nuclear plant is concerned with keeping control over very powerful energy forces that would, if not controlled, render the plant inoperable – yet these are also implicit to the safety of everybody concerned. For example, exacting engineering standards are required to deliver systems that can withstand high temperatures and pressures in the context of being sufficiently robust to avoid release of radioactive materials. Containment walls are also implicit to safety, as is the strength of the reactor-pressure vessel, etc.

Moreover, because of the unique nature of nuclear engineering and the specifications that this involves, there are many specialist parts that are unique to nuclear power technology, and these costs are not reduced through mass production. In some senses nuclear power is still a 'craft' industry given that the design and some of the parts will be plant specific, and not producible from production lines. The number of reactors being built is small which reinforces this 'craft' nature. This leads to a further problem, in that the engineers and technicians necessary to complete tasks are in short supply, or may not even exist at all, and are retiring. If there is a large ongoing programme, such technical expertise can be maintained, but if projects emerge more or less on a one-off basis, then the lack of such expertise may cause big problems. This has been evident in the case of building the French EPRs as discussed in Chapter 6. This lack of relevant technical expertise at both the construction site and in the supply chains could well be a major factor in the failure in the West, at least in recent years, to build nuclear reactors in anything like the time they were supposed to be built.

Indeed, of the countries studied in this book, if recent constructions are considered, only China has seemed able to deliver nuclear power plant construction times consistently under eight years. Even that excludes the French EPR design which China has built at Taishan which has taken longer than 8 years to bring fully online. This issue of construction time matters a lot. It has been speculated that a design such as the French EPR may have costs up to around 30 per cent higher because of additional safety features, over and above those in Generation II designs, according to a nuclear consultant interviewed for Chapter 6 (UK). Such extra costs are associated with features such as the passive cooling system, aircraft protection, and a core catcher. However construction overruns are even more important in driving up construction costs. Certainly, as discussed in Chapters 6 and 4 on France and the USA we can see reports of how the costs of reactors currently being constructed have increased well beyond their initial budgets. We can model the costs of building a nuclear power plant according to the time it takes to construct the plant prior to generation taking place. The calculations underpinning this model as shown in Figure 10.1 are based broadly on the costs for a double reactor (3.2 GWe) EPR project of the type being built at Hinkley C and proposed for Sizewell C in the UK. If construction time is, say, eight years instead of five years, then costs are likely to rise by around three-quarters, that is assuming a relatively modest interest rate of capital borrowed (6.3 per cent is assumed here), as shown in Figure 10.1. If the construction time takes twice as long as expected then costs rise to over double, around 230 per cent of the original projection based on five years' construction time.

The costs of renewable energy (mainly wind power and solar PV) have declined greatly in recent years. The fact that nuclear power is now rather more expensive per MWh means that its proponents are left to argue that a low or zero carbon world cannot do without nuclear power because of the 'intermittency' of renewable energy. Renewable energy proponents argue that various types of storage – both short and long term – can overcome such issues. We do not have resources or indeed purpose to examine such arguments further in this book. However we do have a central objective of discussing the extent to which different nuclear safety

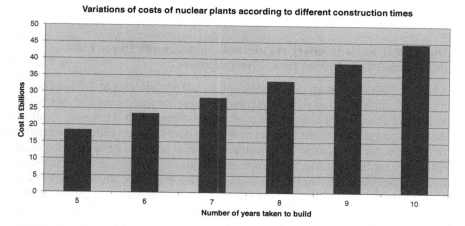

Figure 10.1 Variations of costs of nuclear power plant according to different construction times (5–10 years)

regimes do or do not add to nuclear costs and lead to nuclear power becoming uneconomic.

Then there is the issue over the extent to which more rigorous safety regulations can make nuclear power more expensive and difficult to deliver. At the outset it could be argued that, in addition to the inherent complexity and uniqueness in engineering terms, nuclear power plant designs have been subject to a series of unsettling safety design pressures. These pressures increased during the 1960s and 1970s as nuclear power stations were first deployed in larger numbers. Since Three Mile Island and Chernobyl, and latterly the Fukushima accidents, the nuclear industry has designed, and attempted deployment of, a new generation (Generation III) of 'inherently safe' reactors. Such reactor designs were supposed to solve some of the cost problems suffered by 'Generation II' design reactors, which constitute most of the reactors now in operation around the world. In practice these Generation III reactors have proved difficult to operationalise. However a point to be made here is that the deployment problems are associated with a design choice on the part of nuclear power reactor designers rather than safety regulations per se. The designers respond to concerns about safety. A great deal of guidance on safety standards is produced by the International Atomic Energy Agency (IAEA) which acts in collaboration with the nuclear energy industry at large.

It would, however, be misleading to assume that cost problems are necessarily associated solely with the delivery of new designs of reactors. In Chapter 8, in the case of the UK, there is a detailed examination of the costs of new reactors compared to cost estimates that go back to the end of the 1980s, and in this case little seems to have changed in that today's expected high costs of nuclear construction are on the same level as that experienced 30 years ago.

This leads us on to a discussion of the impact of different levels of safety regulations that exist in different countries.

Do stricter nuclear safety regulations significantly impact the development of nuclear power programmes?

Chapter 3 includes an account of the deployment programmes of different countries, both including and beyond the country case studies covered in this book. Individual chapters include accounts of what is being built. However, in all of the cases going forward the reactors now being developed are called 'Generation III' designs. We can discuss the extent that different levels of strictness of nuclear safety regulations can affect development. Measuring the outcomes seems relatively straightforward. We can assess the relative ease with which new nuclear power stations are built in the comparator countries, and we can examine the rate at which nuclear power plants already in service are being kept online or retired. Of course plant retirements will be influenced by various other factors. However, it will be the case that if stricter safety regulations are a significant factor which is substantially increasing costs then we may be able to observe a) greater difficulty in completing new nuclear power construction and/or b) we may expect a more rapid and numerous retirement rate of existing nuclear power plants.

Comparing strictness of nuclear safety standards requires more technical complexity. It is necessary to select some definable safety policies and technical standards and be able to rank them as more or less stringent. Here we assume that, for example, if regulatory regime A insists that a certain device is fitted to enhance safety whereas another regulatory regime B does not fit them saying that the costs do not justify the benefits, then regime A has stricter standards than regime B.

We have assembled some Tables (10.1, 10.2, and 10.3) to examine the relative strictness of different safety regimes based on the data discussed in the earlier chapters on different states. The focus here is on safety measures that relate to Pressurised Water Reactors (PWRs), although many of these measures will apply to all reactor types. The large majority of all reactors and almost all new reactors are PWRs. The data is drawn from the discussions on safety issues covered in Chapters 4–10. In Table 10.4 we give the number of operational reactors (showing the number that are PWRs) in the different countries that feature in this book.

The most comprehensive data that we have been able to uncover relates to the Western states in our study, namely USA, France, and the UK. Please see Tables 10.1 and 10.2 for details. However, we do have sufficient data to make a wider comparison on the subject of retrofits of passive autocatalytic converters and filtered containment venting systems on existing PWRs. These devices are measures to mitigate serious nuclear accidents (see earlier chapters for more discussion). Please see Table 10.1 for a comparison.

Various safety measures and practices have been selected for inclusion in these tables on the basis that they are, in a review of the relevant literatures, ones that feature prominently in discussions and technical reports about safety. There is discussion of these measures in the different chapters, but, we can add here in order to explain the acronyms that a) FCVS stands for 'filtered containment venting system'. This type of system attempts to ensure that in the event of a severe accident, pressure within the containment vessel can be reduced by venting gases whilst filtering out the radioactivity that would remain within the plant itself. b) PAR stands for 'Passive Autocatalytic Recombiner' which, in the event of a severe accident, attempts to safely 'recombine' hydrogen inside the reactor building that might otherwise explode. c) Independent power generation (and water supply) means that in the event of a severe accident the reactor can continue to be cooled, and therefore the possibilities of radioactive releases and meltdown reduced. Other measures are self-explanatory.

Requirements for fitting safety devices to existing nuclear reactors

It can be seen from the different tables, namely Tables 10.1, 10.2, and Table 10.3, that the USA has, according to the comparisons made, the weakest safety rules. This is set out in more detail in the comparison with the UK and France in Tables 10.1 and 10.2. There are fewer indicators in the comparison including China and South Korea in Table 10.3. However, from what we can see, as for example set

Table 10.1 Nuclear power safety regulations for existing reactors compared in USA, UK, and France (selected measures)

Country	US	UK	France
Discourse	Cost-benefit	Safety preferred over cost (until 'grossly disproportional')	Safety regardless of cost (but according to priorities)
Post-Fukushima action	Task force recommendations only partly accepted by NRC after industry lobbying	Task force established with recommendations accepted by ONR, mainly implemented	Stress tests ordered and analysed leading to 'hardened core' concept implemented for existing plants
PAR	Not required by NRC for PWRs	Fitted	Fitted
FCVS	Not required by NRC for PWRs	Recommended by ONR but not (yet) fitted	Fitted
Independent power generation	Vague requirement by NRC: some guaranteed availability no longer than six hours	Minimum 48-hour guarantee	Available on a permanent basis
Post-Fukushima 'beyond design' technical measures	Not required by NRC	Recommended by ONR	Recommended by ASN

Sources: See chapter texts

Table 10.2 Nuclear power safety regulations for new reactors compared in USA, UK, and France (selected measures)

	USA	France	UK
Indefinite guaranteed power after accident	Not required	Required	Required
Passive Autocatalytic Recombiners (H2 removal)	Not required	Required	Required
Additional cooling systems for reactor core and spent fuel sites	Not required	Required	Required
Double containment	Not required	Required	Not required
Core catcher	Not required	Required	Not required

Sources: See chapter texts

Table 10.3 Nuclear power safety regulations for existing Pressurised Water Reactors compared in USA, UK, France, China, and South Korea (PAR and FCVS)

Country	USA	China	South Korea	UK	France
PAR	Not required by NRC for PWRs	To be retrofitted to PWRs	Fitted to PWRs	Fitted to PWR	Fitted to PWRs
FCVS	Not required by NRC for PWRs	To be retrofitted in majority of cases of PWRs	Recommended to be fitted to PWRs	Recommended to be fitted to PWR	Fitted to PWRs

Sources: See chapter texts

Table 10.4 Reactor numbers in the different countries (showing numbers of PWRs in brackets)

	USA	China	France	South Korea	United Kingdom	Russian Federation
Number of reactors in July 2020 (PWRs in brackets)	**96 (64)**	**45 (43)**	**57 (57)**	**25 (21)**	**15 (1)**	**37 (21)**

Sources: IAEA country profiles, US NRC

out in Table 10.3, the safety standards for retrofitting existing reactors are weaker in the USA compared to Eastern countries such as China and South Korea as well as Western ones such as France and the UK.

We have not done a tabulated comparison including new reactors and safety standards that includes China and South Korea, but from what we can see the safety standards for new reactors are unlikely to be lower in China and South Korea compared to the USA. The USA has, for instance, ruled out increasing safety standards for new reactors in the light of Fukushima, whereas future reactor designs for China and South Korea may well take this factor more into account (compared to the USA).

These tables have not included Russia, partly because of a lack of data about whether Russia's reactor fleet can be compared exactly in the same way as other PWRs. Partly also, there is a reluctance to measure Russian safety standards using exactly the same explicit measures as the other states since Russia's claims to having an equality of nuclear safety standards are undermined by an apparent lack of transparency concerning radioactive discharges in three separate incidents in recent years.

So we can make a general proposition, which is firmly supported by the evidence in this book, that on a series of measures the USA has less stringent mandatory nuclear safety standards compared to other states including UK, France, China, and South Korea.

Now we can move on to the second part of the question of understanding the extent to which nuclear safety rules make nuclear power more expensive and difficult to implement, that is whether the state with the relatively weakest nuclear safety rules (USA) has had more success in maintaining and expanding its nuclear fleet compared to other countries.

In brief, the answer to the question of whether there is evidence that countries with stricter nuclear safety rules have more difficulty maintaining and expanding their nuclear fleets is 'no'. Perhaps the clearest comparison can be made between the USA and France. Both have large nuclear fleets in absolute terms. Both have attempted to build at least one more power plant in recent years. According to the criteria set out in Tables 10.1 and 10.2 France clearly has a stricter set of nuclear safety regulations than is the case of the USA.

Yet it is far from clear that the US nuclear programme is able to either maintain its existing nuclear fleet in operation any better than in the case of France or build new plants any easier. In terms of maintaining the existing fleet the USA has retired a much larger number of nuclear power plants than is the case of France. In fact, one would expect this to be the case since the reactors in the USA were, on average, commissioned at an earlier year than is the case in France (analysis of IAEA country profile data).

However, all that one can say from this comparison with regard to our question is that there is no evidence that the heightened French policy (compared to the USA) of retrofitting existing plants to deal with accident threats is leading to earlier closures of nuclear plants than the USA. Of course there is a story to tell about the economics and politics of retiral (or non-retiral) of nuclear power plants, but we do not have the space to deal with this here. Suffice it to say that markets, taxes, governmental subsidies and energy company policies affecting prices and investment may have a major impact on nuclear plant longevity. These factors are likely to matter much more than regulations covering nuclear safety.

Then there is the case of building new plants. All we can really say is that in both cases there have been great difficulties in building new plants. Indeed in the case of the USA two out of the four plants that have been started this century have actually been abandoned, partly built. None, as of the time that this volume went to press, have been brought online. Construction cost overruns have mounted as a result.

Of course this does not mean to say that the strictness of nuclear regulations has no effect on costs, but it is to say that the effects cannot be of fundamental importance to maintaining and expanding/replacing a nuclear fleet. Indeed there are arguments to suggest that the very lack of consistency in, and the legalistic battles over, nuclear regulation in the USA with the nuclear industry often stalling or defeating regulation may have actually harmed the nuclear programme. The clearest example of this was the argument about aircraft protection of new nuclear plants which we covered in Chapter 4.

There is certainly no evidence that other countries in this study have suffered greater delays in new plants or more early power plant closures (relative to the size of the fleets) than is apparent in the case of the USA. Indeed, with regard to the levels of nuclear safety regulation, US exceptionalism seems to be marked in the aftermath of Fukushima. The UK, France, China, and South Korea all seem to have increased to varying degrees the number and quality of safety standards rather more than is the case of the USA. It may be argued that the Russian system has weaker safety standards (certainly in terms of opacity compared to the USA), but then even in Russia construction times have lengthened in recent years.

Understanding regulatory difference

In trying to account for the differences in regulatory outcomes we distinguish between the nature of the nuclear safety institutions themselves and the cultural context. We stress the key influences of contextual cultural factors governing attitudes to risk in explaining differences between the country cases studied in this book. The theory underpinning this analytical position is discussed in Chapter 2. This theory enables us to categorise and then compare the patterns of cultural bias that are dominant in the different contexts in the country case studies.

The nature of the formal institutions of nuclear safety regulation do not pose much of a clue to explain the differences compared to cultural context as measured by our framing of cultural theory. Certainly in most of the cases there has been a drift towards greater formal independence of the nuclear safety agencies from their governments this century.

The exception in this general pattern is the USA, where the relationship has remained the same. The US NRC is open to extensive influence from the Government in the sense that the Commissioners are appointed by the President on a partisan basis. On the other hand the US system, different to the much more opaque practices of consultation of the other countries' agencies, has a system of consultation before rules are adopted or changed. Yet the context in which the NRC operates is one where the nuclear industry has considerable ability to influence the NRC through the courts and also through lobbying of Congress, especially via friendly representation by Republican Representatives and Senators. It may be that the US nuclear safety system is, by and large, a system that authorises what the nuclear industry is doing with regard to safety rather than what the nuclear safety authority (NRC) would otherwise decide what is necessary.

At the other end of the scale, in terms of sources of influence on nuclear power policies, is South Korea, discussed in Chapter 7. Here 'bottom-up' influences have become important. Until relatively recently, in the case of South Korea, dominated for most of the second half of the 20th century by a conservative, often authoritarian, industrial elite, such a statement would seem strange. But in recent years, perhaps linked to the falling respect for the industrial hierarchy amongst the general public, anti-nuclear politics has been linked to opposition to the industrial hierarchy. Bottom-up egalitarian politics has been in evidence. The concept of energy citizenship has been associated with local renewable energy and energy conservation measures. Indeed such was the recourse to bottom-up politics that the Moon Government, elected in 2017, established a deliberative process to decide policy on nuclear power in general. In parallel, the independence of the nuclear regulatory agency was increased and safety retrofits were required.

Perhaps the US and South Korean cases form the clearest contrast in this study. The USA's political context seems dominated by regulatory individualism. That is a basic opposition to the notion of regulatory action by the state and a strong belief in opposing state action to intervene in industrial policy to deal with environmental risks. The dominant cultural bias in the US nuclear safety regime is towards individualism and against egalitarianism. By contrast the South Korean political context is heavily influenced by egalitarian presumptions. These include great engagement with grass roots actions, opposition to industrial hierarchies, and support for and practice of grass roots decision-making through deliberative processes. The involvement of and activism by grass roots people in environmental decision-making is a hallmark of 'strong' ecological modernisation. Curiously the current status of the nuclear safety regimes in the USA and South Korea seems to be the opposite of what has been observed earlier by Jasanoff and Kim (2009). Rather than, as observed before, South Korea being developmental and the US being concerned with containment, now South Korea seems more oriented towards containment, and the US nuclear regime oriented, in desire at least, towards development.

By contrast France and the UK have reserved decision-making about nuclear power policy to governmental and regulatory hierarchies. These are infused with a long-standing bias towards precautionary safety policies, albeit incorporated into a system oriented to support nuclear power as an industry. Concerns about nuclear safety have been diverted away from opposition to nuclear power per se by the establishment and reinforcement of nuclear safety regimes. This is redolent of weak ecological modernisation, a concept that has been discussed in Chapter 2. In the case of weak ecological modernisation aims of civil society groups are incorporated in discussions between government, its agencies, and the industrial corporations without the civil society groups. Concerns about safety are finessed away by a process of technical discussions, in this case about safety. In France and the UK, given the relative lack of anti-nuclear opposition in recent decades, this strategy appears to have worked.

By contrast in China, dominated by a strong hierarchy, an avowedly authoritarian state, there has been an extensive amount of bottom-up resistance to nuclear power. This is discussed in Chapter 5 on China. This resistance to nuclear plants has intensified since the Fukushima accident, and slowed down the Chinese nuclear programme. Whether one can ascribe the notion of weak ecological modernisation to the case of Chinese nuclear safety policy is a moot point since China lacks the democratic civil society conditions that go along with ecological modernisation in its original European setting. However, as Chapter 5 discusses, the anti-nuclear opposition exists outside the remit of the officially sanctioned NGO system and seems to have had considerable success in averting the siting of local nuclear projects of different sorts. Certainly the Chinese nuclear power programme seems to be building new nuclear power plants faster than other countries, and thus at a cheaper cost compared to the West. One suggestion that may help to explain cost differences between the West and China (discussed towards the end of Chapter 8 on the UK) is that up until now there have been less stringent health and safety practices applied to construction of power plants in China, and also a much greater availability of relevant construction workers in China.

In Russia, as discussed in Chapter 9, the authorities seem to have more success in repressing local anti-nuclear movements compared to China. Russia's nuclear system is strongly hierarchical with military and civil nuclear functions fused. This fusion undermines Russia's claims to have a safe nuclear system since its desire to keep military secrets secure leaves a large information deficit about, in particular, instances of radioactive leaks. It may be significant that in Russia the post-Fukushima debate has been about raising Russian safety standards to meet IAEA levels, whereas in the other states debate has centred on the desirability of raising standards beyond IAEA minima.

This fused military/civil hierarchical system wherein anti-nuclear opposition is, or has been, marginalised has laid claim to having a successful export programme for its nuclear reactors. Despite this, however, Russia's recent experience is that construction times for new nuclear power stations are averaging over eight years. This indicates that the economic prospects for nuclear power are not optimal even in Russia, although in that country there is little competition from renewable energy sources. Given that Russia's export strategy may rest heavily on achieving nuclear constructions within planned timeframes (i.e. five–six years), the prospects for Russian nuclear exports may not prove to be as rosy as Rosatom hopes. If the projects suffer cost overruns then host countries may find themselves heavily in debt, something which will reduce enthusiasm for signing up to buying Russian reactors.

The economic prospects for nuclear power seem to be dragged down by its inherent engineering complexity. This complexity seems largely a product of nuclear designers' attempts to incorporate safety criteria in a cost-effective manner, but which seem to backfire through producing increasing complexity when new plants are built. This slows down construction times and thus leads to very large increases in cost. This problem is also partly a function of the fact that nuclear construction engineering is an extremely specialised task. Because of this there is a dearth of such requisite skills, such a dearth only partially ameliorated where there is a large critical mass of nuclear construction activity in any one country that is guided by a centralised authority. In that sense the nuclear safety regulations may have little direct effect on nuclear programmes. This is ironic since supporters of the US nuclear industry complain that their progress is stifled by safety regulation, and yet their safety rules appear to be weaker than other countries covered in this book.

References

Jasanoff, S., and Kim, S. (2009) 'Containing the Atom: Sociotechnical Imaginaries and Nuclear Power in the United States and South Korea', *Minerva*, 47(2), 119–146.

Index

Printed in the United States
By Bookmasters